Political Augustinianism

Political Augustinianism

Modern Interpretations of Augustine's Political Thought

Michael J. S. Bruno

Fortress Press
Minneapolis

POLITICAL AUGUSTINIANISM

Modern Interpretations of Augustine's Political Thought

Nihil Obstat: Reverend John P. Cush, S.T.L.
Diocesan Censor

Imprimatur: Most Reverend Nicholas DiMarzio, Ph.D., D.D.
Bishop of Brooklyn
Brooklyn, New York   November 26, 2013

Cover image: Historiated initial "I" depicting St. Augustine (vellum), Master of San Michele of Murano (early 15th century)/Musee Marmottan Monet, Paris, France/Giraudon/Bridgeman Images

Cover design: Laurie Ingram

Library of Congress Cataloging-in-Publication Data

Print ISBN: 978-1-4514-8269-0

eBook ISBN: 978-1-4514-8758-9

Manufactured in the U.S.A.

This book was produced using PressBooks.com, and PDF rendering was done by PrinceXML.

This book is lovingly dedicated to my father,
Michael J. Bruno.

Contents

Foreward

Robert Dodaro

"Political Augustinianism," the subject of the present volume by Father Michael Bruno, involves a chronological, analytical and comparative reading of twenty-five scholars whose writings span the period from the beginning of the twentieth century until today and who have treated Augustine's political theology and ethics along with its relevance in the modern world. No treatment of this question has ever covered the breadth and provided the detailed analysis of the various positions assumed by these authors as has this effort by Michael Bruno. He provides a summary of the important theological and ethical considerations that each of these scholars incorporates into his interpretation of Augustine's political thought. He also compares their positions, thus providing readers of this book with a careful, indispensable map detailing the principal points of a discussion that began 110 years ago in France, England and Germany, and which today has become an important conversation in the Catholic and Protestant communities of North America.

This book is both theological and historical; it traces and examines a century-long, focused conversation by scholars of Augustine concerning a controversial area of his thought and its modern theological applications. Giants in the field of Augustinian studies, such as Étienne Gilson, Henri-Irénée Marrou, Reinhold Niebuhr, Paul Ramsey, Joseph Ratzinger (Pope Benedict XVI), Robert Markus, Rowan Williams and Oliver O'Donovan are studied in these pages in relation to the various hermeneutical approaches with which they and other scholars accommodated Augustine's thought to the political realities of their times. Hence, Michael Bruno's work can be read not only as a modern history of the scholarly treatment accorded to Augustine's political thought in itself, but as a commentary on the development of a large swathe of Catholic and Protestant political theologies through the twentieth century and into the twenty-first. Epochal geopolitical events, such as two World Wars, the "Cold War," the decolonization of over half of the globe, a series of international economic depressions and recessions, the global nuclear weapons race, the founding and development of the United Nations Organization, various human and civil rights movements and anti-discrimination campaigns, international terrorism and now the global reach of a violent form of Islamic fundamentalism, considered together with the Second Vatican Council have provided scholars with a modern context for various reappropriations of Augustine's thought in relation to Christianity and political theory, church and state, grace and political virtue. Michael Bruno's work demonstrates that these central themes in Augustine's political writings as found in the *City of God* as well as his letters to public officials and various sermons, have maintained their capacity to provide a foundation for Christian theological and political ethical reflection throughout the most turbulent events of modern political history.

Finally, the book is written with enormous clarity of expression; it is synthetic and analytic at the same time, and it is supported by an exceptionally broad survey of the relevant literature. Michael Bruno demonstrates a capability to express sober theological and historical judgments concerning the wide ranging survey of theological viewpoints he assembles in this work. Moreover, it must be unequivocally asserted that his work represents an original and vitally useful contribution to the ongoing debate within Catholic and Protestant circles concerning this topic.

Professor Robert Dodaro,
Faculty of Sacred Theology
Pontifical Lateran University
January 16, 2014

Abbreviations

AAS   *Acta Apostolicae Sedis*. Vols. 1ff. Vatican City: Typis Polyglottis Vaticanis, 1909-present.

CG   R.W. Dyson. ed. *St. Augustine of Hippo: The City of God Against the Pagans*. Cambridge: Cambridge University Press, 1998.

CSDC   Pontifical Council for Justice and Peace, *Compendium of the Social Doctrine of the Church*. Washington D.C.: USCCB Publishing, 2004.

DH   Vatican Council II. Declaration on Religious Freedom *Dignitatis Humanae* (December 7, 1965). *AAS* 58 (1966): 929-946. Official English translation in *The Documents of Vatican II with Notes and Index: Vatican Translation*, Strathfield, Australia: St. Pauls Publications, 2009: 391-402.

FR   John Paul II. Encyclical Letter *Fides et Ratio* (September 14, 1998). *AAS* 91 (1999): 5-88. Official English translation published by Libreria Editrice Vaticana, Vatican City, 1998.

GS   Pastoral Constitution on the Church in the Modern World *Gaudium et Spes* (December 7, 1965). *AAS* 58 (1966): 1025-1120. Official English translation in *The Documents of Vatican II with Notes and Index: Vatican Translation*, Strathfield, Australia: St. Pauls Publications, 2009: 125-198.

LG

Dogmatic Constitution on the Church *Lumen Gentium* (November 21, 1964). *AAS* 57 (1965): 5-75. Official English translation in *The Documents of Vatican II with Notes and Index: Vatican Translation*, Strathfield, Australia: St. Pauls Publications, 2009: 17-76.

Acknowledgments

No project is accomplished without the assistance of many people, and so at the opening of this work, I would like to offer a word of gratitude. I thank with all my heart my parents, Michael and Rosalie, as well as my family and friends for their patience and support throughout my studies, especially when those studies have taken me far from them. I would also like to express my gratitude to His Excellency, The Most Rev. Nicholas DiMarzio, Bishop of Brooklyn, for his confidence, support, and the very opportunity to undertake this project. I am indebted to Professor Robert Dodaro, O. S. A., who directed and guided this work from its earliest stages. I am truly grateful for his friendship and counsel.

I would like to thank Msgr. James Checchio and the entire community of the Pontifical North American College for the tremendous support and encouragement offered to me, both during this project and throughout my time in Rome. My classmates and friends from the college have been a source of strength and a true grace in my life. The faculty and staff of the college were a source of encouragement, and were of great assistance during this project. I am also grateful for the fraternity and encouragement of my brother priests of the Diocese of Brooklyn, who supported, advised, and prayed for me during this project. I thank His Excellency, The Most

Rev. Enrico del Covolo, and the community of the Pontifical Lateran University, especially Msgr. Nicola Ciola, Professor Lubomir Zak, and the members of the Faculty of Sacred Theology.

I am indebted to Fr. Joseph Zwosta, Fr. Daniel Champoli, and Fr. Christopher Seiler for their input and for proofreading parts of this work. I thank Lewis Ayres of Durham University, Peter Iver Kaufman of Richmond College, and Charles Mathewes of the University of Virginia, who took an interest in this project and offered me valuable feedback. I am grateful for Michael Gibson, Lisa Gruenisen, and the editorial staff at Fortress Press for their assistance in bringing this project to publication. I am also grateful for the advice and counsel of Rev. Msgr. John J. Strynkowski, Vicar for Higher Education, and Professor Richard Gribble, C. S. C., of Stonehill College. Finally, in writing this work I gratefully recall all of my teachers through the years, especially the members of the Missionary Franciscan Sisters of the Immaculate Conception, the Xaverian Brothers, the Congregation of Holy Cross, and the Society of Jesus, many of whom have since gone to their eternal reward. I remain forever grateful to them and for the education I received through their ministry.

I have dedicated this work to my late father, Michael J. Bruno, who with my mother, Rosalie, guided, encouraged, and supported me in every endeavor. It was my father who first led me to St. Augustine, giving me at a young age my first copy of *The Confessions*. This book, therefore, is a fruit of the love and sacrifice of my parents, and I pray that it is a fitting tribute to a great man and a wonderful father. *Requiescat in pace.*

Introduction

Status Quaestionis

Augustine's consideration of faith, politics, and society has largely been rendered synonymous with his work *De Civitate Dei*. This work, written at the beginning of the fifth century c.e., is among the most theologically and historically influential works in the history of Christianity. However, this identification has led to an often generic reduction of Augustine's social and political thought to what is often called the theory of "two cities." This simplified notion attributed to Augustine presents an obfuscation of the true theological foundations of Augustine's insight, and is typically summarized as a patristic antecedent of modern conceptions of Church and state. Unfortunately, many political scientists, philosophers, and even theologians see in this reduction a fair summary of the contributions of St. Augustine to Western political and social thought, and fail to plumb the depths of his ideas, which have remained the object of study and debate since his death in the fifth century. In this present study of contemporary Augustinian interpretations, it is my hope that, at the very least, the complexity and implications of Augustine's thought will become clearer, and that my work will aid in a more nuanced and informed consideration of the Bishop of Hippo in various halls of the contemporary academy.

It must be stated at the outset that the scope of Augustine's work normally cited in the consideration of his political and social thought, especially his *City of God* and a number of his letters and sermons, was not directly political. As we will see throughout this study, Augustine's focus in general remained directly on the journey of the pilgrim soul in the *saeculum*.[1] The discovery of political and social implications to Augustine's work has been, therefore, the work of interpreters both contemporary to Augustine himself and those that emerged after his death. As R. W. Dyson explains, "Insofar as the elements of Augustine's political, social and historical thought are represented in the *City of God*, they are present, if one may so express it, in much the way that the fragments of a pot might be present at an archaeological site. They have to be identified, sorted out from large masses of other material, and assembled."[2] Such a task was deemed necessary in order to clarify the relationship of the Church and the Roman Empire, and later the Church and the Gothic kingdoms, in the wake of the imperial collapse of Rome. As John Rist has synthesized:

> There can be good Christian emperors, but there is no guarantee that a Christian government will behave in a Christian fashion, and after a brief period of hesitation Augustine resolutely refused the Constantinian option—leading towards Caesaropapism—of any 'sacralization' of the state. Yet he spelled out no clear political alternative and the key problem of 'political Augustinianism' was not yet on the table: that is, whether the 'fullness of (secular) power' should reside with the Church (in practice the pope), with the Empire or its successors, however desacralized they might become, or with neither.[3]

1. Joanna Scott, "Contemporary Influence of Augustine's Political Thought," in *Augustine Through the Ages: An Encyclopedia*, ed. Allan Fitzgerald, O. S. A., (Grand Rapids, MI: Wm. B. Eerdman's Publishing Co., 2002), 658. For an extensive treatment of this theme, see Miles Hollingworth, *The Pilgrim City: St. Augustine of Hippo and his Innovation in Political Thought* (London: T&T Clark, 2010).
2. CG, xv.

The question of the rightful placement of power seemed a natural one to examine within Augustine's work. Therefore, Dyson has identified four significant points in *City of God*, all of which have been important to subsequent interpreters and which will aid our study here as well. First, Augustine asserted that earthly government though necessarily flawed remained "indispensable" to the securing of peace and order in human society.[4] Second, Augustine had acknowledged that political community existed according to the divine will, and was endowed with limited authority and power from God, the source of all power.[5] Third, Augustine recognized the heroic deeds and natural virtues of many celebrated heroes of Rome, all the while pointing out the misguided love and transient nature of their virtue.[6] Finally, Augustine recognized that the imperfect Christian state, though sinful and earthly, "can nonetheless provide a milieu within which the Church can do her work effectively and the Christian life can be lived by its citizens."[7]

The debate over the role of secular authority and its relationship to the Church during the Middle Ages made reference to these basic concepts in Augustine's thought.[8] Indeed, as the Church asserted its authority over secular matters, it cited the Bishop of Hippo. This connection would lead to the thesis of Henri-Xavier Arquillière,

---

3. John Rist, *What is Truth? From the Academy to the Vatican* (Cambridge: Cambridge University Press, 2008), 258.

4. *CG*, xxiv. We will discuss throughout this work the significance of that earthly peace and the limitations of human government in obtaining it. My discussion of Robert Markus will build upon this point as well.

5. *CG*, xxv. This observation will be significant in the work of Arquillière and Combès, who identify the importance assigned to this point throughout the Middle Ages.

6. *CG*, xxvi. This will be an important point in Robert Dodaro's distinction of Augustine's view of pagan and Christian virtue.

7. *CG*, xxvii. This argument will be of significance in the considerations of John Milbank, Charles Mathewes, and others.

8. *CG*, xxix.

often called "political Augustinianism."[9] Rist clarifies the link between Augustine and this movement:

> Insofar as political Augustinianism has a theoretical basis—and in this resides much of its claim to be Augustinian—it is that politics is a branch of morality, that in politics as in private life all decisions are going to affect the state of one's immortal soul . . . the leading politician, whether king or emperor, is no different from the ordinary man; he can and should be told when he sins.[10]

This debate evolved, however, with the disconnect introduced by Marsilius of Padua and later William Ockham between political authority and morality, as politics was reduced to functionality and "utility."[11] As Rist notes, this turn in the debate was inevitably "pointing towards the emergence of an independent secular authority."[12] This latter concept of secular authority and the rise of the modern state created new debates in Augustinian interpretation. It will become evident that the last century in particular has been a fertile period for such interpretations, ranging from questions of Augustinian hermeneutics to applications of Augustine's thought in the contemporary public square. We turn now, therefore, to the task at hand and seek to clarify the various interpretations that have emerged, their historical development, and potential movements forward.

---

9. This theme will be discussed at length, as well as its progression.

10. Rist, *What is Truth?*, 259. Rist agrees with Robert Dodaro's assessment that Augustine's concern was not the relationship of the Church and government, but the attitude and disposition of the Christian in political office.

11. Ibid., 266.

12. Ibid.

The Question of Augustine's Political and Social Vision

During his address to the Federal Parliament of Germany in 2011, Pope Benedict XVI sought to reflect upon the role and duty of the politician in light of contemporary challenges. To do so, Pope Benedict cited Book XIX of St. Augustine's *De Civitate Dei*, noting:

> Naturally a politician will seek success, without which he would have no opportunity for effective political action at all. Yet success is subordinated to the criterion of justice, to the will to do what is right, and to the understanding of what is right. Success can also be seductive and thus can open up the path towards the falsification of what is right, towards the destruction of justice. "Without justice–what else is the State but a great band of robbers?," as Saint Augustine once said.[13]

This reference to Augustine's *City of God*, made in a speech to the German Parliament, points to a now century-old trend of interpreting and analyzing the thought of St. Augustine on issues related to both society and politics. The distinction between these two realms is important to keep in mind throughout this work. The political realm in this context implies those institutions which focus on governing and the obligations such governance brings upon citizens, e.g., taxes, military service, and other civic activities. The social realm here refers to the association of human beings in general, namely the various non-political communities in which each human being is a member. While the political elements of Augustine's thought are often commented on, it is important to remember that he focused on these social groupings as well, especially the family and the local community created by multiple families. While political life is necessarily social, it remains true that not every form of social life is political in nature. However, both realms would be of concern

13. Pope Benedict XVI, Address to Federal Parliament in Berlin's Reichstag Building: Politics at the Service of Rights and Justice, September 24, 2011. Original German text in *AAS* 103 (2011): 663-669; official English translation in *L'Osservatore Romano*, September 28, 2011, 7.

to Augustine of Hippo, inasmuch as the Christian must navigate through both on this earthly pilgrimage.

Furthermore, Augustine's work offers what can be called a "systematic" approach to the various questions surrounding these distinct realms of human community. Such a systematic response points to the fact that Augustine consistently addressed these concerns in reference to his larger theological concepts and the pressing theological challenges presented to him by Stoicism, Pelagianism, and Donatism. Therefore, the systematic nature of Augustine's thought on human society and political life cannot be understood in a modern sense, but rather as the integral connection of Augustine's social and political views in relation to his historical context and theology. Augustine's responses to social and political questions, many of which continue to emerge today, were not formed in a vacuum, but rather were formulated in light of the larger questions he grappled with, namely Christ and Revelation, nature and grace, sin and redemption, history and its fulfillment, and the Church and imperial rule.[14] Necessarily, Augustine's systematic response to political and social questions also conveys the components of a Christian ethic for particular circumstances, especially when the Christian is called upon to participate in social and political activities. However, this ethic, like his views on social and political issues, is not programmatic, but rather integral with his theological and pastoral concerns. While Augustine's systematic approach and the ethical principles that he developed in social and political matters have been debated for nearly a century, as we will see in this discussion, they continue to spark new interpretations and raise new points of debate.

14. While I am singling out political and social questions in this thesis, I will attempt to integrally present these questions within the larger arguments of the scholars who have participated in this debate.

Augustinian interpretation of political and social issues developed and evolved over the course of the twentieth century. In 1921, the Anglican priest and theologian John Neville Figgis, who had been a leader in the Christian Socialist Movement in England, surveyed both the physical and ideological devastation caused by World War I and turned to St. Augustine. Eugene McCarraher has commented on what might have drawn Figgis to Augustine, "Figgis wrote, like Augustine, in the smoky twilight of a civilization racked by war and despair."[15] Figgis built his work upon that of Ernst Troeltsch (1865-1923), especially Troeltsch's *Augustin, die christliche Antike und die Mittelalter*, where he argued that the Bishop of Hippo established a "Christian cultural ethic" centered in the human pursuit of the *summum bonum* and fraternal charity.[16] Figgis embraced this idea and advocated for Augustine's relevance by demonstrating the possibilities of this "Christian cultural ethic" in post-war Europe. He argued, therefore, that Augustine's *City of God* remained essential for the student of political thought and was a relevant study for modernity in general.[17]

While Figgis wrote immediately after World War I, the discussion of Augustine's political and social thought became synonymous both positively and negatively with another author, namely H. X. Arquillière and his 1933 work, *L'Augustinisme Politique*. Arquillière's work, its immediate influences, and the responses it provoked, form the initial scope of this work. In fact, the English rendering of Arquillière's title, namely "Political Augustinianism," will refer

---

15. Eugene McCarraher, "Enchanted City of Man: The State and the Market in Augustinian Perspective," in *Augustine and Politics*, ed. John Doody, K. Hughes & K. Paffenroth (Lanham, MD: Lexington Books, 2005), 267. McCarraher sees a direct link between Figgis and the Radical Orthodoxy Movement. See *Augustine and Politics*, 269-271.

16. Eric Saak, *Highway to Heaven: The Augustinian Platform Between Reform and Reformation, 1292-1524* (Leiden: Brill Publishing, 2002), 6.

17. John Neville Figgis, *The Political Aspects of S. Augustine's 'City of God'*, 2nd ed. (Gloucester, MA: Peter Smith, 1963), 115.

throughout this project to Arquillière's specific argument and also to the trend he has spurred in Augustinian interpretation. It is of no surprise that the center of this discussion remains Augustine's concept of two cities, the city of God and the city of man. The nature of these two cities, as well as their rapport, if any, is the question which lies at the core of most of the works we will discuss. However, as we will later see, the entire question around Augustine's two cities would be transformed in 1955 by the proposal of Henri-Irénée Marrou of a *tertium quid*, a point of encounter between the two cities. Marrou's assertion is transformative, as it paved the way for new approaches in Augustinian interpretation. Among these new approaches would be that of Robert Markus and his work, *Saeculum: History and Society in the Theology of St. Augustine*.

From the very beginning of this debate, therefore, it is clear that interpreting Augustine's political and social thought has also implied an attempt at drawing "Augustinian" social and political principles, which can be applied to the contemporary situation of the interpreter. Therefore, the authors we will discuss and the debates that have emerged between them are focused not only on the nature of Augustine's ideas themselves, but also the relevance his principles hold for the relationship of the Church and civil society and the role of the Christian in a secular state. These attempts in applying Augustine's principles, while at times derided by historians and classicists, have been influenced by the context and challenges of the era of each author who has taken up this task. For example, in the aftermath of both World Wars, Augustine's ideas were reflected upon anew and various interpretations emerged. In recent years, Augustine's vision has once again played an important role in the discussions of war, terrorism, and even the evolution of European identity. In the United States, for example, Augustine's name still emerges most frequently during wartime, as debates over the meaning of "just war" immediately recall the thought and legacy of the Bishop of Hippo. It is important, therefore, to recognize that the contemporary discussion of Augustine's social and political vision has been influenced by the history of contemporary theology and the history of the twentieth century in general.

The French voice, for instance, which dominated the beginning of this endeavor, largely gives way to the thought and influence of Reinhold Niebuhr and other Anglo-American thinkers after World War II. Even within the English-speaking world, however, Niebuhr's "realist" interpretation would not be the last word. Robert Markus's concept of *saeculum* in Augustine provoked further discussion, and subsequently led to numerous responses from various authors, including John Milbank and the Radical Orthodoxy movement. Furthermore, a new effort has emerged to recapture the theological context and nature of Augustine's vision of two cities. While this effort was taken up initially by writers such as Ernest Fortin and James Schall, it has more recently been advanced at the turn of the twenty-first century by others like Peter Iver Kaufman and Robert Dodaro. As this study will attempt to show, the discussion of Augustine's political and social thought has been a fruitful area of patristic, theological, and philosophical debate over the past century. This work, therefore, seeks to offer a new systematic presentation of the insights, challenges, and applications that have emerged from this century-long discussion.

Purpose and Method

The nature of this study by necessity is both expository and analytical, as it seeks to present systematically the various interpretations of Augustine on issues of social and political life and examine the hermeneutical and contextual questions that undergird such interpretations. This project, therefore, has a threefold purpose. Firstly, it is our goal to critically review a substantial and representative part of the literature of twentieth and twenty-first century applications of Augustine's political and social thought. Furthermore, we will evaluate the positions taken by the scholars in question by relating them critically. This will allow a demonstration of the contrasts both in interpretation and application of Augustine's principles on issues of social and political life. By comparing their interpretations, we also enter the hermeneutical dimension of this discussion, one that allows us to examine which hermeneutics have been utilized and how deftly they have been applied. Finally, throughout this discussion we will discuss the historiography of the political Augustinian debate as a whole, in order to shed light on its origins, its development, and its current status. Here, we will address the question of why this discussion has experienced a "continental drift" primarily from the French towards the Anglo-American academy, and also why Marrou's *tertium quid* sparked so much interest in the English-speaking world. Also, this last question of historiography will bring us to the current attempt of recent thinkers to capture an "authentic" Augustinian hermeneutic towards political and social questions.

Such a historical evaluation of these Augustinian interpretations is in itself a systematic process, requiring both the synthesis and analysis of numerous works. While one might initially separate the historical and systematic tasks, in reality, the evaluations here attempt to employ both tasks integrally. What is presented here, therefore, is not simply another voice in the debate itself, but a systematic view of the discussion of Augustine's political thought and its progression from the turn of the twentieth century until the present. I have sought to present the thought of various scholars, demonstrate points of interconnectedness and conflict, and analyze both the substance of each argument and its relationship to the debate in general. The first four chapters, therefore, will present the interpretations of Augustine's social and political thought from Arquillière's initial "political Augustinian" project to recent efforts in the new millennium. In the first chapter, focusing on the concept of "l'augustinisme politique," we will discuss the influence of Étienne Gilson, the concept's introduction by Arquillière, and subsequent responses by Combès and Marrou, especially his *tertium quid*. Subsequently, in chapter two we will move to the early American engagement of Augustine's thought, which remained for several decades largely overshadowed by the realism of Reinhold Niebuhr and the responses that emerged to his approach.

After discussing the post-World War II shifts in this debate, we will observe in chapter three and chapter four the emergence of a contemporary Anglo-American contribution, led initially by Robert Markus and his introduction of an Augustinian *saeculum*. We will examine also the significant responses to this theory offered by other authors. Among these respondents are John Milbank, Jean Bethke Elshtain, Peter Iver Kaufman, Robert Dodaro, Charles Mathewes, and other important contemporary voices. Also examined among these authors will be the voices of Joseph Ratzinger and Rowan Williams, both of whom examined this topic as theologians and have in fact returned to it in recent years. Finally, having laid out the origins of this discussion, its first major advancements, and the contemporary debate it has inspired, the last chapter will focus upon the hermeneutical questions that pervade this area of Augustinian interpretation and will explore some important contemporary applications of Augustine's thought. In this last chapter as well, the contemporary theological discussion of Augustine's ideas will be connected to some significant Magisterial texts which focus upon the relationship of the Church and the Christian to civil society.

Clarifications

Before going any further, it is important to note that the scope of this study has prevented entrance into certain related discussions in Augustinian scholarship. First, the focus of this project relates directly to the "political Augustinian" movement initiated by Arquillière's work. As a result, interpretations of Augustine connected to the early twentieth century shifts in the German theological school, especially in the work of Otto Gierke, Albrecht Ritschl, and Adolf von Harnack, are outside of the scope of this work. While those authors are influential on the work of Figgis and others, they are not widely engaged in Arquillière's *L'Augustinisme Politique*.[18] Also, these works and much of the late-nineteenth-century scholarship on Augustine were largely "archaeological," and generally did not apply principles of Augustine's thought on contemporary challenges. While certainly deserving of a comprehensive treatment of their theological contributions, such a study is simply outside of the goals of this project. Also, in reading this work, it must be remembered that as the discussion advances, the distinctions among authors will become increasingly evident and points of debate will emerge with greater clarity.

Also, Augustine's concepts of just war and original sin are themes that I have attempted to engage respectfully and integrally where necessary. However, I remain conscious that the debate around them remains far beyond what can be possibly included in this work. These concepts have their own collections of literature and their own independent historiographies, which cannot be adequately recounted

18. Arquillière references Gierke and Harnack in his bibliography, but only once does he cite Harnack in the text of his work. See *Henri-Xavier Arquillière, L'augustinisme politique: Essai sur la formation des théories politiques du Moyen Âge* (Paris: J. VRIN, 1955), 131.

in this work. Therefore, where relevant, these themes and others have been included and discussed, but in no way does their inclusion constitute an exhaustive study. Also, it must be noted that this work seeks to be a systematic theological discussion; it is not a patristic study of Augustine. As a result, our focus remains the course of Augustinian interpretation and the application of Augustine's work in contemporary theology over the course of the last century. From this perspective, I believe it can safely be argued that the future prospects of Augustinian interpretation and the application of Augustine's social and political vision are assured. Finally, throughout the literature of this debate, many authors use the term "state" to describe the human political community within the earthly city. However, it must be noted that Augustine did not share a modern conception of state, but rather experienced the political reality of the Roman Empire. As a result, in the application of Augustine's ideas, the use of the term state is not meant to be anachronistic, but rather part of an attempt at applying Augustine's principles to contemporary political realities.

1

French Interpretations of Augustine's Social and Political Thought

The twentieth century was marked by two World Wars, a Cold War, economic depression, decolonization of over half the globe, social and political upheaval, and new challenges posed by new technologies, not the least of which was the development of nuclear weaponry. From this tremendous amount of turbulence, and in light of unparalleled human bloodshed, there arose varied responses based upon the application of Augustine's social and political principles. While at times unnoticed, we must remember that a tremendous amount was written by twentieth century thinkers who sought wisdom and guidance for their troubled historical contexts from the Bishop of Hippo. However, those efforts often yielded different conclusions, and from those differences a debate, which is the topic of this project, emerged. The evolution of this discussion of Augustine's political and social thought, therefore, reflects the wider history of theology in the twentieth century, as a utopian and optimistic liberal theological approach quickly yielded to a dialectical and realist school.

Furthermore, within Catholicism, the interpretation of Augustine's thought moved from a traditional understanding of continuity with the Scholastic interpretation of Augustine to a political and social reduction of the Bishop of Hippo's work. Such a reduction saw the removal of Augustine from his larger theological context, and sought to draw from his corpus political and social principles often without their theological context. Henri de Lubac was a consummate critic of this shift, and so he serves as a voice of dissent in a number of sections throughout this chapter, especially where the reduction of Augustine's thought can be observed. Finally, the mid-twentieth century, especially the 1960s and 1970s, proved another crossroads for this entire discussion and the context for an Anglo-American shift. This shift will be treated at the end of this chapter with a discussion of its origins.

We will begin examining the work of Gustave Combès, who writing after the First World War, interpreted Augustine's *De Civitate Dei* under the lens of political authority and the question of its nature and origins. At the end of the 1920s, Étienne Gilson interpreted Augustine within a Thomistic context, viewing Augustine's commentary on political and social questions within the categories of nature and desire. Providing us with a general moniker for this line of Augustinian interpretation, Henri-Xavier Arquillière and his notion of "Political Augustinianism" connected Augustine to the Gregorian Reform and posited that Augustine's thought was foundational for the modern state. Arquillière's work provoked debate and further discussion, especially in the work of Henri Irénée Marrou. Marrou in the middle of the twentieth century would examine the relationship between Augustine's two cities, offering the possibility of a *tertium quid*, which would be another source of future reflection and exegesis. Finally, Henri de Lubac engaged these various interpretations of Augustine, and cautioned against hermeneutical tendencies that strayed from Augustine's fundamental goal, namely conversion of the soul to God.

Gustave Combès

Gustave Combès in his 1927 work, *La Doctrine Politique de Saint Augustin*, presented what has been characterized as a "traditional" interpretation of Augustine's *City of God*. Miikka Ruokanen describes the significance of this categorization, writing "according to the traditional school, the political authority among men is based on the just order of nature given in the creation . . . in *De Civitate Dei* political order is understood as an inherently good order of life. . . ."[1] The work of Combès and the traditionalist school has been related by Ruokanen and Robert Markus to the earlier work of Otto Schilling, especially his *Die Staats- und Soziallehre des hl. Augustinus*, and the later legal analysis of Anton-Hermann Chroust.[2] The work of Combès is, therefore, of significant importance in understanding an early school of interpretation in post-World War I Europe. However, it is also an interpretation often debated among Marrou, Markus, and other subsequent interpreters. As a result, Combès's interpretation is important in understanding the progression of this debate as a whole.

1. Miikka Ruokanen, *Theology of Social Life in Augustine's De Civitate Dei* (Göttingen: Vandenhoeck & Ruprecht, 1993), 11.
2. Otto Schilling, *Die Staats- und Soziallehre des hl. Augustinus* (Freibourg: Herder, 1910). Anton-Hermann Chroust, "The Philosophy of Law of St. Augustine," *The Philosophical Review* 53, no.2 (1944): 195-202.

Combès Augustinian Interpretation of Political Authority

The central element of Combès's argument remains the nature and origin of political authority, which would also prove to be his interpretation's most controversial legacy. In Augustine's reception of Cicero's definition of a republic as a "multitude united in bonds of harmony," harmony is identified as a "union of hearts" that creates a *compositio voluntatum*.[3] This composition of wills is both moral and material, and for Combès it is consistent with man's very nature, which tends to the union of hearts, wills and interests in order to create a *pactum societatis*. This social tendency in man from which society emerges, grows into "a reciprocal engagement," where "rights are recognized, needs are met, and a code of obligations and sacrifices are agreed to."[4] The origin of power, therefore, in Combès's reading of Augustine, lies in nature and is manifested concretely in human society from its most primitive and earliest manifestation, the family. Combès clearly states that for Augustine, "Political authority derived from the familial authority."[5] To justify this interpretation, Combès cites Augustine's *Contra Iulianum* IV, 61:

> But we must recognize the different forms of command and of obedience. The soul commands the body and all the passions; but it commands the body as a king his citizens, a father his children, and all the passions like a master to his slaves: it reprimands them, and tames them. The king, the general, the magistrate, the father, the victorious nations exercise their authority over citizens like the soul over the body.[6]

---

3. Gustave Combès, *La Doctrine Politique de Saint Augustin* (Paris: Plon, 1927), 78. English translation is my own.

4. Ibid., 78.

5. Ibid., 79.

6. Ibid., 80. *Contra Iulianum* IV, 12:61. Nam ut animus corpori dicitur imperare, dicitur etiam libidini: sed corpori, ut rex civibus suis, aut parens liberis; libidini autem, ut servis dominus, quod eam coercet et frangit. Sic regum, sic imperatorum, sic magistratuum, sic patrum, sic populorum imperia civibus sociisque praesunt, ut corporibus animus.

Combès argued that Augustine put forward a hierarchy of authority that included three levels (soul and body, father and family, and king and citizenry), but all three were grounded in one source: the divine will manifested in the social nature of creation. Relying on Augustine's *De Libero Arbitrio* I, 15, Combès argued

> The power belongs to God, he knows the order of all causes, but it does not follow that all depends upon his will . . . He is the author of all powers, but not all wills. Evil wills, indeed, do not come from him, because they are against the nature that comes from him.[7]

The divine will combined with free human will, therefore, transmits and vests authority in human society. However, Combès allies his understanding of Providence to that of Jacques Bénigne Bossuet (1627-1704), who believed it was providence that led to the succession of governments. Indeed, Combès cites the principle, *"Prorsus divina providentia regna constitauntur humana."*[8] Such a view, however, promoted by Bossuet was also problematic, as it led to a secularization of the Christian sense of history and helped to deflate the boundaries of Augustine's two cities.[9] Combès, unlike Bossuet, recognized an ambivalence in Augustine as to the form of governance employed by the subjects of human authority. He argued:

> Monarchy, aristocracy, democracy. These words mean nothing to him. He starts deliberately outside and above human institutions, and from the heights from where he examines them, they all seem to him equally capable of administrating the city. The only requirement: to maintain justice and respect religion. But this reservation having been established, they all recognized the same rights, granted the same benevolence and demanded the same submission.[10]

---

7. Ibid., 82.
8. Ibid., 83.
9. This will be central to our discussion below of Marrou and his effort at establishing a renewed Augustinian based "theology of history."

While the type of government utilized was not essential to Augustine, Combès notes that the necessity of justice remained absolutely essential. It is no coincidence that justice is of central importance in the first five books of Augustine's *City of God*. Augustine believed that justice remained the foundation of power, assuring that any government remains balanced and stable. However, if the subject of authority lacks restraint and allows desires and passions to overcome justice, inevitably tranquility is lost and credibility wavers. As Combès argues, Augustine believed "the great Platonic thesis. Justice being the mother of all virtues, power which denies justice forsakes prudence. Force must be tempered, and condemned in its excess. For it is only a caricature of authority."[11] For this reason, Augustine envisioned the ruler as bearing a duty, a responsibility, and not simply an honor.

Augustine believed that too often love of glory in the exercise of courage and patriotism led directly to vice, as the charge to preserve justice and order leads often to the desire to domination as well.[12] It is for this reason that Combès sees Augustine's call for virtue as central. The exercise of virtue must be encouraged and promoted in both the wielding of power and in the submission of citizens to it. Combès summarizes this vision of power:

> This text has the happy privilege to summarize these expressive formulas of the nature and the roles and purpose of power: power comes from God, it is exercised in the name of God; it is just and merciful in obedience to God and serves God sincerely, it sacrifices itself to collaborate with God, it seeks order, unity, peace, to establish the City of this world, on the model of the City of God.[13]

---

10. Ibid., 86.
11. Ibid., 93.
12. Ibid., 98.
13. Ibid., 109. This virtue perspective will be recovered later in the work of Dodaro and others, and we will return to it in both chapter 4 and chapter 5.

The Reception of Combés's Work

In his work *Theologies d'occasion*, Henri de Lubac cites Gustave Combés as an author who early on recognized the true nature of Augustine's *City of God*. De Lubac notes that Augustine is not concerned with a "state founded on evangelical justice," but rather he is reflecting on the "holy City where God reigns." De Lubac continues, this holy city is "essentially hidden *here below*, even though some of its radiance can be detected, and its invisible borders are constantly changing."[14] In this work, Augustine "takes up, develops and deepens the allegory of the "two ways" that had served to frame the first descriptions of life in conformity with the Gospel . . . The antagonism of the two 'cities,' which Augustine always keeps in mind, has no political overtones."[15]

De Lubac agrees with Combés's analysis of political authority in that both the authority of the divine Law contained in the Scriptures and the positive law decreed by rulers derive from God because "*ipsa iura humana per imperatores et reges saeculi Deus distribuit generi humano.*"[16] De Lubac, like Combés, agrees that Augustine is ambivalent towards the type of government utilized in human society, and notes that no where can it be shown that "theocracy" is the ultimate goal of Augustine's work.[17] De Lubac writes, "In that thin slice of history that Providence gave to Augustine to live, regardless of the emperor in power—pagan, Christian, or apostate, hostile or favorable to his views–he remained 'a faithful subject of the great Roman Empire.'"[18] De Lubac also would have no objection

---

14. Henri de Lubac, *Theological Fragments*, trans. Rebecca Howell Balinski (San Francisco: Ignatius Press, 1989), 245.
15. Ibid., 251.
16. Ibid., 254. "God gives human laws themselves to the human race through the emperors and kings of this world."
17. Ibid., 255.
18. Ibid., 255.

with Combés's assertion that a reflection of Aristotle's idea of justice could be observed in Augustine's use of justice in *City of God*. In fact, de Lubac agrees with Étienne Gilson, who we will discuss below, that a natural law understanding of justice is present in Augustine. Combés as well observes this in *City of God*, and he argued that Augustine's vision is consistent with and expanded in the work of St. Thomas Aquinas.[19]

A critique of this position has been presented by Herbert Deane, who objected to Combés's assertion that positive law must conform to the natural law in order to be valid and hence submitted to by Christians. Combés argues rather that a law not in accordance with the divine or natural law is deemed by Augustine, "only an inert and empty formula, unable to demand an obligation or command. . ."[20] Elsewhere, Combés writes, "Augustine teaches that an unjust law is not a law and hence a citizen must refuse to obey it."[21] Deane argues that such an interpretation is inconsistent with Augustine's later work, especially *De Vera Religione*, which stipulated that a "good and wise" ruler will consider the "immutable rules" of eternal law in legislating.[22] Deane sees the interpretation of Combés as an untenable position. It would require a relative judgment in every case as to whether a law is valid or not, and hence whether the Christian should or should not obey it. This would make governing impossible and it would render civil law irrelevant. Ernest Fortin, however, clarifies the issue by noting, "The Church Fathers did not make any clear-cut distinction between the natural order and the supernatural order or between the natural law properly so called and the divinely revealed law. The tendency was to look upon the realm of morality as a single

---

19. Ibid., 251. Also, See Combés, *La Doctrine*, 105–106.
20. Combés, *La Doctrine*, 152.
21. Ibid., 416.
22. Herbert Deane, *The Political and Social Ideas of St. Augustine* (New York: Columbia University Press, 1963), 90. We will treat Deane independently in the next chapter.

whole and to treat it in the light of those truths which come to us through divine revelation."[23] Deane's concern, therefore, is partly anachronistic, as Augustine's criteria of whether a law was or was not consistent with the "divine law" was not a subjective one, but was based in *id quod in lege et evangelio continetur.*[24]

The interpretation of Augustine's vision of political authority in Combés has also been met with resistance and debate on other points. Combés's assertion that there is a hierarchy of authority manifested in the soul, in the family, and in the state is a clear point of contention. Donald Burt agrees with this premise arguing, "Augustine believed that it was natural for the child to be subordinate to its parents . . . Augustine believed that parental love for the child must be exercised through much command and correction in the early years . . . To refrain from such discipline is to invite chaos."[25] Rowan Williams, as well, sees this conclusion as a fair reading of Augustine, writing, "Augustine makes it plain . . . that the *pax* of the household is to be 'referred' *ad pacem civicam,* even that the *paterfamilias* should derive his standards from the law of the city . . . the *civitas* is itself, like the household, ideally a creative and pastoral community . . ."[26]

However, this point of view is rejected by Robert Markus, who sees the family as an exception to the earthly city in Augustine's vision. Markus argues that such a vision does nothing but allow the political subjugation of others and continue the cycle of domination and pride that Augustine clearly disdains. "The human family differs fundamentally from political society. The family, in Augustine's

23. Ernest Fortin, *Classical Christianity and the Political Order: Reflections on the Theologico-Political Problem*, vol. 2, ed. J. Brian Benestad (Lanham, MD: Rowman and Littlefield, 1996), 226. We will discuss Ernest Fortin in the next chapter.

24. Ibid., 226.

25. Donald X. Burt, O. S. A., *Friendship and Society: An Introduction to Augustine's Practical Philosophy* (Grand Rapids, MI: Eerdmans, 1999), 92-93.

26. Rowan Williams, "Politics and the Soul: A Reading of The City of God," *Milltown Studies* 19/20 (1987), 64.

view, was founded in human nature. In this it contrasted with slavery, an institution brought about by the Fall . . . Political institutions were in their nature more like the latter than the former: that is they belonged to man's fallen state."[27] Miikka Ruokanen also dissents from Combés on this point, arguing that Augustine had neither a concept of a "naturally good structure of political power," nor "an analogy between domestic order and political structure."[28] Ruokanen argues that Augustine's discussion of natural moral law is peripheral to the discussion of "coercive social power in human society."[29] Ruokanen also goes on to reject, as Combés suggests in his work, that Augustine completes Cicero's definition of commonwealth and perfects the idea of "natural justice" by introducing love as its realization. Ruokanen argues, "The very idea of replacing justice with an non-idealistic conception of love, characterized by his understanding of sin, gave Augustine the uniqueness of his own definition and . . . an incredible amount of dynamism and flexibility . . ."[30]

The primary contribution of Gustave Combés, therefore, within this discussion remains his focus on political authority in Augustine's thought, and his theory of political authority emerging from man's most basic relationships. However, Combés also maintained that Augustine was fundamentally ambivalent towards the form of government by which such authority was exercised. However, unlike the accusations of Augustine's later critics, Combés argues with de Lubac that theocracy is not the goal of the Bishop of Hippo, but rather a government striving towards justice. Such ambivalence in the form of government would be a sentiment echoed in various contemporary interpretations of Augustine's thought. Like Combés,

27. Robert Markus, *Christianity and the Secular* (Notre Dame, IN: Univ. of Notre Dame Press, 2006), 58.
28. Ruokanen, *Theology of Social Life*, 103.
29. Ibid.
30. Ibid., 133.

the focus is placed not on the virtue of the government, but on the virtue of those governing. Combés, de Lubac, and Gilson remain in agreement that throughout Augustine's work is a natural law understanding of justice, which allows for an argument of continuity between Augustine and his later Scholastic interpreters. This, however, would be contested by Herbert Deane, Robert Markus and other contemporary authors. Nevertheless, the assertions of Combés, like that of Gilson, would largely be overshadowed in this area of Augustinian interpretation by the debate surrounding a work published six years later, namely Henri-Xavier Arquillière's *L'augustinisme politique*.

Étienne Gilson

In 1929, eight years after the publication of John Neville Figgis's work on Augustine, Étienne Gilson published his own study of Augustine entitled, *Introduction à l'étude de saint Augustin*. [31] Gilson, known for his scholarship in Medieval Philosophy and Thomistic thought, was drawn to Augustine on a philosophical level, as the Bishop of Hippo grounded Western thought in a realism that later would be taken up by St. Thomas Aquinas. Francesca Murphy has noted that, "Augustine, [Gilson] says, conceives the 'natural desire,' not as a generalized wish to catapult from nature into supernature, but as an orientation, a finality, built into human nature by its Creator. God-given faith directs humanity on its journey through nature to God."[32] Gilson, therefore, throughout his work seeks to argue that there is continuity between Augustine's concept of innate truth and the Christian empiricism that would emerge in the Middle

---

31. Étienne Gilson, *Introduction à l'étude de saint Augustin* (Paris: J. Vrin, 1929).
32. Francesca A. Murphy, *Art and Intellect in the Philosophy of Étienne Gilson* (Columbia, MO: Univ. of Missouri Press, 2004), 109.

Ages reaching its height in Scholasticism.[33] This mission, both in his 1927 work and in his 1950 foreword to an English translation of *The City of God*, includes consideration of Augustine's vision of a "Christian society."

Gilson's Interpretation of Augustine's Social Thought

Gilson begins his discussion of Christian life in general by reaffirming the Augustinian principle that all virtuous action finds its end in God. "The virtuous man uses everything, himself included, for the sake of God and he wants a universe in which all beings use themselves, as he does, only in view of God."[34] Drawing from a Thomistic perspective, Gilson's argument would later be echoed by Jacques Maritain in his work *The Person and the Common Good*:

> Because of the [beatific vision], another society is formed—the society of the multitude of blessed souls, each of which on its own account beholds the divine essence and enjoys the same uncreated Good. They love mutually in God. The uncreated common Good, in which they all participate, constitutes the common good of the celestial city in which they are congregated. [35]

True virtue flows, therefore, from the love and freedom man achieves through grace, "which draws his free choice away from the body to fix it upon its final end."[36] Gilson argues that the Christian life, unlike the life of those who have rejected or lack supernatural grace,

---

33. Ibid., 109. Murphy summarizes Gilson's interpretation of the intellect and his philosophical reception of Augustine.

34. Étienne Gilson, *The Christian Philosophy of St. Augustine*, trans. L. E. M. Lynch (New York: Random House, 1960), 167. This idea will be contested by Reinhold Niebuhr, who sees a potential for egoism and pride in finding one's fulfillment in the service of neighbor. His argument will be discussed in detail in chapter 2.

35. Jacques Maritain, *The Person and the Common Good*, trans. John J. Fitzgerald (New York: Charles Scribner's Sons, 1947), 13.

36. Ibid., 168.

is one in which concupiscence, the remnant of original sin, will ultimately be defeated through the merits of Christ. The deflection of any personal merit and achievement in this struggle stands in direct contrast to the pride and vanity promoted in classical society. Such a contrast exhibits the division of humanity into two peoples or cities. "That great host of the impious who lead the life of the earthly man from creation to the end of time, and a people composed of spiritual men, born of grace and called to live in the City of God for all eternity."[37]

Gilson recognizes in Augustine that moral life is always intertwined with social life. He builds upon Augustine's use of Cicero's definition by arguing that man is connected with the city because of love of a common object. "Love of an object spontaneously gives birth to a society which embraces all those whose love is centered in that object of our affection and excludes all who turn away from it."[38] The love of man, therefore determines his citizenship. Gilson explained:

> Since the City of God is the Kingdom of Christ, it is vivified from within by the faith of Christ from which it has its life. It embraces all men who themselves live by this faith, for Christ reigns wherever faith reigns, and where Christ reigns there is also is the Kingdom of Christ. This point is of extreme importance. Henceforth, this new society will find itself constituted by the agreement of wills unified in the love of the same good proposed to them by the same faith. The agreement of hearts presupposes an agreement of minds; that is why the bond of the holy society is a doctrine as well as a love: the love is a love of truth. A truth which can be but a single truth, that of Christ. [39]

37. Gilson, *The Christian Philosophy,* 171.
38. Ibid., 172.
39. Étienne Gilson, foreword for *Saint Augustine, The City of God: Books I-VII*, trans. D. Zema, S. J., and G. Walsh, S. J., (New York: Fathers of the Church, Inc., 1950), lxv.

While both the earthly and heavenly cities share the goal of peace, which they pursue through the ordering of their society, true peace, which satisfies the desires of humanity, is available only through the order of grace. While there might for a time exist an imposed peace in the earthly *civitas,* such peace remains only a false imitation "not even worthy of the name." Gilson argues, "The heavenly city, on the other hand, orders everything with a view to guaranteeing its citizens Christian liberty . . . its order and unity . . . a simply extension of the order and unity reigning in the soul of every just man. This city alone is founded on true order; it alone enjoys true peace."[40] This causes an important question for Gilson, namely if justice is needed for the formation of a society, the impossibility of true justice, even in the Roman Republic, implies that for Augustine no true society has ever existed. Indeed, "there has never been a true society," if Augustine's principles laid out in Book II of *City of God* are to be accepted. This would become a crucial insight in subsequent interpretations, as many future authors accuse Gilson and others of a "Scholastic tendency" of placing true justice and true peace outside of the natural order. As a result, there would emerge a desire in many interpreters and theologians to move beyond this interpretation, which they believe rendered the earthly city incapable of achieving true peace. In reality, Gilson is preserving the eschatological tension in Augustine's vision and far from subverting the civic order, he is recognizing the limits of human society.[41]

Nevertheless, while Augustine's two cities are essentially "incompatible," they must co-exist; living side by side, the citizens of the two cities never, in Gilson's opinion, truly mix together. While seeming to obey all laws and together carry out their common

40. Gilson, *The Christian Philosophy,* 174.
41. This issue of the earthly city's limits will reoccur in numerous subsequent interpretations. While evaded by the realist interpretation, it will be recovered by Peter Iver Kaufman, Charles Mathewes and Robert Dodaro, as we will see in chapter 4.

civic responsibilities, the citizens of the two cities do so for different motives. Even the earthly justice that governs them, which for Gilson, secures the property rights of those who use their goods "for legitimate use," is only an imitation of justice in its perfect form which reigns in the heavenly kingdom. "In that heavenly city wherein the just will have everything they can use, and where they will use it as it should be used."[42]

While Augustine does admit that civic virtue in the earthly city can exist, Gilson notes that the imperfection of its practice remains a testimony to the "supernatural specification" of Christian virtues in their "essence and their end."[43] However, exhibiting openness to the medieval ideal criticized by others, Gilson posits, "A State which could have soldiers, officials and, generally speaking, citizens in accord with the ideal of Christianity, would surely have nothing more to ask for."[44] However, here Gilson appears to depart from Augustine's fundamental argument that the Christian in the earthly city will always have "something to ask for" precisely because his *patria* remains beyond the earthly *civitas*. Gilson does admit that a Christian ruler, indeed a Christian society, does not guarantee in the earthly city a more "perfect" *civitas*, precisely because of the "mixed" nature of both cities.[45] He affirms that the temporal order is kept apart from the spiritual, as eternal law is always immutable and temporal law remains fluid despite the legislator or substance of the legislation.[46]

Confronted with the fact that Augustine simultaneously sees the Church of Christ as the Kingdom of God on earth but not the City

---

42. Ibid., 177.
43. Gilson, *St. Augustine's City of God*, xliii.
44. Gilson, *The Christian Philosophy*, 178.
45. As Robert Dodaro will later argue, building upon Augustine's Christology that such a perfect *civitas* is only created by Christ.
46. Ibid., 180.

of God, Gilson appeals directly to the reality of a "mixed" Church, which will be separated only at the *parousia*. However, unlike the Church, the state bears no corresponding relationship to the heavenly homeland, and is in fact "foreign and indifferent to supernatural ends."[47] Gilson makes this point clearly: "What is to remain then will obviously not be the Church, on the one hand, and the State, on the other; it will be the divine society of God's elect and the diabolical society of the reprobate . . . these two pairs of terms are quite distinct."[48] In a refutation of the application of Augustine's ideas for the creation of a single city or political body, Gilson notes that such a concept is inconsistent with Augustine's stark distinction between the two cities. For Gilson, the City of God alone inspired men with the desire to organize the earth and harmonize it as much as possible with the heavenly city. Gilson argues that, on its own, "temporal human society" could not endow itself with unity or provide a unifying inspiration.[49] Jacques Maritain dissents from Gilson on this point noting that there is a "genuine temporal community" of mankind, which exists beyond political borders. Maritain argues:

> For there exists a genuine temporal community of mankind—a deep intersolidarity, from generation to generation, linking together in solidarity, from generation to generation, linking together the peoples of the earth—a common heritage and a common fate, which do not concern the building of a particular *civil society*, but of *civilization*, not the prince, but culture, not the perfect *civitas* in the Aristotelian sense, but that kind of *civitas*, in the Augustinian sense, which is imperfect and incomplete, made up of a fluid network of human communications, and more existential than formally organized, but all the more real and living and basically important.[50]

47. Ibid., 181.
48. Ibid.
49. Gilson, *St. Augustine's City of God*, lxxx.
50. Jacques Maritain, "The End of Machiavellianism," in *The Social and Political Philosophy of Jacques Maritain*, ed. Joseph W Evans and Leo R. Ward (New York: Charles Scribners's Sons, 1955), 319. It must be recalled that this debate is within the discussion of international community that

Beyond arguing for the hopes of international community, Gilson sought to address the sacralization of the state in the Middle Ages, and related accusations made against Augustine and his Scholastic interpreters. He contends that Augustine neither defined the medieval ideal nor condemned it in advance. In fact, Gilson sees almost a natural progression from the securing of doctrinal unity by the ancient Church into the medieval "sacral era."[51] Indeed, though not explicitly referencing the Donatist controversy, Gilson notes that while the pagan *civitas* could tolerate any theology, the *City of God* could accept only one. "In choosing its own truth, heresy acts as a destructive force, aroused by the devils, to destroy from within the City of God at the exact moment when, by the grace of God, it was beginning to triumph over its enemies from without. Thence did the Church . . . derive the imperious duty of doctrinal intolerance . . ."[52] Gilson sees the medieval state as a response to the fundamental belief that the unity of faith was essential to the state's very existence. Hence, civil intervention was necessary when the unity of faith was threatened. To this point, the Donatist controversy was utilized as a precedent.

Gilson admits the potential problems this solution poses, namely that the city of God requires no such intervention by the state, as the heavenly city and its unity are secured beyond this world. The decision to intervene would also vary according to different situations, and excesses could occur.[53] However, when addressing

---

arose after both World Wars, initially in the League of Nations and later in the establishment of the United Nations.

51. Maritain, "The End of Machiavellianism," 116. "Sacral era" is Maritain's preferred term. Maritain himself saw the end of this era as arising from religious division once again manifested in the Reformation. From a Scholastic context similar to Gilson, Maritain also makes the connection between the securing of theological unity and the medieval concept of sacred and temporal authority.

52. Gilson, *St. Augustine's City of God*, lxx. Here Gilson cites *City of God* XVIII, 51. Also, Gilson notes that this point is significant in the work of Gustave Combès, who will be discussed in the next section.

the issue of the Christian state that would historically emerge after Augustine's death, Gilson seems to give away some of those previously stated cautions:

> What does remain strictly and absolutely true is that under no circumstances can the earthly city, much less the City of God, be identified with any form of State whatsoever. But the State can, and even should, be used on occasion for the Church's own ends and, through her, for the ends of the City of God, is an entirely different matter . . . Although he never formulated the principle explicitly, the notion of a theocratic government is not incompatible with his doctrine, for even though the ideal of the City of God does not include such a notion, it does not exclude it either. [54]

The Impact and Subsequent Evaluation of Gilson's Interpretation

Gilson's work must be read largely as a presentation of the Augustinian roots of Scholasticism. Admittedly, scholastic thinkers sought a more rational and empirical philosophical method, much to the consternation of the Augustinian school. As a result, Gilson's reading of Augustine remains one largely shaped by this Scholastic effort. He explains in his Giffords Lecture around nine years after his study of St. Augustine, "Thus I call Christian, every philosophy which, although keeping the two orders formally distinct, nevertheless considers the Christian revelation as an indispensable auxiliary to reason."[55] It is for this reason that Gilson's work is often joined to the work of Dominican theologian Pierre-Félix

---

53. Ibid., lxxi.

54. Gilson, *The Christian Philosophy*, 182. This argument will be drawn upon H.-X. Arquillière, who will argue for a "political Augustinianism" in continuity with Augustine's thought. Gilson's thesis here of Augustinian ambivalence will also later be contradicted directly by H. Marrou and even later by R. Markus.

55. Étienne Gilson, *The Spirit of Medieval Philosophy: Gifford Lectures 1931-1932*, trans. A. H. C. Downes (London: Sheed and Ward, 1936): 37.

Mandonnet, who wrote at the turn of the nineteenth century.[56] Henri de Lubac described Mandonnet as a defender of Scholasticism "against the reproach of not having known how to distinguish between the domains of science and dogma . . . Augustinianism was characterized in all domains by a tendency to absorb the 'natural' (human) order into the 'supernatural.'"[57] De Lubac notes that while this tendency appears in Gilson's work as well, Gilson's *Introduction* attempted to moderate Mandonnet's position. However, Arquillière, as we shall see below, builds upon Gilson's work to corroborate Mandonnet's interpretation of Augustine's absorption of the natural order.[58]

De Lubac rejects this Augustinian interpretation and argues that Augustine's discussion of justice does not call for a state based on "evangelical justice," and, as a result, Mandonnet, Gilson and Arquillière have all in this way missed Augustine's true meaning.[59] De Lubac notes that Augustine did not seek to write a Christian doctrine of statehood or citizenship in *City of God*, but rather sought to show that there are two loves which lead to two cities, the former built upon love of self and the latter built upon the love of God. These cities remain mixed until the end of the world, and hence that tension is embodied also in each human being. What is required of the Christian in Augustine's view is fidelity, as those who remain faithful are the saints, the citizens of the heavenly city. De Lubac explains:

> As they are in Christian dogmatics, the two perspectives, personal and communal, are mixed, and, according to good interpreters, this results

---

56. See Piette-Félix Mandonnet, *Siger de Brabant et l'Averroïsme latin au XIIIᵉ siècle. Étude critique et documents inédits par Pierre Mandonnet, O. P.* (Fribourg: Libraire de l'Université, 1899).

57. De Lubac, *Theological Fragments*, 236-237.

58. Ibid. See note 8, 237.

59. Ibid., 245. Many of de Lubac's criticisms here will be echoed and expanded upon by Robert Dodaro and other contemporary authors who reject the "Augustinian" nature of the theory of "political Augustinianism."

in a certain vagueness here and there. But it is all the more important to observe that they are interdependent . . . there is no ambiguity of the sort to direct the reader to the wrong road followed by the 'Augustinists'—or their modern inventors. And even today, we are not following the footsteps of Augustine, but very simply the biblical revelation faithfully pursued by Augustine . . . *'Jerusalem, quae aedificatur ut civitas.'*[60]

Gilson is significant, therefore, in the historiography of this discussion for several reasons. First, he demonstrates the early twentieth century effort within Catholic theology that maintained direct continuity between Augustine and Aquinas. He advocated such continuity through the discussion of humanity's ultimate ends in God, the necessity of supernatural grace, the distinction between the supernatural and temporal order, and the necessity of a unity of faith under Truth. Also, Gilson is influential in this debate because of his strong distinction of the temporal and sacred order. While more moderate than Mandonnet, Arquillière interprets this distinction as part of an Augustinian tradition of subverting temporal authority. Gilson, however, in an observation similar to that of Joseph Ratzinger, justifies this distinction by asserting the transient nature of the temporal order, which is relative to earthly legislators and fails to satiate the ultimate desires of man.

What the Church did in the Middle Ages, according to Gilson, is not subvert the temporal order, but attempt to secure a unity of faith not based around a cult of the state, but ordered to truth. While Gilson does entertain the possibility of a theocratic state as consistent with Augustine's theology, Arquillière's accusation of an Augustinian rooted subversion of the temporal order appears an oversimplification of Catholic theology in this period. However, as we will see below, despite the protestations of de Lubac, "political Augustinianism"

---

60. Ibid., 246.

would overshadow Gilson's work and Augustinian interpretation in general during the first half of the twentieth century.

Henri-Xavier Arquillière

The connection between Augustine and his medieval interpreters alluded to by von Gierke and others was finally given a name by the French philosopher Henri-Xavier Arquillière, in his 1934 work *L'augustinisme politique: Essai sur la formation des théories politiques du Moyen Âge.* Arquillière's concept of "political Augustinianism" argues that the work of Augustine subsequent thinkers and churchmen during the Middle Ages—especially Gregory the Great, Isidore of Seville, Gregory VII, and Giles of Rome—all pursued the subordination and subsequent absorption of the civic order by the supernatural order of the Church. Arquillière commented on this tendency, which he observed most especially in the papacy of Gregory VII: "One dominant idea becomes clear, from the early years of [Gregory's] pontificate: he is responsible for the salvation of the world, so the papacy must reign everywhere, as sovereigns among their subjects secure Christian justice, as an essential condition of salvation."[61] For Arquillière, there is continuity between the subsequent medieval conception of the unity of temporal and ecclesial power and the vision of St. Augustine put forward in *De Civitate Dei.*

---

61. *Henri-Xavier Arquillière, L'augustinisme politique: Essai sur la formation des théories politiques du Moyen Âge* (Paris: J. VRIN, 1955), 27. All Translations are my own unless otherwise noted.

Arquillière's Theory of Political Augustinianism

In attempting to trace the thought of Hildebrand, Arquillière notes that Christ himself had recognized the legitimate authority of the state, and that the separation of the political and religious domain was initially consistent with the Gospel itself. Furthermore, the divine nature of political rule was invoked from man's very nature, as the social nature of man created in God's image and likeness implied also the "indispensable conditions for social life." He wrote, "The authority of a chief and the obedience of his subordinates . . . There is the foundation, willed by God, upon which States and nations are based—well before the existence of the Church."[62] However, Arquillière argues that a shift from this view occurred in Augustine, whose vision absorbed the natural order into the supernatural.[63] This transition was accomplished, in Arquillière's opinion, primarily by the placement of true justice and true peace in the heavenly city, and the insistence that only a symbolic resemblance of justice and peace could be present in the earthly *civitas*. Indeed, grace was the only source of any trace of justice and peace, as man's nature without it remained marred by the sin of Adam and unable to promote the virtue and concord characteristic of the heavenly city. As Arquillière comments, "One can still note that for the African thinker, scarred by memories of his youth, nature appears as the generator of sin."[64] There was, therefore, a tendency, Arquillière believed, in Augustine that led to the absorption of natural law into the realm of supernatural justice, "the right of the State into that of the Church."[65] It was this

---

62. Ibid., 37.
63. See Piette-Félix Mandonnet, *Siger de Brabant et l'Averroïsme latin au XIII° siècle. Étude critique et documents inédits par Pierre Mandonnet, O. P.* (Fribourg: Libraire de l'Université, 1899). See also, Étienne Gilson, *Introduction à l'étude de saint Augustin* (Paris: J. Vrin, 1929).
64. Arquillière, *L'augustinisme politique*, 64.
65. Ibid., 54.

"tendency" in Augustine, while not expressly taught by the Bishop of Hippo, which grew into a doctrine for his later disciples.[66]

Augustine maintained rather nuanced distinctions both between rational speculation and faith and nature and grace, which reflected the reality of human life. Arquillière believed that such nuances were lost upon his disciples, who simplified the nuances of the great bishop and theologian. For Arquillère, such confusion and simplification was embodied by Gelasius and later Gregory the Great. Pope Gelasius in the late fifth century argued that while two powers governed men, the sacred authority of the Pontiff and the royal power of the sovereign, the latter remained more powerful as it corresponded to the "supreme judgment."[67] Arquillière notes that this sentiment would be taken up by Gregory the Great and would expand with the entrance of Gothic tribes into Rome. He summarized this movement:

> [Gregory the Great] speaks of the pontiff who, with the help of princes, is concentrated on the restriction of the reign of sin and the promotion of the action of grace. The mission of the religious king had, by its very nature, become paramount in a Christianized society. It captures, from the beginning, the confusion of powers which would mark the Middle Ages, the essentially spiritual character of pontifical intervention. We can say that by introducing Christian morality in politics, by inculcating the duty of kings with the discipline of the Church, Gregory opened an unlimited opening for the interventions of the Holy See.[68]

Arquillière notes that Augustine interpreted the thirteenth chapter of St. Paul's Letter to the Romans as a mandate for Christians to submit to legitimate civil authority and fulfill their civic responsibilities. Augustine believed that the order established by God for man included political rule and the need for submission to that rule.[69]

66. Ibid., 55.
67. Ibid., 40.
68. Ibid., 40.
69. Ibid., 118.

However, unlike many Fathers of the Church, Augustine strongly criticizes the pagan state and its persecution using theological arguments. Here, the Bishop of Hippo applies the notion of Christian justice to the condition of pagan Rome and its inability to access true justice as a result of its public religion. Arquillière writes:

> He applies his concept of justice to the state. He examines the notion of the state itself. He appealed to Cicero, the Stoics. He compares their ideas with the Christian idea of justice. As we have seen he exalts the concept of 'real' justice, that which is born of faith and grace, compared to the Roman state—which worshiped false gods and hence seems unworthy of this name.[70]

Arquillière believed that Augustine had laid foundations for the modern state in his concept of the necessity of obedience to a sovereign despite religion or conduct. Indeed, the modern state would, like Augustine, see the natural order as including political life and seek to build a commonwealth without appeals to revelation or grace. These observations from Augustine's work were not immediately acted upon, and Arquillière argued that this delay was due to the medieval assertion of the spiritual over temporal power. He wrote, "Moreover, the spread of the ancient foundations of the natural state are initially delayed as a result of the new Christianized worldview, until they reappear again and crystallize as the topic of the Modern Age."[71]

Arquillière saw in Gregory the Great the embodiment of the transition from Augustine's thought to "political Augustinianism." It would be Gregory the Great who would assume "secular power" as a result of Rome's fall and the entrance of Germanic tribes seeking imperial legitimacy.[72] The subordination of political authority under

70. Ibid., 119.
71. Ibid., 120.
72. Ibid., 121.

the authority of the Apostolic See would continue for Arquillière with Isidore of Seville, and most especially with Gregory VII. Douglas Kries has summarized Arquilliere's vision of this process, "The slow, even unconscious, erosion of the natural foundations of politics triumphed in the era which saw the ascendancy of the medieval papacy." He continues, "[Augustine's] obfuscation of the boundary between the natural and the supernatural did lend itself to the interpretations of those subsequent Christians who would be more rigorous in drawing out conclusions regarding the subordinate character of the political realm."[73]

The Impact of Arquillière's Work

While Arquillière saw his work in line with the thought of Mandonnet and Gilson, his implication of Augustine, admittedly through his interpreters, as creating the intellectual foundations for the medieval conception of a "sacred *imperium*" has remained a controversial point of debate. Indeed, the needed separation of Augustine from his interpreters has been one of the chief criticisms of Arquillière's concept of "l'augustinisme politique," which began to be cited widely after the work's publication. This problematic identification of Augustine and his subsequent interpreters has been identified succinctly by Ernest Fortin:

> Since the days of Pope Gregory VII, the Church often threatened to absorb the temporal power in accordance with a trend that the late H. X. Arquillière misleadingly dubbed "political Augustinianism.' I say 'misleadingly' because it is not at all evident that the papal absolutism of Augustine's medieval disciples can be traced to Augustine himself. At the same time, the Church was thrust into the position of having to defend

---

73. Douglas Kries, "Political Augustinianism," in *Augustine Through the Ages*, 657.

its own independence against the encroachments of an ever more highly centralized temporal authority . . .[74]

The concept of "political Augustinianism" has been, therefore, both embraced and rejected. Henri de Lubac forcefully dismisses Arquilliére's thesis, noting, "Neither in St. Augustine's work nor even in that of the theologians of the first part of the Middle Ages, whether or not they refer expressly to him, does one find the kind of 'political Augustinism' that so curiously blossomed in the work of Giles of Rome and his emulators . . . In short, the Augustinism in question here is not the work of St. Augustine. It is more like the reverse of true Augustinism."[75] Elsewhere, de Lubac laments, "A limpid and simple explanation based on the thesis of a prestigious book transforms ten centuries of history into a series of consequences whose development, in spite of the novelties it created, appears marvelously uniform."[76] Yves Congar also dissented from the political characterization of Augustine's *City of God*, noting that the work was composed and must be read in an "ethical and spiritual point of view," not as a political program.[77]

In a similar vein, Robert Dodaro has argued that Arquillière's discussion of the natural and supernatural order is itself the wrong question, and has bemoaned the impact of Arquillière's faulty thesis, namely an inevitable controversy derailing the discussion of authentic Augustinian political and social thought.[78] Dodaro argues:

---

74. Ernest Fortin, "The Aristotelian Revolution," in *Classical Christianity and the Political Order: Reflections on the Theologico-Political Problem*, ed. J. Brian Benestad (Lanham, MD: Rowman & Littlefield, 1996), 184. We will discuss Fortin's work in greater detail in the next chapter.

75. De Lubac, *Theological Fragments*, 241. De Lubac presents in this article a systematic refutation of Arquillière's argument, which he calls a "regrettable theory" and a "fiction."

76. Ibid., 259.

77. Yves Congar, O. P., *L'Eglise dans le monde de ce temps*, Tome I (Paris: Cerf, 1967), 85.

78. Gratitude is owed to Professor R. Dodaro for granting me access to an unpublished manuscript of a paper delivered at Ave Maria University in Naples, Florida, in 2005, entitled "Augustine and the Debate Concerning 'Political Augustinianism.'"

In my view, Arquillière asked the wrong question of Augustine's texts. Stemming as it did from the equally maladroit fixation by Mandonnet and Gilson on what they claimed was a lack in Augustine's thought of a formal distinction between the natural and supernatural realms . . . Augustine, in my view, is far less interested than his interpreters in discussing the respective merits of a Christian or secular state.[79]

While many have argued, like de Lubac and Dodaro, that the discussion of Augustine's social and political thought has been taken off course by Arquillière's concern for political categories, which were of minimal importance to Augustine himself, Arquillière's work has influenced others. His focus on Augustine's concept of *res publica* and the question of its need for true justice, drawn from the practice of true religion, has been influential. Henri Irénée Marrou disagreed and responded to Arquillière's work by noting the "mixed nature" of human existence, and suggested the presence in Augustine of a *tertium quid*, namely the reality of a *saeculum* where the two cities overlap.[80]

Arquilliére's argument that there is a subversion of the temporal order in Augustine's thought and an isolation of political matters in his corpus would be embraced and built upon by Robert Markus. Markus would also expand Marrou's *tertium quid*, neutralizing this overlapping space of the two cities of the influences of any belief or value system in his notion of *saeculum*. Markus argued, "The main lines of his thinking about history, society and human institutions in general (the *saeculum*) point towards a political order to which we may not unreasonably apply the anachronistic epithet 'pluralist,' in

79. Ibid., Dodaro posits that Augustine neither secularizes or sacralizes the state, but rather his true concern is the promotion of civic virtue. We will discuss Dodaro's thesis more extensively later in this work.

80. Henri Irénée Marrou, "Civitas Dei, civitas terrena: num tertium quid?" *Studia Patristica. Papers presented to the Second International Conference in Patristic Studies held at Christ Church, Oxford*, vol. 2., ed. Kurt Aland and Frank Leslie Cross (Berlin: 1957), 348. We will discuss Marrou's argument in further detail below.

that it is neutral in respect of ultimate beliefs and values."[81] It must be stated that Markus's insistence on neutrality, or the "secularization," of human society under the guise of Augustinian thought is contrary to Arquillière's thesis. However, his interpretation of Augustine relies and builds upon Arquillière's notion that there is continuity in the "political Augustinian" tradition from Augustine to Gregory the Great. Peter Brown has described the influence of this concept on Robert Markus:

> He [Markus] traced, between late antiquity and the early middle ages, an eclipse of the sense of the autonomy of the *saeculum*—a growing lack of recognition of the role of pre-Christian skills, of respect for the resilience of non-Christian social structures, and a narrowing of the wide diversity of interests and of life trajectories which the late antique world still had offered to believing Christians. By the time of Gregory the Great, the withering of a sense of the secular had led, in his opinion, to a definitive end of the ancient world and to the beginning of the middle ages.[82]

Recognizing the ongoing debate and the varied responses Arquillière's work has inspired, Douglas Kries concludes that while influential, there remains a fundamental ambiguity in Arquillière's thesis. "Arquillière thus implies that there is a sense in which 'political Augustinianism' is something of a misnomer, and a sense in which it is not."[83] This ambiguity has opened the door to numerous contemporary commentators and interpreters of Augustine of Hippo, and has made Arquillière's discussion a significant step forward in the contemporary discussion of Augustine's social and political vision.

---

81. Robert Markus, *Saeculum: History and Society in the Theology of St. Augustine* (Cambridge: Cambridge University Press, 1970), 151. Markus's thesis will be laid out and discussed in more detail in chapter 3.
82. Peter Brown, "Introducing Robert Markus," *Augustinian Studies* 32:2 (2001), 184-185.
83. Douglas Kries, "Political Augustinianism," in *Augustine Through the Ages: An Encyclopedia*, ed. Allan Fitzgerald, O. S. A., (Grand Rapids, MI: Eerdmans, 2002), 658.

Henri Irénée Marrou

The Augustinian scholar and French historian, Henri Irénée Marrou, wrote during the middle of the twentieth century. In the midst of Europe's own crisis and devastation, Marrou like other thinkers set his gaze on St. Augustine, who lived during a period of similar crisis and transition. However, unlike other historians, who envisioned Augustine's age in a negative or diminutive light, Marrou saw it as a pivotal period and helped usher in the historical category of Late Antiquity.[84] Marrou's biographer, Pierre Riché, has noted in his recent work *Henri Irénée Marrou: Historien Engagé*, this unique approach:

> His interest does not dissociate his study [of Augustine] from that of the cultures of civilizations. If he dedicated part of his work as a historian to St. Augustine, this is certainly because of the genius of the bishop of Hippo and the greatness of his work, but probably also because he [Augustine] lived through the crisis of the Roman Empire . . . it led to reflection on revising the standard clichés and substituting the disparaging name of the Lower Empire, with the simple chronological term of late Antiquity. This means that the historian has gone deeper than the scholar.[85]

Marrou and an Augustinian Influenced Theology of History

A crucial moment in the discussion of "political Augustinianism" occurred in the 1954 *Congrès International Augustien* held in Paris. In that congress, Arquillière, Marrou, Joseph Ratzinger, and other Augustinian scholars were present, and the concept of "political Augustinianism" was raised. Marrou's paper presented at that

---

84. This shift opens up the field of study now regularly associated with Peter Brown and Robert Markus.

85. Pierre Riché, *Henri Irénée Marrou: Historien Engagé* (Paris: Cerf, 2003), 8.

congress, "La Théologie de l'Histoire," which hinges on Augustine's *City of God*, is important in both understanding Marrou's own interpretation of Augustine and his influence on so many subsequent interpreters of Augustine's political and social thought.[86] Marrou believed that any philosophy of history had to include a theology of history, namely some way of explaining the continuation of time, which lies beyond our understanding. This need was understood by Augustine himself, who saw a "historical mentality" as essential and indeed unique to Christianity.[87]

> Augustine is much more reserved in his judgments on known history: like him we can identify the limits of our knowledge, and the reasons for those limits. Theology of history is a knowledge that is derived from faith, and as such, *per speculum et in aenigmate*, partial, filled with darkness, and at once ignorant and certain. As a result it would be necessary to explore the deep roots of this mystery of history . . . History has not been completed, and we can no longer think that you can not judge a melody before the final cadence or that it makes sense only in its ending.[88]

The judgment of the "melody" of history before its end, however, is only secured by a theology of history, namely by the Christian understanding that history's climax has broken into time itself.[89] However, Marrou recognized the secularization present within the Christian understanding of history, largely due to problematic interpretations of Augustine. The first such interpretation, as we have observed in the discussion of Combés, was that of Jacques-Bénigne Bossuet, who directly connected the Christian *civitas* and

---

86. Marrou's theology of history" has been comprehensively surveyed by Gianluigi Pasquale, O. F. M. Cap., *La Teologia della Storia della Salvezza nel Secolo XX* (Bologna: Edizione Dehoniane Bologna, 2001), 355-372.

87. Henri Irénée Marrou, "La Théologie de l'Histoire," in *Augustinus Magister: Congrès International Augustinien* (Paris: Études Augustiniennes, 1954), 196.

88. Ibid., 196-197.

89. This would be formulated by Oscar Cullmann, *Christ and Time: The Primitive Christian Conception of Time and History* (Philadelphia: Westminster Press, 1950).

its spiritual society with the visible Church and the building of the *civitas dei* on earth. As Gianluigi Pasquale has noted, "This error formalized by Bossuet—which is part of the consolidated medieval tradition—consisted in a principle of secularization that projected the absolute in the relative, the transcendent in the empirical."[90] The second cause of secularization for Marrou lies in Enlightenment thought, namely the work of R. Turgot and Voltaire, who while preserving an Augustinian dialectic in history, replaced Augustine's categories with the search of "ideas" for the sake of "humanity" and "freedom." Marrou argues that this is a direct "precursor to Hegel."[91]

As a result of this secularization, and at times manipulation, of St. Augustine's vision, Marrou believed that a proper Augustinian vision had to be recovered, and hence the *City of God* had to be revisited. For Marrou, human history in Augustine remains necessarily connected to the economy of salvation. He comments, "The difficulty between Augustine and us is the proper object of his theology, and I think also that of the theology of history, the historical object itself, it is the economy of salvation; the history of mankind, the real adventure, the real issue that history recounts, it is the history of salvation, *Heilsgeschicte*."[92] Marrou argued that while history reached its height and gained its full meaning in Christ, Christ's "mystical body" on earth grows and journeys in history towards its fulfillment in the *parousia*. He explained in his 1968 work, *Théologie de l'Histoire*, which expanded on his initial treatment of the subject, "The duration of our history is the time necessary for the recruitment of the population of saints and the building of the City of God. All of the Fathers agree on this point."[93] As Pasquale points

---

90. Pasquale, *La Teologia della Storia*, 356. Marrou himself mentions Bossuet in his study. See Marrou, "La Théologie de l'Histoire," 196.
91. Ibid., 193.
92. Ibid., 202.

out, "The major coherent approach with which to open the twelve books of *De Civitate Dei* is essentially to see expressed this 'mystery of history.'"[94]

In his rejection of this secularization of Augustine's vision and his subsequent call to recover the theological and soteriological essence of Augustine's *De Civitate Dei*, Marrou directly confronts and rejects Arquillière's concept of *l'augustinisme politique*. For Marrou, such a school of thought is a continuation within Christian theology of the secularization that has plagued it and a deflation of Augustine's theological vision into historical and political banalities. Arquillière's theory for Marrou contributes to the continual misplacement of the true object of history itself and the theology of history, which lies not in earthly fulfillment but eternal salvation. It is not the drama of humanity that is important in history, but the history of humanity's salvation. Augustine's work is an attempt to explain and point out that humanity's history is forever intertwined with the very economy of humanity's salvation in accord with the will of the Creator and Father of history itself.[95] For Marrou, the focus on contemporary issues and the application of Augustine's thought on political and social questions misses the point of Augustine's work. He states his concerns quite clearly at the 1954 Paris congress:

> And we demand in Augustine the interpretation of problems—which preoccupy us: the rights and duties of the state, the rapport between ecclesial and civil power, and who knows what else? Why do civilizations flourish and disappear, why do political regimes, class relations evolve or clash? The misunderstanding [of Augustine] has

93. Henri Irénée Marrou, *Théologie de l'Histoire* (Paris: Seuil, 1968), 40-41. In this later work, Marrou will also open up the category of ontological sense and knowledge, which in the discussion of the person became a point of contact with philosophy. I believe one can see here a bridge to the work of Gaetano Lettieri, whom we will discuss later. See in this work pages 64-66.

94. Pasquale, *La Teologia della storia*, 361.

95. See Marrou, "La Théologie de l'Histoire," 40-41.

persisted for centuries: the drama of what Mgr. Arquillière and his school have called *l'Augustinisme politique* lies in this series of transpositions. It might be useful, before examining Augustine for our own problems, to allow ourselves to listen first to what he himself has chosen to teach us, and what lies, for the Christian, as the central problem.[96]

It is in light of this refutation that Marrou lays the foundations for his concept of a *tertium quid* in Augustine's vision of two cities. It is an attempt to refute Bossuet and the subsequent secularization of Christian history. Within this concept, Marrou sought the recovery of Augustine's fundamental concept of *commixtio*. Marrou argued that while Augustine laid out two cities, he also included a third element in his vision, namely their overlap. The *civitas dei* and the *civitas terrena* remain for Augustine mixed together and cannot be humanly separated. He does note that two loves regulate the two cities, and that the cities remain essentially different. Furthermore, Marrou sees little possibility for optimism in history, precisely because of the evil and sin that govern the earthly city and remains a historical and anthropological reality as a result of original sin.[97] Therefore, while mixed there remains a fundamental tension between the two cities, whose essence is different but whose borders on earth are impossible to draw. Marrou notes:

> . . . and a third element, difficult to designate with specific terms but which is essential to the historical order, which appears to us as the inextricable and provisory *commixtio* (the still unfinished story of the mystery) of the two cites, or as developed elsewhere in Augustine's evangelical terms, this *commixtio* of good grain and chaff, grain and straw, the good and bad of the miraculous catch.[98]

96. Ibid., 202-203.
97. Marrou, "La Théologie de l'Histoire," 198. Here, Marrou, while parting from Niebuhr's concept of original sin, also praises his insistence on a concrete understanding of time and history in Augustine.
98. Ibid., 202.

Marrou argued that the overlap of the two cities in history allowed for more than simply the presence of sinfulness in earthly city, but also it demonstrated the concrete influence of the saints on humanity. "Between them and us is established a communion, a fertile communication. Each one of us can measure how in his Christian life and his awareness of the exigencies that faith require one or another great figure of the passed has influenced us. How they are present among us active and real as the closest of friends and teachers . . ."[99] Marrou, while appearing here to offer a spiritual perspective, in reality presents the object and fundamental theme of Augustine's *City of God*, namely holiness and participation in the history of salvation. This vision of the *tertium quid* as an experience of "fertile communication" and the "exigencies of faith" presents Marrou's vision of the *tertium quid*, and remains contrary to Markus's secularized *saeculum*.

Marrou's *Tertium Quid*

A year after suggesting that a "third element" is present in Augustine's vision of two cities, in 1955 at Christ Church, Oxford, expanded his argument in another paper, "Civitas Dei, civitas terrena: num tertium quid?" Here, Marrou argues that the question of a third element hinges on the textual interpretation of various passages in both Augustine's *De Civitate Dei* and *Enarrationes in Psalmos*, in which the formula *civitas Dei, civitas terrena* appears. Marrou cites Joseph Ratzinger's lament that there has been a "habitual misinterpretation of the famous formula."[100] Marrou cites the intervention of Joseph Ratzinger in the *Augustinus Magister* Conference, who argued that

---

99. Ibid., 366. Pasquale notes that this insight is influenced by Leopold von Ranke's insight that each era of history stands equidistant from eternity. Pasquale, *La Teologia della storia*, 365.
100. Marrou, "Civitas Dei, civitas terrena," 343.

many false interpretations arise from the misunderstanding and manipulation of Augustine's term "mystical."[101] While Augustine uses the term *mystice* to describe the two cities in *City of God*, 15:1, it signifies the "spiritual sense of the Scriptures." Marrou also shares Charles Journet's insight that the *City of God* encapsulates "everything in history, in man who is *secundum Deum* . . . the camp of values belonging to Christ opposing the camp of values belonging to the Prince of this world."[102]

While some have sought the identification of the hierarchical and sacramental Church with the City of God, Marrou, like Journet, is aware that Augustine often reaffirms the earthly assembly of both good and evil, which forms the *ecclesia permixta*. He notes, therefore, that this dynamic is also present in "the assembly of each historical society empirically observed . . ."[103] The empirical reality of *commixtio* in both the Church and amongst the citizens of the earthly *civitas* informs much of Marrou's insight about a possible *tertium quid*. One element of Augustine's *commixtio* put forward by Journet is the presence of *infravalentes* among human societies. While not equal to the supreme *supravalentes* of the heavenly city, they allow for the ordering of civilization and temporal, cultural and human goods. Journet notes, "Underneath the theology of the two mystical cities, St. Augustine himself has pointed out a place of a third city, that is often confused with the city of the devil, and it is the city of man, with its great *infravalentes* (Greek philosophy, Roman valor, earthly peace, etc.)."[104]

101. Ibid.
102. Ibid. Marrou cites here Journet's *L'Eglise du Verbe Incarné*. See *L'Eglise du Verbe Incarné* IV: *Essai de théologie de l'histoire du salut* (Saint Maurice: Editions Saint Augustin, 2004), 78.
103. Ibid., 344.
104. Ibid.

Marrou believed that this insight of Journet had clear implications for understanding the context of human existence and action in light of Augustine's *City of God*. Marrou argues that within "the platonic atmosphere" of Augustine it would be obvious that there existed temporal goods present in history that related to the ultimate goods of the *civitas dei*.[105] The platonic influences of Augustine seem here to be Marrou's as well:

> The property is not defined as property without the use that men make of it. Man on the other hand is one: it is the same man who uses air, water, everything that has been tailored to food, the protection and care of his body and is secondly the subject of a supernatural vocation to eternal happiness or damnation, and it is the use he has made of the same earthly goods that will determine his or her conviction.[106]

There must, therefore, be a space where humanity decides how to use the goods they are given, all the while those goods themselves remain partial manifestations of their fullness in the *civitas dei*. Marrou focuses here on Augustine's treatment of peace. Augustine made clear that the *pax temporalis* could be secured by man, but it remained relative and temporary in light of the *pax finalis*.[107] He elaborates this idea:

> But, and this is essential, these earthly goods retain their positive value, they are goods emerging from the social condition of man . . . The Augustinian doctrine of peace is inseparable from that of *ordinata dilectio*, peace is *tranquilitas ordinis* and order is the hierarchy of beings, who determines the hierarchy of loves, appetites, uses.[108]

Marrou, in light of the concrete historical reality of man and the historical context of his actions, puts forward a *tertium quid*, an

---

105. Ibid., 343.
106. Ibid., 346.
107. Ibid., 345.
108. Ibid., 346-347. Here Marrou cites *City of God* XIX, 13 and also Augustine's discussion of the hierarchy of loves and desires in *City of God* XIX, 14 and XIX, 17.

autonomous third reality called the *saeculum*. It is not a mere coincidence that the term refers to the New Testament word *aiôn*, the new age brought about by Christ. This term used by Augustine in *City of God* XV is central to his understanding of human history after the Incarnation of Christ, as it awaits its fulfillment. Augustine uses this term to describe the history of the two cities, "For the history of the two cities of which we are speaking extends throughout the whole of this time or *age* in which the dying pass away and the newly-born take their place."[109]

Recognizing that during this time good and evil, the city of God and the city of the devil remain inextricably mixed, Marrou introduces this concept of *saeculum*, as human existence in historical time.[110] The *saeculum* is not, Robert Markus would later explain, "a no-man's land between the two cities . . . but it is the temporal life in their interwoven, perplexed and only eschatologically separable reality."[111] This *saeculum* is indeed tense and suffers from the disorder that is inherent in man's condition, but it is also the space where temporal peace can be secured and where the partial manifestations of man's goods can be utilized. It is, therefore, the time of choice and the moment when man exercises his freedom, and hence his citizenship in one of the two cities. Marrou concludes by drawing from his theology of history and the insights of Charles Journet:

> And this is the last word of the Augustinian doctrine, which establishes what we might call the mystery of history: as long as the *saeculum* has not closed its *ordo temporum*, as long as we contemplate history with our eyes of flesh, it appears as an inextricable mixture of good seed and tares–and love as Mgr. Journet has said, the border between the cites of good and evil passes for each of us inside his own heart.[112]

---

109. *CG* XV, 1: 634.
110. Marrou, "Civitas dei, civitas terrena," 348.
111. Robert Markus, *Saeculum: History and Society in the Theology of St. Augustine* (Cambridge: Cambridge University Press, 1970), 71.

The Impact of Marrou's Concept of *Saeculum*

Marrou's introduction of *saeculum* as a *tertium quid* amidst Augustine's two cities must be viewed in light of his larger effort of addressing the secularization of the Christian theology of history. His *saeculum* is introduced to provide an alternative to the conflation of the *civitas dei* and *civitas terrena*, which has steadily resulted from the work of Bossuet, Voltaire and Enlightenment thinkers, especially Hegel.[113] Marrou, as a historian, was aware also of the dangers within Christianity itself of the absence of a *tertium quid*. Marrou observed in late antiquity how the Church had to take a leading role in culture and society in light of a collapsing Roman empire, and he utilizes Maritain's term of "sacral Christendom," to describe the results.[114] Where initially a "cultural symbiosis," as Markus has called it, was possible between Western society's classical tradition and its Christian faith, as the Middle Ages continued such symbiosis became less and less apparent. As Marrou wrote in his work, *St. Augustine and His Influence Through the Ages*:

> The *City of God*, well or ill understood, provides a framework of thought for the builders of that new political and social entity which is Christendom, and for the disputes brought forth by that ever-recurring conflict of the 'two swords,' the two powers of the Priesthood and of the Empire. (How the problems have changed! Not without distortion can the Augustinian solutions be adapted to them.)[115]

Perhaps the greatest impact of Marrou's work, however, lies in its reception and expansion by Robert Markus, who was greatly

---

112. Marrou, "Civitas Dei, Civitas Terrena," 350.
113. Hegel's role in this process is treated by Gianluigi Pasquale, *La Ragione della Storia: Per una filosofia della storia come scienza* (Torino: Bollati Boringhieri, 2011).
114. See Robert Markus, *Christianity and the Secular* (Notre Dame, IN: Univ. of Notre Dame Press, 2006), 78.
115. Henri Irénée Marrou, *St. Augustine and His Influence Through the Ages*, trans. Patrick Hepburne-Scott (New York: Harper Torchbooks, 1957), 158.

influenced by the concept of *saeculum* introduced by Marrou's paper in Paris, 1954. Markus understood this concept of *saeculum* as essential, the necessary "eschatological gap" between the proclamation of the Christian message and submission to it. Markus utilizes the image of two concentric circles:

> Christianity is committed—perhaps uniquely among world religions—to a belief in a Church that is, a visible community of believers distinct from political society. The two will always overlap but never coincide. The inner circle, the Church, is the sacramental anticipation of the future Kingdom which it is charged to proclaim to the world. The outer circle is the secular, the realm which is still in a state of waiting for the proclamation to be heard and received. It may be wider or it may be narrower; but it will always be there until the eschaton.[116]

One major difference, however, between Markus's conception of the *saeculum* and Marrou's introduction of the concept remains Markus's insistence on its neutrality. In his work, *Christianity and the Secular*, Markus connects this concept to John Rawls, as Markus sees the *saeculum* as a neutral public square where all religions and ideologies must equally make a claim to the citizenry and help build "overlapping consensus."[117] Markus speaks of Christianity's place in society, "A secular pluralist society will give it a hearing in open debate, without granting it a decisive or privileged voice."[118] It appears that Markus's interpretation of *saeculum* betrays Marrou's fundamental mission of addressing the secularization of the theology of history. Gilson provides an alternative to Markus's "neutral saeculum" by arguing that the *City of God* is "indifferent." "The City

---

116. Markus, *Christianity and the Secular*, 15. We will discuss Markus's ideas in more detail below.
117. This concept of "overlapping consensus," is used by Markus in Christianity and the Secular, 67. Rawls expresses it in John Rawls, *Political Liberalism* (New York: Columbia University Press, 2005), 13.
118. Robert A. Markus, "Political Order as Response to the Church's Mission," *Political Theology* 9, no. 3 (2008), 322.

of God is a stranger to every nation and ever state . . . it is indifferent to diversities of language, habits and customs, and attacks nothing, destroys nothing which is good and useful."[119]

One consistent criticism, therefore, of Markus's reception of Marrou's concept is the irrelevance of the Church in his vision of the public square. Marrou and Gilson maintain a different interpretation of Augustine, as the origin and end of history is known through "revelation."[120] The *saeculum*, which is itself "created," can never be devoid of the divine or ignore God's revelation. Revelation is the expression of the love of God from which every Augustinian ideal flows. How can such a *saeculum* be Augustinian?[121] The Church remains for Augustine the instrument of salvation, the dispenser of grace, and the authoritative interpreter of the Scriptures. Michael Hollerich has written a succinct critique of this problem in Markus's s*aeculum*. He writes:

> The reader is certainly left with the impression that the church and everything connected with it (sacraments, ministry, discipline, community life) occupied a reduced and even discretionary space in human life . . . The real 'action' was not in the church but in the world (i.e., the *saeculum*). Augustine saw no radical distinction between the church and the city of God . . . The church was nothing but the community of salvation insofar as its social practice, replicating its narration of the story of Jesus, embodied the forgiveness of sins and realized the bond of charity among its members. The church's *raison d'être* was the extension of its practice into the whole of human life, not excepting a putatively 'political' realm reserved for the competency of 'the state.'[122]

---

119. Gilson, *The Christian Philosophy*, 182.

120. Ibid., 183.

121. This question will be addressed later both in the discussion of Markus's ideas and in the analysis of the contemporary debate.

122. Michael Hollerich, "Milbank, Augustine, and the Secular," *Augustinian Studies* 30, no. 2 (1999), 12.

Henri de Lubac remained suspicious of the *tertium quid*, fearing that it would be used to relieve the antagonism of the two cities that is so essential to Augustine's vision. The fact that the cities remained both intertwined and essentially opposite points to the tension that Augustine envisioned for the Christian in an often hostile society. De Lubac, therefore, argued that the perception of the *saeculum* as a middle way and not simply the time and space of human history, was both wrong and threatened Augustine's vision.

> But in itself the antagonism of the two 'cities,' which Augustine always keeps in mind, has no political overtones. That is why certain historians' assiduous search through some of the passages for the outline of a 'third way,' which would reduce the antagonism, is in vain. They are either chasing a chimera or unconsciously professing a blasphemy. What middle way could be possible, what 'intermediate and middle region' between the two cities would be preferable? What Christian would dare to tarnish the Gospel in this way.[123]

De Lubac also argues that a third element is not necessary in Augustine's vision, and could potentially be detrimental to the overall impact of the work. The mystical nature of the two cities precisely shows that they are not political, and as a result Augustine can envision the two cities both opposed and mixed simultaneously without a logical contradiction emerging. It is, therefore, not contradictory to recognize in Augustine's work statements which recognize the presence of "natural law" or the legitimacy of political authority. Such elements are not contradictory with his vision because it is neither a political tract nor a platform for earthly society. In fact, de Lubac notes that Augustine imposes on Christians an obedience to temporal authority that preserves the Christian's "spiritual liberty."[124] Augustine has specifically tried to assure that the

---

123. De Lubac, *Theological Fragments*, 251.
124. Ibid., 253.

Christian does not have to sacrifice his conviction and faith in order to obey the power of the state. As de Lubac notes, it must never be forgotten that the author of the *City of God*, "desires, certainly, the conversion of everyone to the true God, a conversion that would of course affect morals and legislation."[125] De Lubac's analysis, therefore, serves as a stern caution in the interpretation of Augustine's *saeculum*, so that the authentic theological vision of Augustine's two cities will not be marred beyond recognition or lost completely.

"Political Augustinianism" at a Crossroads

Before we move away from the initial, largely French-based, discussion of Augustine's political and social ideas, it is important to address its early phase and the subsequent movement of this debate to the English-speaking world. To understand this shift there are, I believe, two important, intertwined elements in the twentieth century that have determined in each generation the level of engagement with Augustine, namely contemporary philosophical trends and the historical aftermath of two world wars.

The initial reading of Augustine's political and social thought flows from the "liberal school" of Protestant theology at the turn of the twentieth century, which Antonio Nitrola has described aptly as:

> The theological translation of Enlightenment optimism, the consecration of modern subjectivity that proposed itself as a standard without external limitations, especially those of dogmas or ecclesiastical laws. In this way this theology is 'liberal' because it expresses man freed, emancipated, matured, illuminated, recognizing only the authority of reason and the fruit of his research, a man that on the social level is represented by the bourgeoisie.[126]

---

125. Ibid., 254.
126. Antonio Nitrola, *Trattato di escatologia vol. 1: Spunti per un pensare escatologico* (Torino: Edizioni San Paolo, 2001), 38.

This theological school saw the discussion of the "kingdom of God" not in eschatological terms, but as the construction of a human community built on love.[127] It was imbued with an optimism and utopianism that seemed in little accord with the *City of God*. These tendencies can be observed in Figgis and Harnack, with the latter relating the kingdom of God directly to the rapport between God and man's own conscience.[128] Early twentieth century theology embraced the "secularization," of the philosophy of history and indeed hastened it. Arquilliére's theory of *l'augustinisme politique* in some ways reflects this trend and its popularity. The human community, the earthly *civitas*, becomes the object of examination and by many it is seen as the Kingdom of God being built on earth. The early twentieth century saw, therefore, a deflation of the two cities into one, and the eschatological *tension* that pervades Augustine's *City of God* is largely ignored.

World War I, however, changed the tenor of the theological discussion, as man's capacity for evil was seen in the violence that devastated Europe. This violence, the historical reality of war, contradicted and buried the optimism and utopianism so prevalent at the turn of the century. Barth and Bultmann's "dialectical" theology emerged, refusing the identification of the Kingdom of God with human progress or activity and rejecting the liberal theological method.[129] However, this would also lead to a resurgence and reexamination of Augustine of Hippo. Indeed, Figgis, Arquilliére, and Combés would all examine Augustine in this post-war context. While Figgis and Arquilliére retained some of the "liberal" school's tendencies in making Augustine's work programmatic for the human

---

127. Ibid., 39. Nitrola cites here A. Ritschl as a prime example of this shift.
128. Ibid., 40. Nitrola traces here Harnack and the early twentieth century liberal school of theology with detail and clarity.
129. Ibid., 59.

community, their focus and examination of Augustine is itself significant. Reinhold Niebuhr and Paul Ramsey would mark this transition as well. While both retained similar tendencies, their interest in Augustine during a post-war context is revealing. In fact, as we will discuss, Niebuhr maintains a "liberal" Protestant reading, but includes in his interpretation a realism undoubtedly influenced by the post-war experience. Here the importance of the historical context is made clear, as Augustine's reemergence would coincide with the ends of both World Wars. Both conflicts reveal the relevance of Augustine's eschatological vision and for a time quell utopian tendencies. Ernest Fortin noted in his 1972 work, *Political Idealism and Christianity in the Thought of St. Augustine*:

> Two closely related events have altered the intellectual climate of our time and supplied the framework for its liveliest theological and political debates: the resurgence of utopianism among the prophets of radical or egalitarian democracy and the programmatic violence which in recent years has frequently accompanied the demand for a just society.[130]

After World War II and the Augustinian interpretations of Reinhold Niebuhr and Paul Ramsey, among others, Fortin recounts the emergence of the "New Left" and the "revolutionary," at times Marxist-inspired, exegesis of the Gospel message (which we must not forget is also based on a secularized philosophy of history). This trend would later yield to nihilism, which spread throughout Europe and largely relegated the entire Augustinian discussion to specifically Christian circles. As Josef Pieper recounts:

> The wish-image of a reduction into nothingness, of an 'an-nihil-ation" in the most extreme sense, was, within the area of Western tradition, probably first formulated by Nietzsche. For him nihilism is not just an intellectual position, not merely the theoretical 'conviction of the absolute inability of existence to endure,' 'not only the result of

---

130. Fortin, *Classical Christianity*, vol. 2, 31.

contemplating the 'in vain' and not only the belief that everything is worthy to go to destruction.' . . . the notion of an end in the absolute sense . . . has penetrated the collective consciousness of the modern world.[131]

In the middle of the twentieth century, therefore, I believe a crossroads can be found in the contemporary discussion of Augustine's political and social thought. While in much of Europe a secularized–Marxist concept of history caused a dismissal of Augustine's vision, Marrou's *tertium quid* provided a continued outlet for numerous English-speaking thinkers to continue Augustinian interpretations in a challenging and anxious contemporary period. Other Christian thinkers like Ratzinger, Fortin, and Schall would challenge the upheaval of this period and would defend the eschatological sense of Augustine's vision and the role of the Church within the economy of salvation.

In the 1960s and 1970s, therefore, Augustinian interpretation became a polarizing field. In this context, Arquilliére's *l'augustinisme politique* was given renewed interest, as it aided a "programmatic reading" of Augustine and helped some condemn so-called "Medieval" tendencies and interpretations. In 1968, with violence and revolt engulfing the streets of many world cities, political and social ideology was influenced once again by a "liberal" utopianism similar to that of the early twentieth century. The philosophical context of this movement differed with a strong tendency towards anarchism and nihilism. The secularization of the Christian philosophy of history and the conflation of Augustine's two cities were reignited. For example, one can see the potential for such a conflation in Gustavo Gutiérrez's influential work, *A Theology of*

131. Josef Pieper, *The End of Time: A Meditation on the Philosophy of History*, trans. Michael Bullock (San Francisco: Ignatius Press, 1999), 60.

Liberation, which cites Augustine's *City of God*. It is also a tendency in the work of Graham Ward, who will be discussed later in this work.

In Gutierrez's work, *City of God* is cited in order to justify the relegation of theology to a "critical reflection" of historical praxis. As Gutierrez argues in *A Theology of Liberation*, "The Augustinian theology of history which we find in *The City of God*, for example, is based on a true analysis of the signs of the times and the demands with which they challenge the Christian community."[132] This reading of Augustine was consistent with theological trends of the period, and seems to justify the fear of de Lubac that the eschatological tension of Augustine would be diminished. In Gutierrez's work, the earthly city is rendered the object of theology, and Augustine's theology is utilized as a precedent for the political and social analysis of present history. However, such an interpretation of Augustine can be problematic, as creation seems to become the focus and the *civitas dei* can be rendered purely an earthly reality. As Gutierrez explained, "It is a theology—which is open—in the protest against trampled human dignity, in the struggle against the plunder of the vast majority of humanity, in liberating love, and in the building of a new, just, and comradely society—to the gift of the Kingdom of God."[133] While the prophetic call against the "trampling of human dignity" remains an essential Gospel concern, the ramifications of the concept of "Kingdom" here seem to justify de Lubac's fears in the interpreting of Augustine's concept of two cities.[134]

---

132. Gustavo Gutiérrez, *A Theology of Liberation*, trans. and ed. Caridad Inda and John Eagleston (Maryknoll, NY: Orbis Books, 1988), 5.

133. Ibid., 12.

134. This was one problematic element identified by the Congregation for the Doctrine of the Faith in its 1984 Instruction, "Thus there is a tendency to identify the kingdom of God and its growth with the human liberation movement, and to make history itself the subject of its own development, as a process of the self-redemption of man by means of the class struggle." See Congregation for the Doctrine of the Faith, Instruction on Certain Aspects of the "Theology of Liberation" AAS 76 (1984), 876-909.

While many movements tended to unify Augustine's two cities in the mid twentieth century, others sought different interpretations of Augustine's vision. Most prominently among these thinkers is Robert Markus, who embraced Marrou's *saeculum* as a way of introducing a neutral and secularized public square.[135] This effort was characterized by the desire for an autonomous secular authority free from any "private" influence. However, while Markus sought to expand the overlap of the two cities in the *saeculum*, other thinkers moved in the opposite direction, namely the complete separation of Augustine's two cities. Most notably among these authors were Jacques Ellul and William Stringfellow, who would separate the two cities and reject the very notion of a secular political order.[136] Markus's thesis and any possibility of a sustained rapport of the two cities in a *tertium quid* is an impossibility for Ellul and Stringfellow. Ultimately, for them, Christianity will fundamentally and inevitably be rejected by the city. The Christian must subsequently separate himself completely from any attachment to it in order to remain faithful to the Gospel. Ellul explained:

> The whole affair will boil down to our rejection by the city. We will be expelled from the city, unless as Jesus promised, we are thrown into the very heart of the city, into prison. Then our collaboration with the builders must stop. But we may be inducted voluntarily to leave the city, to break off cooperation, to take a position of refusal . . . This takes place when every means is blocked for the Christian to fulfill the sole destiny of man and his work, to give glory to God. When there is no longer any means of turning man's work to the glory of his Creator, when there is no longer possible in Babel any mark of the revelation of God's character in Jesus Christ, then life is no longer possible for the Christian. He must

---

135. This effort will be discussed in detail in chapter 3. While much of Markus's work provides groundbreaking insight into Augustine's thought, his interpretation of *saeculum* has sparked much controversy and debate.

136. See especially Jacques Ellul, *The Meaning of the City* (Grand Rapids, Eerdmans, 1970) and William Stringfellow, *An Ethic for Christians and Other Aliens in a Strange Land* (Waco, TX: Word Books, 1973).

flee, cut himself off from the city . . . I am not referring simply to religious ceremonies and the like, but also to the 'secular' acts of laymen and especially a certain state of mind among men.[137]

Babylon and Jerusalem are seen here as the two opposing forces in the world, and there remains no relationship, no overlap between them. As Rosemary Radford Reuther synthesized this strain of Augustinian interpretation, "The role of the Christian is to witness to the eternal and unbridgeable antagonism between the two . . . No final synthesis of Christian hope and a redeemed political order is expected. The role of the Christian in this world is endless resistance; a final incompatibility separates messianic hope and human historical community."[138]

The complexity of Augustine's own context and the instability present during his lifetime have inevitably contributed to the continued interest in his *City of God* over the course of the twentieth century. Augustine, who lived during a turbulent period, has remained an attractive point of reference during a turbulent contemporary age. As Miles Hollingworth helpfully reminds us, "His political ideas were, in the first instance, the impression left by a Pauline theology of discipleship upon the social and political pretensions of Rome, but they have in turn gone on to become the preeminent alternatives to the kinds of moral and political argument that do not take full account of man's limitations as a rational creature."[139]

---

137. Ellul, *The Meaning of the City*, 182.
138. Rosemary Radford Reuther, "Augustine and Christian Political Theology," *Interpretation* 29, no. 3 (1975), 264.
139. Miles Hollingworth, *The Pilgrim City: St. Augustine of Hippo and his Innovation in Political Thought* (London: T&T Clark, 2010), 208.

2

From Realism to Justice Ethics

The Early Anglo-American Reception of the "Political Augustinian" Discussion

Having discussed the emergence of Augustine's political and social thought in the French-speaking world, especially the popularity of the theory of *l'augustinisme politique*, the first major American interpreters took up the question in a similar context but utilized different methods. Largely influenced by the aftermath of World War II and the Cold War, the discussion of "political Augustinianism" took on an increased urgency, as important questions were asked about the structure and nature of human society, the rights and responsibilities of the state, and the need to restrain man's capacity for evil even with force. As a result, the initial American interest in Augustine's political and social vision would serve as an important bridge from the largely Scholastic questions surrounding the French discussion of Augustine's thought with the contemporary political and ethical analysis drawn from Augustine's corpus of work.

Reinhold Niebuhr and Paul Ramsey viewed Augustine in a realist lens, and dominated the American school of interpretation for decades, especially in light of the post-war political crisis and the Cold War itself. Herbert Deane, however, would argue that a more pessimistic interpretation of Augustine was necessary, especially in light of Augustine's anthropology and his limited expectations for human society. Finally, Ernest Fortin dissented from both of these views, and presented an interpretation of Augustine's vision centered on virtue. Fortin also presented an alternative to the often critical views of the Donatist controversy so frequent in Augustinian scholarship. Each of these authors plays a crucial role in influencing the burst of later contemporary commentators on Augustine's thought and, as it will become evident in chapter three and four, each of these early tendencies will be manifested by their successors in Augustinian interpretation.

Reinhold Niebuhr

It can be safely argued that no American theologian was more influential in American politics after World War II than Reinhold Niebuhr.[1] Niebuhr took up the question of the social and political thought of St. Augustine, but with influences much different from those of Figgis and the French thinkers we have discussed previously. Niebuhr's influences included the Social Gospel Movement and the philosophy of John Dewey, especially the former's democratic idealism and the latter's humanistic and secular philosophy.[2] As Arthur Schlesinger has commented, "Certainly the social philosophy

---

1. The reemergence of Niebuhr was documented sympathetically by John Patrick Diggins. See John Patrick Diggins, *Why Niebuhr Now?* (Chicago: University of Chicago Press, 2011).

of Dewey and the commandments of the Social Gospel fused happily in a common conviction that human and political tensions, however widespread or exasperating, could be dissolved in the end by reason or by love."[3] Another factor in Niebuhr's Augustinian interpretation was his consistent rejection of "natural law" theory in Christian ethical thought, an element that was essential to Gilson, Maritain, and others.

Niebuhr's theology and embrace of Augustine was defined by a realism that emerged in response to war. As John Diggins summarized, "[Niebuhr] warned that Christians would be tempted to invoke Jesus' Sermon on the Mount to justifying refusing to take up arms against evil . . . a religious aversion to violence seemed to him a delusionary conceit, the bad faith of a conscience trying selfishly to retain its innocence in an amoral and power-driven world."[4] This realist interpretation has reemerged and led to a resurgence in Niebuhr's influence, especially in light of the American War on Terror after the attacks of September 11th. As Diggins explains, "Niebuhr was always willing to forgive his fellow Americans, but he asked them to be mindful of a question that goes to the heart of ethics and their moral responsibilities: How much evil might an American do in attempting to do good?"[5]

Niebuhr would summarize his Augustinian interpretation in his essay "Augustine's Political Realism."[6] Considered ground-breaking by Richard Fox, a Niebuhr biographer, Fox notes, "That essay was a finely nuanced exploration of Augustine's insight that the

---

2. Arthur Schlesinger, Jr., "Reinhold Niebuhr's Role in Political Thought," in *Reinhold Niebuhr: His Religious, Social, and Political Thought*, ed. Charles Kegley and Robert Bretall (New York: The Macmillan Co., 1956), 130.

3. Ibid.

4. John Patrick Diggins, *Why Niebuhr Now?* (Chicago: Chicago University Press, 2011): 4.

5. Ibid., 9.

6. Reinhold Niebuhr, *Christian Realism and Political Problems* (New York: Charles Scribner's Sons, 1953).

Neoplatonist quest for self-realization had to be confronted with Paul's Biblical view: self-love was the source of sin."[7] This essay, therefore, forms the primary source of Niebuhr's interpretation of Augustine, and despite its brevity remains an influential work among contemporary Augustinian commentators.

Reinhold Niebuhr's Understanding of Augustinian Realism

Realism for Niebuhr is the "disposition to take all factors in a social and political situation, which offer resistance to established norms, into account, particularly the factors of self-interest and power."[8] This is contrasted by idealism, which holds to moral norms and principles instead of self-interest with disregard or indifference to the realities of human life. Niebuhr, however, believed that these realities "offer resistance to universally valid ideals and norms."[9] For Niebuhr, the distinction between realism and idealism is centered more on "disposition than doctrine," and for that reason Augustine emerges, in his opinion, as the West's first realist. Augustine envisions the complexity and social dynamics present on every level of society within his *City of God*. In Niebuhr's view, therefore, Augustine proves himself to be open to the complexity of both the individual and human society in general. For Niebuhr, "Christianity's ethical ideal is an impossible one. We aspire to it while shackled to the lust for power and the passion for possession."[10]

Niebuhr argues that the capacity for Augustine to perceive such tension was not coincidental, as Augustine's realism emerged directly

---

7. Fox, *Reinhold Niebuhr: A Biography* (New York: Pantheon Books, 1985), 255.
8. Niebuhr, *Christian Realism*, 119. James Schall picks up on Niebuhr's use of Machiavelli as an extreme realist in his work, James Schall, *The Mind That is Catholic* (Washington D. C.: Catholic University Press, 2008).
9. Ibid.
10. Diggins, *Why Niebuhr Now?*, 116.

from an economical theology fundamentally grounded in Scripture.[11] This biblical faith, Niebuhr asserts, taught Augustine of evil's origins within the self, and was opposed to the rationalistic division of mind and body. This latter school placed sin within the body, and allowed man to be neatly divided between lustful flesh and a noble virtuous mind. Such dualism, however, is not present in Augustine's anthropology, as the Bishop of Hippo believed that humanity was an integral unity of body and mind. Niebuhr comments on this concept of man's integrity in Augustine, "The self has, in fact, a mysterious identity and integrity transcending its functions of mind, memory, and will."[12] This concept of a "transcendent freedom of the self" was central to Niebuhr's theology and caused him to reject two extremes: the ancients and the moderns. The ancients saw in human nature a universal mind and the body, while the moderns attempted to reduce anthropology to nature alone. Both were insufficient at capturing the Scriptural vision of humanity in light of such "transcendent freedom," and so Augustine can be claimed by neither. Gerald Schlabach comments:

> For Niebuhr, the transcendent, the eternal—the realm wherein an ethic of pure mutuality through pure self-sacrifice could function—was like Kant's noumenal realm. It was ultimately real, but currently inaccessible to all but a very few; even for them, Jesus' ethic constituted a 'tangent toward eternity' and out of history.[13]

Niebuhr observes a direct connection in Augustine between his anthropology and his understanding of evil as "self-love," *superbia*. It is pride which causes us to abandon our true end, God Himself.

11. Ibid., 121.
12. Niebuhr, *Christian Realism*, 121. Niebuhr asserts that Augustine was influenced by Neo-Platonism's concept of transcendence, but rejected Plotinus's tendency to eliminate the particular self in a "realm of undifferentiated being." To demonstrate this he cites Augustine's *De Trinitate* 15, 22.
13. Gerald Schlabach, "Is Milbank Niebuhrian despite himself?" *Conrad Global Review* 23, no. 2 (Spring 2005), 35.

Pride for Niebuhr is the replacement of God with our individual self, or what Niebuhr calls our "egocentricity."[14] However, Niebuhr does not share the traditional concept of original sin often drawn from Augustine's theology, namely "a dynamic progress of sin from individual to species to individual."[15] In fact, in Niebuhr's discussion of Augustinian realism he seeks to avoid any use or reference to the concept of original sin. Peter Kaufman considers this an attempt at rendering Augustine's theology less severe and leaving room for the possibility of some "progressive justice" through the efforts of the state.[16] Geoffrey Rees has examined and critiqued Niebuhr's views on original sin, and has concluded that unlike Augustine, Niebuhr seeks to place the concept "within the realm of the voluntary."[17] Niebuhr confirms this in his work, *The Nature and Destiny of Man*: "Here is the absurdity in a nutshell. Original sin, which is by definition an inherited corruption, or at least an inevitable one, is nevertheless not to be regarded as belonging to [man's] essential nature and therefore is not outside the realm of his responsibility."[18]

Niebuhr, therefore, although advocating for man's transcendent freedom over any temporal and natural process, understands original sin as originating not in man's nature but his anxiety (a term he admittedly takes from Augustine), namely his temporal-historical context. Rees explains, "The temptation to sin arises in freedom, but the anxiety fueling that temptation is as much backward-looking as it is forward-looking, because the self cannot account to itself the origin of its own freedom."[19] Niebuhr cannot accept a concept of sin

14. Ibid., 123.
15. Geoffrey Rees, "The Anxiety of Inheritance: Reinhold Niebuhr and the Literal Truth of Original Sin," *Journal of Religious Ethics* 31, n.1 (2003), 84.
16. Peter Iver Kaufman, "Christian Realism and Augustinian (?) Liberalism," *Journal of Religious Ethics* 38, no. 4 (2010), 700.
17. Rees, "The Anxiety," 80.
18. Reinhold Niebuhr, *The Nature and Destiny of Man: A Christian Interpretation*, Vol. 1, *Human Nature* (New York: Scribner's and Sons, 1941), 242.

based in a past event that affects all of humanity, as such a concept would contradict an "individualism that isolates the self precisely on the ground of justice in moral accountability."[20] In his opinion, therefore, original sin could not be outside of man's responsibility because ultimately such a concept would misrepresent human freedom and limit it by assuming a preconception of sinfulness. Fundamentally, Niebuhr's rejection of a traditional Augustinian concept of original sin seeks to preserve two fundamental truths, "Man in his essential nature is a sinner, yet at the same time he is free and responsible."[21] While we aspire to the good, to that which is transcendent, Niebuhr affirms that we inevitably cannot escape the reality of sin and pride, which influences our choices.

Niebuhr admits that we always have our anxieties and temptations, but humanity sins in freedom and is knowledgeable of its guilt. He believed that humanity's sinfulness in freedom "disallows out of hand any possible literalistic interpretation of original sin."[22] Rees explains:

> Niebuhr recognizes that [the doctrine of original sin] is never anything more than a starting point for the hard work of practical engagement; anything less and it is just another instance of the form of all sin, another dodge of human responsibility. At the same time, however, Niebuhr is compelled to purge 'literalistic illusions' from his discussion . . . because he assumes the necessity of freedom to the just assignment of responsibility, where freedom is only imagined in an absolute unidirectional relation to futurity. [23]

While parting with the traditional understanding of original sin that is central to Augustine's anthropology, Niebuhr does admit that human pride enters every community, and is a corrosive element emerging not from the body, but from the self manifesting its will.

---

19. Rees, "The Anxiety," 82.
20. Ibid., 85.
21. Alexander Burnstein, "Niebuhr, Scripture, and Normative Judaism," in *Reinhold Niebuhr*, 421.
22. Rees, "The Anxiety," 87.
23. Ibid., 95.

However, this perspective eliminates any social sense of sin, and empties the Augustinian conception of human pride and sinfulness. Niebuhr's concept of original sin, therefore, bespeaks an individualism that pervades much of his thought. The individual self cannot for Niebuhr be subject to any societal or anthropological category, which mitigates its personal responsibility. The problematic consequences of this position have been laid out by Edward Santurri:

> This Augustinian conception of the 'universal ruin' of humanity is missing from Reinhold Niebuhr's account of original sin, because Niebuhr's interpretation is governed by his belief in an individualism that isolates the self precisely on the ground of justice in moral accountability . . . So Niebuhr ultimately disallows any social or species perspective on sin . . . [24]

Niebuhr and Augustine's Two Cities

Niebuhr sees the "social effects of human egocentricity" as essential to Augustine's concept of two cities. However, Niebuhr's analysis of Augustine's vision, like his view of original sin, remains fixed on the social concrete reality of man and lacks the reflection on the heavenly city that is so central in Augustine's *City of God*. As Kaufman explains, "The late antique African bishop nudged Niebuhr to look for the formula for leavening the city of this world with the love of the city of God."[25] Niebuhr saw that Augustine's two cities were commingled on the three levels of human community: family, commonwealth, and world. However, the two cities, while comingled, maintained on each level a fundamental tension. The *civitas terrena* is dominated by self-love with contempt for God, while the *civitas dei* is characterized by love of God with contempt for self.[26] Indeed, Niebuhr applied this interpretation concretely to the

---

24. Edmund N. Santurri, "Global Justice after the Fall: Christian Realism and the 'Law of Peoples,'" *Journal of Religious Ethics* 33, no. 4D (2005), 85.
25. Kaufman, "Christian Realism," 699.

global community in the wake of the Second World War. Niebuhr could only speak with guarded optimism, but posits in Augustine the potential for a "world community" formed with great difficulty. "Augustine is a consistent realist in calling attention to the fact that the potential world community may have a common human reason but it speaks different languages . . ."[27]

In focusing on the *civitas terrena*, Niebuhr sees Augustine's realism as defined by an emphasis on "the tensions, frictions, competitions of interest, and overt conflicts," which plague every human community. Diggins comments, "Niebuhr denied that humankind could transcend its sinfulness and cited Saint Augustine in asserting that what is called peace in this world must be gained by strife."[28] For Niebuhr, the family itself is no exception to the consequences of this realism, as treachery and conflict can exist on that most fundamental level of community no less than the others. There is, therefore, always a brokered "armistice" in the earthly city between competing factions, which are united not, as Cicero believed, around a compact of justice but in common love or interest. Such an armistice, however, must be preserved by an imposition of power, which Niebuhr sees as implicit in Augustine's analysis of the imperial city's rule over the provinces.

> This realism has the merit of describing the power realities which underlie all large scale social integrations whether in Egypt or Babylon or Rome . . . it also describes the power realities of national states, even democratic ones, in which a group, holding the dominant form of social power, achieves oligarchic rule, no matter how much modern democracy may bring such power under social control.[29]

26. Ibid.
27. Niebuhr, *Christian Realism*, 125. This concern for global community is a common concern also of the thinkers we have discussed in Chapter 1, arising from a post-War context.
28. Diggins, *Why Niebuhr Now?*, 44.
29. Ibid., 126.

Niebuhr differs with many commentators by arguing that the themes of power and interest do not infringe upon justice, but rather are necessary correctives to Cicero's concept of moral consent. Hobbes and Luther had endorsed state power as a result of a realist pessimism drawn from Augustine and a fear of the potential of anarchy. However, in the wake of fascism in Europe and the aftermath of the War, Niebuhr noted that neither Hobbes nor Luther had placed enough restrictions upon the will of the ruler, and left their interpretations of Augustine open to tyrannical dictators. Niebuhr calls for a balance in political realism, namely that "the dangers of tyranny are weighed as realistically as the dangers of anarchy."[30] One contemporary Protestant theologian, Daniel Williams, explains:

> The development of democratic processes of persuasion is extremely valuable; but it may lead men to feel that they are free from the temptations and brutalities of conflict when actually they have only covered them up . . . they have transferred their vices to larger and larger groups. Beneath the facade of peaceable economic relations there lies a struggle for power which may erupt into overt conflict.[31]

Niebuhr's understanding of the *civitas terrena* is based in a common patristic concept of a "natural order," which he calls a "primitive social norm." This norm, regulating communal property relations and social cohesion of the human community, is necessarily criticized by later civilizations. However, Augustine's concept of primitive social norm in his *civitas terrena* meant that man's governance over others was not part of the divine created order and, as a result, no government or civilization can be sanctified. Indeed, Niebuhr's famous dictum is understood better in this light, "Man's capacity for

30. Niebuhr, *Christian Realism*, 127.
31. Daniel Williams, "Niebuhr and Liberalism," in *Reinhold Niebuhr: His Religious, Social and Political Thought*, ed. Charles Kegley and R. Bretall (New York: The Macmillan Co., 1956), 200.

justice makes democracy possible; but man's inclination to injustice makes democracy necessary."[32]

Niebuhr's brief discussion and interpretation of the *civitas dei* highlights the "comingled" nature of the two cities, but recognizes that the city of God manifests man's true transcendent nature with God as his end. It is this city that prevents Augustine's realism from falling into cynicism or nihilism, as man's nature is not based in his normative behavior on earth: "The corruption of human freedom may make a behavior pattern universal without making it normative. Good and evil are not determined by some fixed structure of human existence."[33] While the egoistic demonstration of self-love reigns in the earthly city, it is true love that offers man a healthy existence and peace in his communities. Recognizing the uniqueness of Augustine's rendering of love, rather than justice, as the norm of community in his discussion of the City of God, Niebuhr sees Augustine as truly conscious of the "power and persistence of egotism, both individual and collective."[34]

Augustine, Niebuhr believes, achieves the balance between a monastic tendency towards individual perfectionism and the Christian sense of duty in the perfection of earthly peace. In his realistic approach, Niebuhr argues, Augustine avoided the medieval tendency towards a justice based in rational natural law and the modern sentimentalism that often characterizes Christian liberals. Niebuhr's problem with the former is its insensitivity towards changing human contexts and conditions, and the latter while based in the other extreme has failed in a similar way. Augustine's success, therefore, is based in his reliance on Scripture: "His conception of the radical freedom of man derived from the biblical view, made it

32. Reinhold Niebuhr, *The Children of Light and the Children of Darkness* (New York: Scribners, 1950), xi.
33. Niebuhr, *Christian Realism*, 130.
34. Ibid., 131.

impossible to accept the idea of fixed forms of human behavior and of social organization, analogous to those of nature, even as he opposed the classical theory of historical cycles."[35]

For Niebuhr, earthly peace can only be secured by a larger love or loyalty that focuses one's self interest towards larger groups and communities. Niebuhr associates directly a sense of justice present in society and the spirit of love in man, as it is this common sense of justice that allows for the presence of sacrifice and collective interest. It is the duty of the Christian, therefore, to perfect human society with the "calculations of justice" that promote mutual responsibility and secure the earthly peace. "Thus the loyalty of a leavening portion of a nation's citizens to a value transcending national interest will save a 'realistic' nation from defining its interests in such narrow and short range terms as to defeat the real interests of the nation."[36] These "competing assertions of interest" are necessary because passions and self-interest inevitably threaten and seek to undermine loyalty and national interest. Put simply, for Niebuhr religious idealism is not enough. "Individuals can 'refine and purge' their egoistic impulses, acting responsibly and benevolently toward one another, but selfishness, dishonesty, and hypocrisy invariably predominate whenever individuals organize themselves into groups, nations, classes, and races."[37]

Niebuhr's Divergence from Augustine

Niebuhr departs from Augustine's ecclesiology, and more specifically the identification of the Church as *societas perfecta*. Admitting this association, Niebuhr notes that Augustine posited numerous

35. Ibid., 133.
36. Ibid., 137.
37. Diggins, *Why Niebuhr Now?*, 43.

reservations upon the identification of the Church and the Kingdom, and in this way the Reformation finds an Augustinian heritage. However, Niebuhr also rejects Augustine's concept of an *ecclesia permixta*, noting that his concept of grace prevents the vision of the redeemed turning to Christ and yet not "freed from the corruption of egotism which expresses itself, even in the lives of the sense."[38] There is, therefore, little treatment of the concept of mediation in Niebuhr's interpretation, which is the continuation of his understanding of original sin. Niebuhr defended Luther's concept of *iustus et peccator simul*, by interpreting Augustine's *ecclesia permixta* as based not in coexistence in the Church but in the "conflict between love and self-love in every soul."[39] Augustine's insistence on *ecclesia permixta* becomes for Niebuhr an internal, individual reality within the Christian. Here, Niebuhr's individualism and insistence on transcendent freedom shape his interpretation of Augustine. As John Diggins describes this preference: "Augustine defined perfection in history as contemplation of the eternal, and he instructed humanity to aspire to the *civitas dei* . . . But Niebuhr focused instead on the perils of this world . . . And while sin is not a necessity, it is natural and universal . . ."[40]

Even the love of neighbor, which Augustine saw as ultimately directed towards God, is problematic for Niebuhr. Niebuhr sees such a motive of love, as "emptying the meaning" of meeting one's neighbor's need.[41] He recognizes that in the New Testament *agape* is sacrificial, but such sacrifice for Augustine is directed to the only immutable end of man, God himself. Niebuhr commented that Augustinian *amor dei* assumes a level of humility that recognizes

38. Niebuhr, *Christian Realism*, 138
39. Ibid.
40. Diggins, *Why Niebuhr Now?*, 116.
41. Niebuhr, *Christian Realism*, 140.

humanity's smallness in front of their ultimate end. However, the danger of this tendency is that such a love of God falls into the egoism it must contest, as humanity seeks its self-realization in confronting the needs of others. As Diggins has commented, "Not afraid to contradict Jesus, Niebuhr notes that a concern for the physical basis of life cannot be left to a 'naive faith in God's providential care.'"[42] Instead of man's every act having God as its end, Niebuhr subscribed to a biblical sense of acting before God and being renewed by him in history.[43]

While Augustine's insistence on a divine end was a prevention of idolatry, Niebuhr believed that the self-realization caused by love was a betrayal of the sacrificial nature of *agape* and inconsistent with man's true nature. While Thomas Aquinas and others saw love as a natural impulse directed to the Creator, Niebuhr affirmed that while attempting to exercise *agape* humanity will inevitably "backslide" into sin.[44] However, like Augustine, Niebuhr recognizes the value of man's daily responsibilities and domestic duties as significant moments in defining his choice towards the transcendent. Niebuhr rejects the divorce of transcendence from human experience, and sees this division as a methodological problem in contemporary theology. Niebuhr argues:

> We must be clear about the fact that all the illusions about man's character and history which made it so difficult for either the classical or the modern age to come to terms with the vexing problems of our togetherness, seem to stem from efforts to understand man in both his grandeur and his misery by 'integrating' him into some natural or rational system of coherence. Thereby they denied the mystery of his transcendence over every process which points to another mystery

---

42. Diggins, *Why Niebuhr Now?*, 22.
43. John Halvorson, "The Kingdom and Realism in Ministry," *Word and World* II, no.2, 113.
44. Diggins, *Why Niebuhr Now?*, 30.

beyond himself without which man is not only a mystery to himself but a misunderstood being.[45]

Niebuhr's fundamental lesson from Augustine is the separation of power and virtue, which Augustine achieves in his two cities. Niebuhr's concern, however, remained not the goal of membership in the heavenly city, but the reality of the earthly city and the sinful factors that drive it. As Diggins concludes his study of Niebuhr, "Niebuhr addresses the realities of human affairs and demonstrates that until we consider certain Christian insights about human nature, we can never understand the nature of power in history."[46] It is the search for those insights which drew Niebuhr to Augustine initially, and which has caused his interpretation of Augustine to remain influential.

Niebuhr's influence can be felt throughout this period of Augustinian interpretation. Similar to John Neville Figgis after World War I, Reinhold Niebuhr looked to Augustine after World War II and rejected the aversion to violence voiced by many during the war. Therefore, unlike Gilson, Combès, and others who sought continuity with a Thomistic based natural law theory, Niebuhr's realism sought the evaluation of concrete historical circumstances in determining moral responsibility. He insisted that Augustine's *civitas terrena* captured the inevitable conflicts and tensions present among every human community, and hence caused Augustine to remain relevant in the development of a post-war Christian ethic. However, while relevant, Niebuhr also saw Augustine and traditional Augustinian interpretations as problematic. Niebuhr's concept of original sin, for example, broke with Augustine's concept of the Fall, as he believed this mitigated personal responsibility for sin and the importance of man's concrete reality. A proponent of Luther's

45. Niebuhr, *Christian Realism*, 143.
46. Diggins, *Why Niebuhr Now?*, 117.

theology of grace, Niebuhr also rejected the notion of *ecclesia permixta* as contradictory to the primacy of grace. Finally, Augustine's view that the ends of man's actions lie in God alone was seen by Niebuhr as devaluing the interpersonal encounter and the role of charity in the Christian life.

Here is perhaps the greatest break of Niebuhr with previous Augustinian commentators. Neibuhr's concern was not human self-realization, but rather the daily embrace of responsibilities through the exercise of man's "transcendent freedom." Such freedom was an essential category in Niebuhr's thought, as unlike a natural law theory or notion of the *summum bonum*, it accounted for man's historical reality and the important Christian insights into human nature and human relationships. This aversion to connecting Augustine to the concept of natural law would become a standard element in the thought of numerous contemporary theologians, especially seeking the promotion of a secular public sphere. As we examine their works below, it will become a clear theme and a contemporary trend in several authors and their Augustinian interpretations.

Paul Ramsey

Paul Ramsey, a prominent Christian ethicist and Protestant theologian, was both an heir and respondent to the Niebuhrian tradition in the mid-twentieth century. Ramsey recognized in Niebuhr the transformation of ethics from one based on the recognition of human sinfulness to an "Evangelical ethics" based on man's relationship to God.[47] This transition was based on a rejection of any form of ethical idealism and the relative acceptance of contingencies in every moral act. Niebuhr believed an action had

47. Paul Ramsey, "The Transformation of Ethics," in *Faith and Ethics: The Theology of Reinhold Niebuhr*, Paul Ramsey, ed. (New York: Harper and Row, 1957), 140-141.

to be judged as a response to particular circumstances. Ramsey commented on Niebuhr's ethics:

> A relational value-theory firmly grounded in related being fits into a context with a number of other approaches which Niebuhr makes to an understanding of the nature of man, of the 'good for' him and of his responsibility . . . In brief, to be ethically responsible means to be a respond*ing* being in relation to other beings.[48]

Ramsey, however, while respectful of Niebuhr's contribution also recognized the need within Protestant theology to recover a level of ethical principle distinct from the relativism that so characterized Niebuhr's realist ethics. Ramsey himself notes that "general justice" is actualized and specified for political choice and action only in the various views of the word common good held by different people.[49] Methodologically, therefore, Ramsey remains more open to the utilization of idealistic moral principles within his system, and this leads to a different reading of Augustine than that of Reinhold Niebuhr. Ramsey himself wrote at the beginning of his *Basic Christian Ethics*, "It is the author's conviction that, especially in formulating social policy contemporary Christian ethics must make common cause with the ethics of philosophical idealism . . . comparable to Augustine's *use* of Platonism and Aquinas' *use* of Aristotle . . ."[50]

Ramsey's Ethics of Love

It can be said that much of Ramsey's ethics remained in dialogue with the discussion of moral ends in Reinhold Niebuhr. Niebuhr saw

---

48. Ibid., 144.
49. Paul Ramsey, *The Just War: Force and Political Responsibility* (Lanham, MD: University Press of America, 1968), 28.
50. Paul Ramsey, *Basic Christian Ethics* (Louisville, KY: Westminster John Knox Press, 1950), xxxiii. Emphasis added by the author.

Augustine's placement of God as the end of every moral action as problematic and ending in an egoistic search for self-realization. As a result, he sought to preserve the essential ethical meaning of the human encounter with one's neighbor in God's presence. Ramsey, therefore, enters the discussion of moral ends, and morality in general, by focusing on the "ethics of biblical love." In developing a theology of *agape*, Ramsey seeks to fulfill the ethical need for Christian principles and recover the eschatological element of the moral act. "Love for neighbor comprises the full meaning of absolute, unhesitating obedience to God . . ."[51] He continues, noting the eschatological and urgent nature of Jesus' teaching of love of neighbor, "The least that needs to be said is that there are crucial teachings of Jesus whose meaning has been so decisively affected by his kingdom-expectation that they can be torn from their context only at great peril of complete misunderstanding or with exceeding carefulness to conserve their original meaning."[52]

Using terms similar to Niebuhr, Ramsey calls *agape* the "primitive idea of Christian ethics," namely the entrance point into any ethical discussion.[53] Here he replaces, like Niebuhr, the Aristotelian centrality of natural law, by arguing that love is to be the basic and central ethical standard. He argues, "While love frees from the law it binds a man even closer to the needs of others, even as Jesus Christ was bound; and precisely that which alone frees also binds."[54] Indeed, for Ramsey the Christian must not be concerned with "what" the good is, but "whose" good will be chosen, and this "is the main, perhaps the only, concern of Christian ethics . . ."[55] To justify his position, Ramsey invoked Augustine's interpretation of Romans 1:16,

51. Ibid., 34.
52. Ramsey, *Basic Christian Ethics*, 35.
53. Ibid., xvii
54. Ibid., 88.
55. Ibid., 115.

by noting that the Bishop of Hippo believed that only those who have faith truly have a properly informed conscience.[56] However, when Augustine turns to the soul's desire for its true end, Ramsey observes a betrayal of the centrality of *agape* in the morality of the Christian. As Davis has summarized, "This [desire], according to Ramsey, betrays Augustine's adherence to a neo-platonic theory of transcendence and results occasionally in an 'insufficiently Christianized element' in the bishop's ethics . . . to vacillate between enjoying the neighbor and using him in the pilgrimage to God."[57] Ramsey, like Niebuhr, saw Luther as a more reliable source on this theme and, like Luther, prefers Augustine over Aquinas and other "natural law" theorists.

> Nothing in Ramsey's ethics rules out finding ethical norms or rules in secular philosophy or morality in general. But natural justice, like the text of the Bible, must be shaped and formed by *agape*. Ramsey labels his own system as a "mixed agapism: a combination of *agape* with man's sense of natural justice or injustice.[58]

While recognizing a biblical basis for such a strong insistence on *agape* in a Christian moral system, Charles Harris and others have dissented from this view and pointed out problematic elements in Ramsey's system. Harris has noted that it is a "radical altruism," which separates Christian love and ethics from other systems, and hence "Ramsey's proposed solution to the requirement that love be supreme is the view that radical altruism overlays and qualifies a basic religious regard for the sanctity of life."[59] Therefore, as Harris

56. Ibid., 86.

57. Scott Davis, "'Et Quod Vis Fac': Paul Ramsey and Augustinian Ethics," *The Journal of Religious Ethics* 19, no. 2 (1991), 36-37.

58. Michael McKenzie, "Christian Norms in the Ethical Square: An Impossible Dream?" *Journal of Evangelical Theological Society* 38, no.3 (September 1995), 421.

59. Charles E. Harris, Jr., "Love as the Basic Moral Principle in Paul Ramsey's Ethics," *Journal of Religious Ethics* 4, no. 2 (1976), 255.

argues, it is not agape, but the sanctity of all human life, which grounds such altruism and truly informs moral decision-making. He continues, "One possible interpretation of love is that it more effectively functions as a subsidiary moral principle which stipulates that whatever the good is, we should be more concerned with its application. . ."[60] While dissenters to Ramsey's project are numerous, the main source of his Augustinian interpretation emerges in his discussion of "just war."

Ramsey on Just War and Augustine

Ramsey from the outset makes a clear distinction between action taken in self-defense and action made on the behalf of others. Ramsey, recognizing the sacrificial nature of *agape* argued that "self-defense is the worst of all possible excuses for war or for any other form of resistance or any sort of preference among other people."[61] Indeed, any urge to self-defense is based in the egoistic love of self, and contradicts the Gospel's call to service. Augustine's ethic was framed by the death of Christ, and the *agape* demonstrated by Jesus on the cross truly separated Christians concretely from their pagan counterparts. As Scott Davis summarizes, "Self-defense cannot help but become an excuse for judging in our own favor, and as such an instance of avoiding the gospel insistence on service of the neighbor. Thus it should never feature in a Christian argument for resistance."[62] However, Ramsey did see a clear mandate for the Christian to come to the aid and protect others from injustice and undue harm. He comments in his work *The Just War*, "I say, the use of power, and possibly the use of armed force, is of the *esse* of politics

---

60. Ibid., 254.
61. Ramsey, *Basic Christian Ethics*, 173.
62. Davis, "Paul Ramsey," 37.

and inseparably connected with those higher human goods which are the *bene esse* of politics in all the historical ages of mankind . . ."[63]

Ramsey makes a distinction between the individual acting out of self-defense and the individual as "the instrument of the political will of the community."[64] In the latter case, the individual acts not just in accord with one's own will or for one's own self-preservation, but on behalf of the community which has deemed the action necessary. Just as political community is necessary for the public good, so too must an individual carry out their responsibility to the community in fulfillment of his mandate. The fact that the community requires the use of force is not surprising for any reader of Augustine, who as Ramsey noted, justifies coercion of the Donatists by seeing such coercion as an extension of *caritas*.[65] Ramsey clarified this connection of *caritas* with the need at times to utilize force:

> To summarize . . . love for neighbors threatened by violence, by aggression, or tyranny, provided the grounds for admitting the legitimacy of the use of military force. Love for neighbors at the same time required that such force should be limited. The Christian is commanded to do anything a realistic love commands (and so sometimes he must fight). But this also prohibits him from doing anything for which such love can find no justification (and so he can never approve of unlimited attack upon any human life not closely cooperating in or directly engaged in the force that ought to be repelled).[66]

Ramsey also applies *agape* in the discussion of the protection of non-combatants and conscientious objectors. As Davis notes, "Ramsey has developed, through the interpretation of Augustine, not merely a set of disembodied principles about the conduct of war, but

63. Ramsey, *The Just War*, 8.
64. Davis, "Paul Ramsey," 53.
65. Ibid., 54.
66. Ramsey, *The Just War*, 144-145.

a paradigm of the way in which the transforming action of Christ generated specific principles which then become binding on the Christian conscience."[67] Ramsey, therefore, viewed in Augustine's consideration of war not simply the emergence of a formula for moral rectitude during wartime, but rather an appeal to the Christian's conscience while participating in a war. This "paradigm" centered on the Christian conscience includes, therefore, strict limitations on the mandate that is given to combatants and demands the protection of those non-combatants, who find themselves knowingly or unknowingly in harm's way. Ramsey's argument is clear, "If a man cannot irresponsibly forsake those who need to be saved from an oppressor, neither can he directly and indiscriminately attack innocent people in order to restrain that same oppressor."[68] For Ramsey, writing after World War II, this principle directly applied to the dropping of the atomic bomb on Hiroshima and Nagasaki, which killed, injured, and devastated thousands of non-combatants. He lamented:

> The means that nuclear war against the civil centers of an enemy population, the A-Bomb on Hiroshima, or obliteration bombing perpetrated by both sides in World War II were all alike immoral acts of war; and that Christians can support such actions only by dismissing the entire western tradition of civilized warfare . . . [69]

Conscientious objection is also a concept Ramsey sought to protect, as it derived from a consideration for the "common humanity" of those who have a "conscientious scruple against such service."[70] Ramsey deeply admired the Second Vatican Council, and wrote on the implications on the ethics of war present in *Gaudium et Spes*.

67. Davis, "Paul Ramsey," 54.
68. Ramsey, *The Just War*, 145.
69. Ibid., 145.
70. Paul Ramsey, "The Vatican Council on Modern War," *Theological Studies* 27, no.2 (June 1966), 195.

Appreciating the Council's acceptance of the need for authority in any community, Ramsey believed, "It ought to be possible for the government directing the energies of all toward the common good partially to humanize the effects of war by granting alternate national service to conscientious objectors."[71] The Council, to Ramsey's approval, put forth that military service is a moral act, "falling among those things that may be objectively required for the common good . . ."[72] There is the need, therefore, to defend the rights of citizens who objects against an abuse of authority, and who exercises their duty "to disobey any civil authority that oversteps the limits drawn by natural law and commands him to do something contrary to the gospel."

Ramsey's Anthropology and Concept of Virtue in the Light of Augustine

Unlike Niebuhr and Barth, who rejected independent ethical principles in theology, Ramsey's primary mission was to fill what he perceived as an untenable void by establishing some of those very ethical principles in American Protestant theology. If some appeal to natural law or ontology was necessary, Ramsey felt that both Luther's and Calvin's embrace of natural law justified its use (although he sought to avoid any appeal to Thomistic metaphysics).[73] His method, therefore, lends itself to a strong reliance on Augustine, to whom Ramsey appealed on several important themes. In his examination of the question of sin and grace, Ramsey recognized an "American" trend towards "anthropological" arguments and an aversion to what

---

71. Ibid., 196.
72. Ibid.
73. One sees here a continuation of Niebuhr's method and an implicit opposition of other Protestant theologians, such as Paul Tillich, who make use of Thomas's understanding of *analogia entis*.

he calls "Christocentric thought."[74] He posited, "Perhaps our American theology, composed in large part of independent anthropological and ethical statements, and some forms of European theology, content to be without a full length doctrine of man or an ethic even in a dependent position, are both responsible for this sad misunderstanding."[75] Ramsey recognizes that Augustine, in responding to Pelagius, argued that grace is a "power or quality infused into and transforming human moral character."[76] It is God's response to man's first disobedience, the consequences of which include on the part of man "an unwillingness even to be forgiven."[77] Indeed, Ramsey here sets aside metaphysical elements in this discussion and shows a Niebuhrian influence by noting that the Augustinian concept of sin remains "within the will and disobedient spiritual pride" of man.[78] Ramsey wrote:

> Substantial grace perhaps repairs any loss that man has suffered; but only God's *humilitas* meets man's rather substantial pride. At the same time the humility of God appears objectively as Christ for us, kissing the lips and dwelling in the heart only through the decision of faith.[79]

Ramsey, however, sought to clarify an apparent vacillation in Niebuhr's thought on man's natural knowledge and capacity for virtue. Davis explains, "[Niebuhr] sometimes suggests that persons can naturally recognize the requirements of love and be called to account for their failures to respond to those requirements . . . There is danger in such a position because severing the necessary connection of insight to faith runs the risk of leaving human freedom radically indeterminate."[80] For Ramsey, Augustine's affirmation of the

74. Paul Ramsey, "God's Grace and Man's Guilt," *The Journal of Religion* 31, no. 1 (Jan. 1951), 22.
75. Ibid., 22.
76. Ibid. 35.
77. Paul Ramsey, *Nine Modern Moralists*. (Englewood Cliffs, NJ: Prentice Hall, 1962), 39.
78. Ibid., 54.
79. Ramsey, "God's Grace," 36.

uniqueness of Christian love and knowledge is a necessary extension of revelation in Jesus Christ, and Niebuhr's position posed an evident threat to that relationship between revelation and Christian love. Indeed, as Donald Yeager has pointed out, "[Niebuhr] had little patience with the notion of Scripture as transhistorical revelation and even less patience with the notion of Scripture as universal law."[81]

Augustine, in Ramsey's interpretation, while arguing in continuity with the classical pagan notion of virtue affirms also that Christ sets the standard, which man can either accept and flourish or reject in pride.[82] It is through God's grace offered in Christ that humanity can achieve conversion, and ultimately begin to educate the will and order life according to God and not self-reliant pride. Davis summarizes this concept, "Christ, for the convert, is a master who uncovers the reality of human loves and then imparts to the Christian the discipline necessary to pursue proper love . . . ."[83] In Augustine, therefore, Ramsey found both an account of Christ's grace and an acceptance in continuity with man's nature. By affirming this aspect of Augustine's theology, Ramsey rejected Niebuhr's assertion that everyone is fully aware of God's presence, but interpreted that presence differently.[84] Augustine, Ramsey observes, saw a uniqueness in the transforming power of Christ.[85] The faith of the Christian, therefore, necessarily provides a distinct knowledge and disposition in one's relationships.

Ramsey affirmed, in light of Augustine, that any attempt at Christian ethics must include recognition of Christ's transformative

80. Davis, "Paul Ramsey," 43.
81. Donald Yeager, "On Making the Tree Good: An Apology for Dispositional Ethics," *Journal of Religious Ethics* 10, no.1 (1982), 116.
82. Davis, "Paul Ramsey," 45.
83. Ibid., 47.
84. Yeager, "On Making the Tree," 107.
85. Such a uniqueness alluded to here by Ramsey will be expanded and clarified later in the work of Robert Dodaro, whom we will discuss in chapter 4.

and redemptive role, and the uniqueness of the knowledge and love revealed by Him. In this way, Ramsey sought to recover the Christocentric vision obscured by Niebuhr and Barth in their dismissal of independent ethical principles and recapture the balance Augustine had put forward. Ramsey commented:

> The humility of God, then, is the 'chiefest remedy by which the swelling of our pride may be cured'; and the suffering of God is the remedy by which despair of the forgiveness of sins may be cured. These conditions God preveniently establishes, or so Christians believe, for the redemption of men, who were otherwise by sin plunging deeper into sin and guilt.[86]

Augustine's insistence on the transformative nature of Christ's grace touches upon Ramsey's treatment of human society and his interpretation of Augustine's *City of God*. Ramsey admits that Augustine posits true justice as a characteristic of the heavenly city alone; however, he notes that justice is struggled for and partially present in the earthly city. Ramsey recognizes in Augustine the reality of the Christian bound up with a common agreement among citizens in a society collaborating and working towards specific objects. This consensus, building on Cicero's idea, means that individuals will combine their will to accomplish various causes.[87] However, Ramsey argues that no natural law analysis can assure the justice of a cause or end, and so Christian ethical principles, most especially *agape*, must inform the consciences of Christians in their participation in society.[88] The reality that society's ends can themselves be misguided and inconsistent with the common good is for Ramsey a "structural defect" in human political life in the earthly city.

---

86. Ramsey, "God's Grace," 36.
87. Paul Ramsey, *War and the Christian Conscience* (Durham, NC: Duke University, 1961), 29.
88. Davis, "Paul Ramsey," 51.

The potential for this defect has numerous ramifications for Ramsey. Building off of Niebuhr's realism, he affirms, therefore, that the preservation of peace and the assurance of earthly justice at times require force. Political life, therefore, necessarily at times includes force. Commenting on the encyclical of Pope John XXIII, *Pacem in Terris*, Ramsey points this out, noting the reality that the search for justice by nations and among mankind is plagued continually by the defective search for the common good:

> Obviously, if men clearly and impartially apprehend justice in the midst of their disputes, if human society is to such great degree a spiritual activity, if the 'whole' reason for authority and power is to realize a common good, and if disarmament can be based simply on trust, it may be believed a ready achievement for the common good of nations to be extended to their mutual pursuit of the universal common good . . . there is a 'structural defect' . . . [89]

To demonstrate the tension of the citizen of the earthly city, Ramsey points to Augustine's teaching on human sexuality. Even in marriage, even when genuine goods are agreed upon and sought, there remains a "failure of rational control" and the persistence of sinfulness.[90] Augustine realized that as marriage demonstrates, "good cannot be effected in a fallen world apart from evil."[91] As a result, Christians who refer to Christ's transformative *agape* and enter the "sacramental bond" of marriage are differentiated from their pagan counterparts, as sexuality in such a transformed context "is raised to a higher power."[92] Ramsey writes, "The picture Augustine gives us is of the whole of humankind, consciously or unconsciously going on after Christ with increasing momentum by the providence of God

---

89. Ramsey, *The Just War*, 81.
90. Ramsey, "Paul Ramsey," 57.
91. Paul Ramsey, "Human Sexuality in the History of Redemption," *Journal of Religious Ethics* 16, no.1 (Spring 1988), 66.
92. Ibid., 72.

toward its ultimate end and goal."[93] Indeed, the end of marriage, like the end of humanity itself, is to join the angelic choirs in praise of the Triune God. As Ramsey recognized, Augustine saw the Christological mystery as informing communal life on all levels for, "The beginning was understood by him from the End who had appeared in the midst of history."[94]

As we have shown, Paul Ramsey serves as both a conduit of Niebuhr's realist thought and also as a critic of that system's lack of general ethical principles. Therefore, he tempers Niebuhr's rejection of the divine end of all human actions by seeking to recover the New Testament notion of "kingdom" and hope. Agreeing with Niebuhr's view of agape as the central element of Christian ethics, Ramsey builds upon Niebuhr's aversion to natural law ethics by preferring instead the centrality of agape. However, perhaps Ramsey's greatest contribution to this discussion is his advocacy of Augustine's thought on just war and the centrality of the Christian conscience as a limiting force against war's evils. Ultimately, Ramsey can be viewed as attempting an interpretation of Augustine that recovers a Christocentric theological mindset, while remaining in the sphere of Niebuhr's realist theological shift.

Herbert Deane

Herbert Deane was a political scientist and professor of government, but retained throughout his career an interest in the political and social impact of Augustine of Hippo. His work, *The Political and Social Ideas of St. Augustine*, sought first to collect and present systematically important Augustinian texts that expose elements of his political and social thought. Deane recognized the necessity for

93. Ibid., 58.
94. Ibid., 82.

such a project stating, "Genius [Augustine] had in full measure, but system-building and architectonic skill were not his forte; he is the master of the phrase or the sentence that embodies a penetrating insight . . . but not the patient logical philosopher."[95] Deane's sources throughout his work consist primarily of *De Civitate Dei, Enarrationes in Psalmos, In Ioannis Evangelicum Tractatus,* and the *Confessions.*[96] Like Machiavelli, Rousseau and Hobbes, Deane believed Augustine to be a pivotal thinker not only for his genius, but because of the instability and historical upheaval of his day. Augustine is by virtue of his context and his thought a bridge between the Classical and the Christian civilizations of Western Europe, and, as Deane notes, he was impelled "to examine anew fundamental issues of social and political life."[97] For Deane, the essential task of Augustine is to somehow reconcile the classical concept of an earthly society that promotes virtue and goodness in its citizens with a Christian apocalypticism that limited the state to the punishment and suppression of evil. This task would gain greater urgency in light of the Christianization of the empire, and would be forever shaped by Augustine's placement of the true and noble *civitas* beyond the earthly realm:

> [Augustine] made definite and clear the sharp cleavage between the Christian view of the nature and functions of the state and the classical doctrine that it was the highest and noblest form of human association, which existed to make possible the good life for its citizens and to form and educate them so that they might become truly human, that is, good and virtuous men who had realized their fullest potentialities.[98]

---

95. Herbert Deane, *The Political and Social Ideas of St. Augustine* (New York: Columbia University Press, 1963), viii.

96. It would be Robert Dodaro and other later authors who considered the importance of adding Augustine's *Epistulae* to this systematic discussion.

97. Deane, *The Political and Social Ideas*, 4.

98. Ibid., 11.

Deane's Interpretation of Augustine's Anthropology, Ecclesiology, and Soteriology

Deane focuses in the beginning of his work on Augustine's theology and psychology of fallen humanity, noting that, unlike many of his contemporaries, Augustine exhibits extraordinary perception towards the social and political elements of human nature. Indeed, Deane views the concept of "original sin" as the rebellion and disobedience of man towards his creator, and argues that Augustine connects it directly to man's pride and "presumptuous desire."[99] Deane, in sharp contrast to Niebuhr's opinion, interprets in Augustine's concept of original sin a pattern of transmission that includes all people from their birth. Hence, humanity is left sharing the lot of its first parents. And thus, it is clear that Augustine held that by God's grace a certain number would be saved. This concept of election, Deane asserts, would be connected to his anti-Pelagian insistence on man's soteriological dependence on God.

> The primary motive for Augustine's constant insistence that sinful man is absolutely dependent for his salvation upon God's free grace is, I believe, his conviction that pride is the root of sin, and that the most insidious form of pride is that of the man who attributes to himself and to his own efforts his good works or his progress in spiritual life. If pride is the root of sin, sin can be overcome only by complete humility and by attributing to God any good that man does.[100]

Like St. Paul, Augustine had a deeply interior sense of man's dependence on God for his salvation, as such was his personal experience of conversion as a younger man. His early life was devoid of any hint of a claim towards salvation, and indeed his experience caused him to embrace the centrality of God's soteriological action in the Incarnation. However, Deane argues that Augustine's conception

99. Ibid., 16.
100. Ibid., 20.

of the elect excludes many Christians from sharing the fruits of the Incarnation of Christ: "Indeed, as we shall see, only a minority of those who are Christians, that is, baptized members of the visible, sacramental Church, will be saved . . . Among those who have been predestined and chosen . . . are a number of men who lived before the Incarnation."[101] The implication of this doctrine is that not even Augustine himself can identify those members of the City of God among the visible members of the Church on earth. The concept, therefore, of *ecclesia permixta* for Deane is a necessary consequence of Augustine's concept of election and predestination.

For Deane, the two cities are an extension of Augustine's soteriology, namely the category of salvation and redemption, and anthropology. Unlike Niebuhr, Deane asserts that the *civitas dei* is the assembly of saints, which Augustine identifies in a limited manner with the Church visible. However, Deane notes that the Kingdom proclaimed by Christ, the City of God, is not of this world, and Augustine sees no intention by the Lord in intermingling or associating it with any earthly state, city or association.[102] Although bearing more resemblance than the earthly city, Deane notes that the visible Church is not simply an earthly extension of the *City of God*. This distinction allowed Augustine to combat the "Puritan sectarianism" of the Donatists, whose ecclesiology of a "pure" Church stood in stark contrast to Augustine's *ecclesia permixta*.[103] Citizens of the heavenly city, therefore, remain pilgrims journeying in a foreign land to their home country, heaven itself. However, citizens of the earthly city remain bound to this world and its transient satisfactions. Deane writes, "No one can be a member of both societies; either God

---

101. Ibid., 24.
102. Ibid., 29. This stands in contrast to the interpretation of Milbank, as we will discuss in the next chapter.
103. Ibid., 35.

is loved with all the heart and all the soul and all the mind or the world is loved."[104] Indeed, towards the end of his life as more and more people entered the Church's number, Augustine maintained that such growth did not mean a growth among the citizens of the heavenly city. "His words give no support to the hope that the world will gradually be brought to belief in Christ and the earthly society can be transformed, step by step, into the kingdom of God."[105]

Deane's Interpretation of Augustine's Psychology of Fallen Man and Its Repercussions

The source of what has been called Augustine's so-called "pessimism" is his opinion that only a small minority of people actually respond to God's grace and convert from their pride. Deane notes, "This handful of saints cannot in this world be certainly distinguished from the crowds of sinners among whom they live, work and die . . . we are dealing, for the most part, with fallen, sinful men. It is they who set the tone and fix the imperatives of earthly life and its institutions."[106] The human soul in its natural and healthy condition is created to love God and moves toward God, by using the things of this world but loving only his Creator. In deviating that love of God to other things humanity "forgets its origin and destination, and becomes enmeshed in the charms and pleasures of the sights and sounds seen and heard on the journey . . ."[107]

While earthly life has in Augustine's view temporal blessings, such as health, wealth, honor, friendship, and family, none of these things are the highest or necessary good. These temporal goods must be used by the pilgrim citizen of the heavenly city, who must remain

104. Ibid., 31.
105. Ibid., 38.
106. Ibid., 39.
107. Ibid., 41.

cautious not to become controlled by the desire for these goods. This caution is necessary because the degenerate lustful use and desire of temporal goods remains the characteristic of the earthly citizen, or in Hobbes's term the "natural man."[108] Deane argues that senseless pride, unbridled egoism, and insatiable cupidity all characterize such a creature, and the result of the interaction of multiple such people is necessarily conflict. "The world in which these men live and struggle, despite its appearance of solidity and reality is an empty, shadowy realm, far removed from the abode of true happiness and true satisfaction."[109]

This *cupiditas* in Augustine's view yields to the *libido dominandi*, which rages over man in all of his relationships, at home and in society. As Deane notes, "Augustine's picture of fallen man, ridden by avarice, lust for power, and sexual desire, is a somber and pessimistic portrait, which calls to mind the views of human nature expressed by his followers at the time of the Reformation, Luther and Calvin, and by Machiavelli and Hobbes."[110] His is a "grim realism" that recognizes the true Christian as a rare breed among the human race. As a result, the human world is marred by sin and "misplaced love," which distorts the good of the natural world and leads directly to conflict, tension, and war. Deane notes of Augustine's lament that such a condition renders human beings often incapable of understanding the true sentiments of others, and can destroy even the consolation of friendship.[111] Deane, while noting the darkness of Augustine's psychology, also sees the hope which tinges the Augustinian vision. Deane explains:

---

108. Ibid., 47. Deane makes a direct association that I believe is problematic between Augustine and Hobbes, ignoring the differences between Augustine's vision, which includes grace, and Hobbes's concept of "natural man."
109. Ibid., 48.
110. Ibid., 49.
111. Ibid., 63–64.

His picture man's life on this earth is a somber one; life is indeed a hell on earth, filled with suffering, sorrow, disappointment, strife, and bitterness, and ended by death . . . Augustine's pessimism and despair are not ultimate . . . they are the means by which the ultimate triumph of good is being accomplished. At least for the true Christian, the end of the drama is not death or futility, but the perfect peace and felicity of eternal life with God.[112]

Deane on the Augustinian Concepts of Justice and Morality

For Augustine, the state and political order are "remedial institutions" emerging after the Fall to keep sinful man in check. However, in a manner similar to Ramsey, Deane underscores that man's natural sociability is governed by the law of love, which is at the heart of the Christian ethic. "Religion and morality—man's obligation to obey and love God and his duty to love and serve his fellow man—are this indissolubly linked by Christian teaching."[113] This is distinct from any human moral code or legal system, as the only true virtue exhibited by man in Augustine's view is that which is addressed to God. While Niebuhr and his school are cautious against natural law interpretations in Augustine and the divine ends of human action, Deane shows no such trepidation. He argues that such a natural law is "innate" and follows from man's rational being without special revelation. The law in question, the "golden rule," is also for Augustine the "eternal law of God," and their source is not reason alone, but divine Truth.[114] Unlike Combès, Deane sees a separation from this law and the civil laws of the earthly city, for the true justice of the Divine order is not the often inconsistent justice of man. "God's law, the basic principles of morality and justice, is eternal and

112. Ibid., 66–67.
113. Ibid., 80.
114. Ibid., 87.

unchanging, but the specific, detailed customs and positive laws that govern human relationships may differ from to time to time and from place to place in accordance with circumstances and needs."[115]

This divine law is often overshadowed on earth by man's sinfulness and pride, and Augustine notes that the unity and concord forged by God's grace is a rare occurrence in human society. However, by virtue of Christ's entrance into the world and His death on the cross, repentance and life are offered in the face of such captivity to sin rampant in humanity. While grace alone brings about true conversion only in a few, it can never be forgotten that order, stability, and peace emerge among the masses from divinely ordered human institutions. "These institutions, such as private property and the entire legal and political order are divinely ordained as both punishments *and* remedies for the sinful condition of man . . . the earthly peace and order that they make possible are no longer natural and spontaneous, but must be maintained by coercion and repression."[116]

While Deane admits that Augustine conceived of "vestiges" of heavenly justice in the formation of human institutions, peace and order would also require coercion and punishment to combat man's pride and sinfulness. Indeed, human civilization and governance depend upon the order and peace of society, which is built upon a conception of justice and a "mutual understanding and good faith."[117] However, the justice, peace, and concord of the City of God are not the same as their shadows in the earthly city, and Deane points out that the external conflicts in society are matched by internal conflicts with the human person. Human cooperative efforts, therefore, must be maintained with a legal code, a system of punishment and

---

115. Ibid., 91.
116. Ibid., 96.
117. Ibid., 98.

deterrence that at least promotes temporal peace and the attainment of earthly necessities until the end of the world and the separation of the cities.[118]

For Augustine, Deane asserts, the citizens of the heavenly city obey the laws of the earthly city as long as there is no conflict with the divine law, and they are charged with helping to maintain through their efforts the "peace of Babylon." Augustine recognizes that the laws of the earthly city are responsible for securing the earthly possessions and property of the subjects of a particular society, which by their nature are not governed by divine law. Morally, Augustine sees those who misuse property as wrongfully possessing it, but he maintains that the legal order must remain neutral over the use of private property. "All that the laws can do is to prevent men from appropriating property that legally belongs to others and to punish anyone who commits theft or fraud."[119] Augustine, Deane notes, is rather neutral towards wealth and possessions, but cautions that the seeking of such things can be a clear and sinful distraction for the Christian. "The true Christian, whether he is rich or poor, should love God alone, and put his trust only in Him and not in any earthly good . . . The true Christians who happen to be wealthy 'possess riches' but 'are not possessed by them.'"[120]

Deane and Augustine's Vision of State and War

Deane believes that Augustine has an essentially "modern" conception of the state, recognizing that it requires coercive force and that its absence causes anarchy and lawlessness.[121] While no earthly state possesses true justice, Augustine sees no expectation

118. Ibid., 103.
119. Ibid., 41.
120. Ibid., 109.
121. Ibid., 117.

of such justice except in the city of God. The reason for this is clear, "Augustine is insisting that true justice can be found only in a community or commonwealth made up of individuals who serve and love God, *as a result*, possess true justice."[122] As a result, Augustine removes piety and justice from the discussion of governance's legitimacy. "While this or that man who happens to be a ruler or an official may be pious and just, the state itself—the political order—can never be truly just . . . the actions of the state cannot be a direct embodiment of Christian precepts of righteousness."[123] Deane notes that the fear and coercion used by the state is understood by Augustine, who realizes that even the most well-ordered state is still only a shadow of its heavenly counterpart. The "Christian state" is not a possible solution to this dilemma because it can never truly exist in the earthly city. The mixed nature of the earthly citizenry is a fact, and as a result, the coercion and punishment of the state remains necessary. Political power, for this reason, has a divine origin; Christians and non-Christians must pay their taxes, fulfill their obligations, and abide by the laws of the state always cognizant of the providential nature of history. For Augustine, the alternative, namely anarchy, would be nothing more than the unleashing of the evil self-seeking pride of human beings, which would threaten the tenuous harmony of the earthly order.[124]

Deane observes in Augustine's writings the admonition that despite the moral character or religion of the ruler, the Christian must obey him, inasmuch as there is no conflict with the commands of God. Even here Augustine does not call for rebellion or uprising, but martyrdom, which is "passive disobedience with complete acceptance of the consequences."[125] Indeed, what compels the Christian citizen

---

122. Ibid., 119. Emphasis added by the author.
123. Ibid., 134.
124. Ibid., 144. Here Deane sees a commonality between Augustine and Hobbes, in their concern for the protection of the civil order.

is not the favor of an earthly potentate, but the ruler of heaven and earth. For Augustine, "no ruler could ask for a better or more virtuous citizen than the true Christian."[126] It is the Christian who stands unbothered by the treatment of any human superior because of the "inner freedom" of mind and soul gained through a reliance on God's grace. Deane, however, criticizes here what he sees as a "paternalistic" streak in Augustine's conception of the ruler:

> The king may be a good and wise father, or a cruel and tyrannous father, but in either case his subjects must not only obey but honor and respect him. Augustine does not conceive of the citizen as mature, rational persons who have a right to be consulted about their wishes. Most of them are willful, passionate children, who must remain permanently under the firm tutelage of a stern master.[127]

In similar terms to his discussion of the "state," Augustine treats the issue of war as "the punishment imposed upon a state and upon its rulers when their behavior is so aggressive or avaricious that it violates even the norms of temporal justice."[128] Because of sinful pride, competing interests, and perverted desires for wealth, conquest or revenge, Augustine sees war as a horrible but inevitable reality. While inevitable, however, it is always an evil for which man alone is responsible. While falling under God's Providence, Augustine makes clear that the responsibility for war itself and its horrors lie in humanity. While we often choose to use our freedom in such a heinous way, the outcome and aftermath of such events remain utilized by God's providence.[129] Augustine, who knew firsthand the effects of war and its calamities, was not hesitant in noting that officials or rulers who assured peace and prevented the plague of war

125. Ibid., 149.
126. Ibid., 150.
127. Ibid., 153.
128. Ibid., 156.
129. Ibid., 157.

through other more diplomatic means deserved "greater honor and glory than the just warrior."[130]

Deane notes that if war was to be fought, Augustine puts forward criteria to judge whether the cause is just. While a defensive war was to be considered just, an offensive war also could be just if one party refused to make reparations for crimes committed. Deane writes, "Augustine thus narrowly limits the scope of offensive wars that can be regarded as just, and he knows that few of these conflicts between nations in human history fall within these limits."[131] When presented, however, with the pacifism of the Manicheans, Augustine rejected it on the grounds that war is at times necessary to prevent and end wrongdoing and injustice. Deane notes that it was not death that was the supreme evil for Augustine, but anarchy and disorder. The Christian was granted no exception by Augustine for fighting in a just war and answering the call to arms made by his king or ruler. Here, a break is observed with others in the early Church, whom Deane argues forbade any Christian participation in the coercion of others by force. However, Augustine believed that war carried out without desire for revenge or pleasure was ultimately an "act of love and benevolence" fulfilling the law of Christ.[132]

The realism of Augustine is manifest in his acceptance that "dreadful choices" at times must be made. "If a statesman feels—and he may well do so—that his primary duty is to secure the existence and safety of the state whose affairs he is directing, he may have to act in a manner that is morally objectionable, in ways in which he would never think of acting in his personal relations."[133] The only exception for such a dilemma is present in the peace and harmony

130. Ibid., 159.
131. Ibid., 161.
132. Ibid., 164. This concept was also treated by Paul Ramsey in his discussion of Augustine's concept of "just war."
133. Ibid., 167.

of the heavenly city. To prevent such discord and in light of his experience as a citizen within a crumbling Roman Empire, Deane notes that Augustine would actually prefer a world of smaller states satisfied with their boundaries and resources.[134]

Deane finishes his examination of Augustine's corpus by discussing Donatism and the coercion approved by Augustine at the beginning of the fifth century. Deane, after thoroughly laying out the situation and documentary evidence surrounding Donatism, argues that Augustine limited state punishment to the leaders of the schism, especially those who committed violent acts against Catholics. "Augustine insists that it is not only right for the public authorities to punish wrongdoing, since in so doing they are acting as ministers of God, but that such punishment is an act of love which is intended to lead to the correction and reform of those who are punished."[135] However, Deane notes that Augustine's opinions evolve in his corpus from an early insistence on limiting intervention to civil discourse to the approval of a state operated forceful coercion in support of the Church. For Augustine, such action does not change a man's evil will, but it is an attempt to change his conduct. Deane sees Augustine's justification of coercion in this case as strained, noting his appeals to Christ's purification of the temple to justify his actions. Also, Augustine's call for obedience to secular governance becomes more stringent in light of the controversy.[136] He argues, "Coercion in and of itself is neither right nor wrong; what must be considered when coercion is applied to anyone is 'the nature of that to which he is coerced, whether it be good or bad. . .'"[137]

Deane, like numerous other commentators of Augustine, reflects upon the long-term impact of the coercive effort against the

134. Ibid., 171.
135. Ibid., 189.
136. Ibid., 190.
137. Ibid., 197.

Donatists. He argues that Augustine's defense of intervention grew into a larger principle that bound Christian rulers to utilize their power and authority in matters of doctrine. Heterodoxy became not just an ecclesial matter, but an offense against the state. Deane notes that this merging of authority is exceptional to Augustine's larger vision, but inevitably sees it as one element of concordance between the Constantinian imperial project and the bishop of Hippo. "[Augustine] not only recognized and accepted the fact that rulers were using their power to defend the Church, but he set forth, by argument and appeal to the Scriptures, a thoroughgoing defense of these activities."[138] Deane, like Arquillière, argues that Augustine's position germinates in the Middle Ages under Popes Gregory VII and Boniface VIII. The reality is that in the suppression of heterodoxy the State and its officials now became agents of the Church. "The political authorities are reduced to the status of 'the secular arm,' the coercive instrument by which ecclesiastical decisions are enforced upon dissident and recalcitrant members."[139] Therefore, Deane argues that Augustine's attitude towards the state collides with the political and legal coercion of the Donatists. Deane, like others after him, found difficulty in what he saw as Augustine's attempt to reconcile the use of the "blunt weapons" of the political system against the interior beliefs and ideas of a particular group. Deane posits:

> To defend the Church's appeal to the State to punish heretics and schismatics by imprisonment, fines, and exile as a labor of love toward errant sinners, to argue for this policy on the basis of the analogy with a father's loving correction of his son, to speak of the successful results of the state's coercion as 'consequences of the Lord'–all these demonstrate the grim conclusions to which even a very wise man can be led by zeal for the promotion of orthodoxy.[140]

138. Ibid., 215. As we will discuss later, Ratzinger will distinguish between Augustine and Eusebius on this theme.
139. Ibid., 216.
140. Ibid., 220.

Deane concludes his work by noting the relevance of Augustine's realistic political theory, which has no room for utopian dreams or visions of perfection. While many of his ideas are in step with classical and early Christian attitudes towards the state and society, Augustine differentiates himself in a number of ways. He places upon Christians a positive duty to participate in the State's governance and fulfill the obligations it places upon each of its citizens. His vision of war includes the possibility of a "just war," and the first truly systematic defense and criteria of just warfare. His encouragement of the Christian to take on positions of public leadership was a novel one, as he noted the need for the Christian to fulfill his duty even in difficult and ethically dubious circumstances. Necessities of office, therefore, were not a disqualifying element for Augustine.[141] Finally, Deane believed that Augustine permitted secular authority to take action in the preservation of Christian orthodoxy despite the theocratic risks and potential inconsistencies with his larger vision.

Deane, in a manner consistent with Arquillière, attributed the long hiatus in discussing Augustine's political thought as the result of a "sacralized" Western Christian empire and the subsequent Gregorian papacy that would contest imperial influence. While Augustine's ideas were largely misinterpreted and selectively chosen at the expense of his larger vision, it would be the Reformation, in Deane's opinion, that would open the minds of "modern" man to Augustine's imperfect politics. Deane maintained that Luther, Calvin, Hobbes, and Machiavelli all would draw from and at times exaggerate ideas from Augustine's corpus. However, writing in the early 1960s in a Cold War context, Deane saw Augustine's work as increasingly relevant once again.

I say only that in our era of war, terror, and sharp anxiety about man's

141. Ibid., 226–227.

future, when, again, a major epoch in human history may be drawing to a close, we cannot afford to ignore Augustine's sharply etched, dark portrait of the human condition . . . The intellectual equipment we employ as we face our dilemmas will be needlessly restricted if it has no place for Augustine's powerful and somber vision.[142]

Ernest Fortin

The twentieth century Catholic political philosopher, Ernest Fortin, enters the discussion of Augustine's political vision, as part of his larger examination of the confrontation between Christianity and classical thought. Fortin, who recognized the impossibility of a "perfect" reconciliation between the two, sought to examine the influence of the two major thinkers in this confrontation, namely St. Augustine and St. Thomas Aquinas. Their work, he believed, was seminal for Western culture and needed to be reconsidered in light of the failure of numerous "modern secular" alternatives. Daniel Mahoney, in his foreword to Fortin's collected works commented on the added urgency that Fortin held in recovering the Augustinian and Thomistic principles drawn from their confrontation with classical thought.

> Late modern and postmodern thought genuflects before the altars of science and history and, more dangerously, of idiosyncratic, ungrounded commitment. Fortin does not see the victory of these modern forms of the synthesis of faith and reason as being good for philosophy, religion, or decent common life. A world of thought and action dominated by 'irrational philosophers and rational theologians,' as Lessing strikingly formulated it, leads to a postmodern world of vulgar relativism and perspectivism.[143]

Fortin was fascinated with Augustine, who saw great potential in the ideas of Plato, but encountered those ideas often through the

---

142. Ibid., 243.
143. Daniel Mahoney, *Classical Christianity and the Political Order: Reflections on the Theologico-Political Problem*, ed, Brian J. Benested (New York: Rowman and Littlefield, 1996), ix.

work of Cicero. This influence would be of central importance in understanding Augustine and causes Fortin to state the underlying context of his Augustinian interpretation quite clearly, "[Augustine] thus appears if not as the originator at least as the foremost exponent in ancient times of a new tradition of political thought characterized by its attempt to fuse and reconcile elements derived from two originally independent and hitherto unrelated sources, the Bible and classical philosophy."[144]

Augustine on Virtue and Civil Religion

Fortin sees the political doctrine of Augustine centering on the discussion of virtue. While man's sociality is natural, his perfection and fulfillment can only be achieved by entering into relationships with others. Hence, the citizen's relationship to the state must be characterized by the virtue of justice, which Fortin calls the "cornerstone of civil society."[145] It is this virtue that orders society, regulates the various relationships within it, and preserves the peace and common good. Fortin bemoans the reduction of modern political and social ethics to a discussion of rights secured by law, and sees Augustine as providing a contrary vision of rights emerging from the virtue of justice.[146] Augustine's break with the classical tradition he inherited, in Fortin's view, was that he recognized that the philosophical ideal of the just city was impossible to achieve without providing a remedy for man's inherent weakness and fallen nature. "By asserting the eminent desirability of perfect human justice and at the same time its practical impossibility, philosophy discloses its

---

144. Ernest Fortin, "The Political Thought of St. Augustine," *History of Political Philosophy*, 3rd edition, ed. Leo Strauss and Joseph Cropsey (Chicago: University of Chicago Press, 1987), 176-205 in *Classical Christianity and the Political Order*, 1.
145. Ibid, 5.
146. Ibid., 6. This question of individual rights will shape much of the later debate over Augustine's vision present in chapter 5, and as we will observe it will also spark a call to recover an authentic Augustinian hermeneutic.

own inherent limitations; it thus proclaims at least implicitly the need to supplement human justice by a higher and more genuine form of justice."[147] The condition of "original justice" for Augustine signified that justice ordered all things according to reason in a hierarchy both within and outside of man himself. As the body was ruled by the soul, so are virtuous subjects ruled by wise rulers.[148]

The present state of affairs, however, remains one marked by sin, especially the desire for dominion and power over others. The common good and the pursuit of justice have been replaced with desire and the pursuit of selfish interests. As a result, the nature of political leadership reflects this shift by becoming remedial and punitive, in order to check man's disordered pursuits. Fortin describes the Augustinian vision of this degradation from man's original condition:

> It is a state of permanent revolt, which has its source in man's initial revolt against God. The prototype of this revolt is original sin, the sin committed by Adam and transmitted in a mysterious way to all his descendants . . . the freedom that man once enjoyed in pursuit of the good has yielded to oppression and coercion. Coercion is apparent in the most typical institutions of civil society, such as private property, slavery, and government itself, all of which are necessitated and explained by man's present inability to live according to the dictates of reason.[149]

The fundamental remedy for this sinful condition cannot be found in a society riddled by human sinfulness, but only in the grace given to humans freely and without any merit of their own. The Church emerges for Augustine as a refuge in the midst of chaos, alone in its search for the good and without equal as the distributor of grace and instrument of salvation. The task of civil society is,

147. Ibid., 6. Fortin's ideas here, in my opinion, serve as an important introduction to the later work of Robert Dodaro and others, who will expand on Augustine's concept of virtue.
148. Ibid., 7.
149. Ibid.

therefore, necessarily reduced in Augustine from its classical ideal.[150] "At best, civil society can by its repressive action maintain relative peace among men and in this fashion insure the minimal conditions under which the Church is able to exercise its teaching and saving ministry. Of itself it is incapable of leading to virtue."[151]

Augustine, therefore, necessarily views Roman society, both in republican and imperial form, as lacking true justice and hence the essence of a true city. While valuing Rome above other nations, Augustine notes that the object of its love remained a purely earthly desire for human greatness and vainglory. The "heroic virtues" of the Romans heralded in literature and myth were nothing but "resplendent vices." "To the degree to which the Romans renounced pleasure and the gratification of their lower appetites, they were entitled to some reward. God granted this reward when He allowed Rome to assert her supremacy . . . But the argument stops here."[152] Fortin explains that, for Augustine, Christ's coming has "eclipsed the brightest beacons of the ancient world," and has heralded a new category of heroism, one based in exemplary virtue and sacrifice. This heroism, embodied by the martyrs, seeks no earthly goal, but the heavenly reward promised by Christ.

Augustine and the Two Cities

The concept of the two cities is considered by Fortin to be Augustine's most distinctive contribution to the discussion of the nature of civil society. Recognizing the multiplicity of nations and

---

150. While they do not necessarily share ecclesiological viewpoints, Fortin's observation here parallels the observations made by John Milbank, which we will discuss in chapter 3.
151. Fortin, "The Political Thought," 8. Fortin demonstrates that temporal law is itself limited and not reflective of true justice, as it is an adjustment to the evils present within society and secures only limited justice.
152. Ibid., 14.

cultures in existence, Augustine draws from sacred Scripture and notes the existence of two societies to which all people of all time belong: the city of God and the earthly city. The analogous use of the term "city" does not point to an existing city or kingdom, as Constantine's *basileia* or the Israelite theocracy. Rather, the earthly and heavenly cities are divided in a manner corresponding to "the distinction between virtue and vice, with the implication that true virtue is Christian virtue."[153] The citizenship of these cities is determined by no terrestrial category, but only by the ends pursued by their citizens. This breaking down of categories was transformative and threatening to Augustine's pagan contemporaries. It risked in the view of some, Fortin notes, a "stripping" of the city's status, importance, and value. It also blurred distinctions between "friend and foe," and dissolved the defensive identifications that protected the city.[154] Augustine, however, while maintaining the necessity of civil society, saw no pragmatic end as greater than the true virtue and true justice offered to the citizen of the heavenly city.

Indeed, the heavenly city remains the community of believers and the assembly of disciples of the true God. Fortin explains, "It is made up entirely of godly men and its whole life may be described as pious acquiescence in the word of God. In it and in it alone is true justice to be found . . . its pattern is laid in heaven and because its perfect state is achieved only in the afterlife . . ."[155] While at times generally equated with the Church, Augustine maintains that the Church is

---

153. Fortin, "The Political Thought," 19.
154. Ernest Fortin, "Political Idealism and Christianity in the Thought of St. Augustine," from *Political Idealism and Christianity in the Thought of St. Augustine* (Villanova, PA: Villanova University Press, 1972) in *Classical Christianity and the Political Order*, 40. Fortin here responds indirectly to the accusations of Arquillière and others that Augustine somehow subverted the temporal order. In reality, Augustine recognizes the need for civil society, but rejects the claim that it is man's highest end. The temporal order is real and needed, but it is not man's ultimate goal.
155. Ibid, 40.

an *ecclesia permixta*. Fortin here parts from the harsh interpretation of this concept in Deane. Rather, Fortin believes that this concept signifies that "anyone dedicated to the pursuit of truth and virtue may be said to be implicitly a citizen of the city of God, and anyone who abandons virtue for vice is ipso facto excluded from it."[156]

Fortin, however, argues that the city of God does not void the importance and necessity of civil society. While true justice and true virtue are only attainable in the heavenly city, Augustine sees civil society as "supplementing it," providing the means of achieving the goal of citizenship in the city of God. "Civil Society itself continues to be indispensable in that it procures and administers the temporal or material goods which men need here on earth . . . instruments to promote the good of the soul."[157] Fortin sees Augustine's vision of "twin citizenship," as more than mere coincidence. Indeed, the Bishop of Hippo maintained that as citizens of the earthly city, Christians had to fulfill all political obligations and civic responsibilities. However, the hearts and minds of Christians must be molded and shaped by no other influence except the Gospel.[158] This reservation of heart and mind to the Gospel is precisely because the Christian's final goal is not simply membership in civil society, but citizenship in heaven. In placing man's true end outside of the city's jurisdiction, Augustine broke with classical tradition. However, as Fortin notes as well, "to the problem of human living it may be viewed as a prolongation and fulfillment of that tradition."[159]

Fortin, as we have mentioned, maintains in his reading of Augustine the necessity of the Christian to participate and take up his obligations in civil society. When clashes between Christians and pagans occurred under Gratian and later at Rome's defeat to Alaric

156. Fortin, "The Political Thought," 20.
157. Ibid.. Fortin here is willing to speak of these functions more positively than Kaufman.
158. Fortin, "Political Idealism and Christianity," 47.
159. Fortin, "The Political Thought," 20.

in 410, Augustine maintained the impossibility of invoking one's allegiance to God as a justification for shirking civic responsibility. Christianity was not "subversive nor conformist," and so both anarchism and legitimism were excluded as possible Christian opinions. Fortin notes, "In a spirit of moderation and charity it simply teaches that Christians should bear with equanimity the inescapable evils of life without ceasing to toil unwearyingly for the suppression of those evils of life which can be successfully overcome by human effort and perseverance."[160] Relying on St. Paul's letter to the Romans, especially chapter 13, Augustine saw no problem with the Christian fulfilling his responsibilities as a citizen of the civil society and his vocation as a disciple of Christ. Indeed, both roles were necessary by virtue of the Christian's earthly existence and supernatural fulfillment. Such a combination was readily understood by Augustine as well. Fortin, therefore, concludes:

> Indeed, Christianity is to be understood above all as a faith rather than a divinely revealed law governing all of one's actions and opinions and called upon to replace the human laws under which men live. It is compatible with any political regime and, in temporal matters, it does not impose a way of life of its own, different from that of other citizens of the same city . . . . The only practices to which it is opposed are the ones that reason itself denounces as vicious or immoral.[161]

While ecclesiastical and civil authorities seem to be at odds in Augustine, Fortin maintains that Augustine envisions a relationship based in a combination of Christian wisdom and political power. This resolution is discussed in the context of the Christian prince in Book V of *City of God*.[162] Fortin observes here Augustine's call for the Christian who serves in office and wields temporal power to act "in accordance with Christian principles and for the common good of his

---

160. Fortin, "Political Idealism and Christianity," 47.
161. Fortin, "The Political Thought," 24.
162. Here Fortin draws on *City of God* V, 24.

subjects." Unlike other early commentators, Fortin sees no evidence for the claim that Augustine anticipated the medieval sacrilization of temporal power, or the concept of "two swords." Fortin contends, however, that Augustine also did not hold a concept of church and state, which Markus and others have claimed can be seen emerging from Augustinian principles. The relationship of sacred and secular in Augustine is ambiguous precisely because Augustine's priority was not in laying out constitutional principles that are so often sought and referenced today. Fortin notes:

> Given the highly contingent and unpredictable circumstances of the Church's existence in the world, it is doubtful whether Augustine ever seriously considered the possibility of articulating in any but the most general way the nature of the relations between these two societies.[163]

Fortin, like other commentators, addresses Augustine and Donatism, but here again notes that Augustine likely had no concept that his decision to coordinate state intervention would serve as a medieval precedent. Fortin seeks to provide context that is frequently absent from other interpretations of Augustine, in that the controversy in question had "paralyzed" the Church in North Africa. Furthermore, initial hopes of avoiding imperial involvement were dashed by Donatism's emergence as a "nationalist movement."[164] Donatists, Fortin argues, were not a quiet fold, but agitated other Christians and threatened both the spiritual and social unity of North Africa. Augustine turned to civil authorities as a last resort, largely due to the "the political nature" of the situation, not because of the theological dispute. Fortin points to the limitations Augustine placed on the use of this force, namely that the faith was not to be forced. He ordered that fervent Donatists should be separated from unwilling and unknowing participants, and he condemned excessive

163. Fortin, "The Political Thought," 21.
164. Ibid.

severity. Fortin writes, "What was for [Augustine], a mere concession to necessity or at most an emergency measure designed to cope with a specific situation was later invoked as a general principle to justify the Church reprisals against heretics and apostates."[165]

Fortin further defends his argument by noting that, unlike Eusebius, Ambrose, Prudentius and Orosius, Augustine did not join in the exaltation of "an era of unprecedented peace and prosperity under the auspices of Christianity . . ."[166] Like Joseph Ratzinger, Fortin observes that while Augustine marveled at genius in human society and the importance of art and industry within the empire in which he lived, Augustine never wavered from his view that material and even political progress did not equate to an increase in moral progress. Fortin maintains that Augustine rejected the optimism of some of his peers, who believed evils would decrease and diminish under Christian rule. He writes, "Considered in its totality, the life of earthly societies appears not as an orderly progression (*procursus*)toward a determinate end, but as a simple process (*excursus*) by which the two cities run out their earthly existence, with its characteristic mixture of successes and failures but no guarantee of salvation in this world."[167] Fundamentally, the solution that Augustine puts forward remains "transpolitical," as he placed man's perfection as a Christian and a human being beyond the reaches of civil society.[168]

---

165. Ibid., 22.
166. Ibid., 26.
167. Ibid., 26-27. As we will observe in chapter 3, the contrast between Eusebius and Augustine is central to the analysis of Joseph Ratzinger on this question.
168. Fortin, "Political Idealism and Christianity," 49.

Augustine and the Problem of Modernity

Ernest Fortin directly confronts the claim made most prominently by Reinhold Niebuhr and Herbert Deane that a Western tradition of political realism emerges from the work of St. Augustine. However, Fortin adds to this list of "modern" interpretations Hannah Arendt, who saw Augustine as the "first philosopher of freedom," Langdon Gilkey, who called him "the father of the modern historical consciousness," and Charles Taylor, who argued that Augustine bridges Plato with Descartes.[169] All of these thinkers, Fortin asserts, pivot their claims on Augustine's reception of Cicero's definition of republic or commonwealth, and the necessary consensus towards common ends. However, Fortin argues, Augustine in reality has rejected Cicero's definition, as actual cities sparsely exhibit such a common collaboration and are incapable of perfect justice or virtue. Also, Cicero's definition requires a "morally neutral" agreement on the objects of their love, but this would undercut Augustine's own vision of the fallen nature of man and his political and social realities. As a result, Fortin argues, "Augustine was neither the starry-eyed idealist for which he has been taken by some, nor the hard-nosed realist for which he has been taken by others . . . his relationship to modernity is on the whole rather different from the one to which much of modern scholarship has accustomed us."[170]

To explain how human beings can live in imperfect conditions and still hold onto ideals of perfection to which they are called, Fortin makes clear that Augustine kept his distance from the classical options offered to him. Augustine does not utilize Cicero's concept of *ius gentium*, where the state mediates between the natural and civil rights of its citizens, and in fact never even uses the term.[171]

---

169. Ernest Fortin, "Augustine and the Problem of Modernity," is a previously unpublished work in *Classical Christianity and the Political Order*, 141.
170. Ibid., 142.

Furthermore, Augustine does not appeal to conceptions of primary and secondary natural law as Aristotle does, nor the absolute and relative rights of the Platonic tradition. Rather, Augustine embraces the biblical principle of the universal love of God and neighbor. He recognized the irreplaceable and necessary nature of civil society, and the justice, though limited, that it was capable of providing. Fortin notes, "One does not serve one's neighbor by abandoning him to his lot and withdrawing from society altogether, but by working for the betterment of that society."[172]

Fortin considers Augustine's rejection of Cicero's ideal as resulting from his concept of natural law and virtue. This is because Augustine does recognize the presence of the natural law, but argues in *De libero arbitrio* that it imposes as a duty the possession of all virtues, especially theoretical wisdom.[173] Augustine, however, admitted that such wisdom and such a capability was rare, and hence he found no grounds to support the concept of *ius gentium*. This, Fortin notes, would imply that certain people are perfectly just, who are not. Augustine, therefore, holds what Fortin calls a "premodern position," which consists of "high ideals and moderate expectations."[174] Augustine is not a "modern thinker," whose ideals are small and whose expectations absolute, but rather he remains opposed to modernity's conception of society in orientation and in principle. Where modernity has focused on the discussion of rights deriving from choice and based in a vision of man's limitations, Augustine and the classical tradition he inherits focused on virtue and its promotion within the state. As J. Brian Benestad has summarized, for Augustine and for his contemporaries, "Good government helps make for good human beings."[175]

171. Ibid., 144.
172. Ibid., 146.
173. Ibid., 148.
174. Ibid., 148.

In light of contemporary biases and the prevalent influence of modern political philosophy, Fortin questions the true openness of contemporary authors towards Augustine, who largely characterize pre-modernity with an intellectual bias. Many of these authors, therefore, hold to Augustinian interpretations that are anachronistic; for example, the claim is often made that Augustine is a precursor to modern democratic values. It is true that Augustine had a unique grasp of the human condition and the role of civil authority as a remedy of that condition, but that is far from the Enlightenment concept of social contract. Also, a fundamental difference that we will return to later in this study is that Augustine's vision of freedom is not based in choice, but in truth. Fortin, therefore, concludes:

> The charges of naive idealism, moral intransigence, or religious fanaticism once commonly leveled at Augustine are part of a caricature indulged in for the specific purpose of casting discredit on a premodernity that his critics had already rejected on extratheoretical grounds, whether it be the revulsion inspired by the Spanish Inquisition, the sixteenth century wars of religion, or the seventeenth century witch hunts.[176]

Conclusion

It is evident that the initial American encounter with Augustine's political and social thought was heavily influenced by the impact and trauma of both World Wars and the first use of nuclear weapons in an armed conflict. While the realism of Niebuhr was widely subscribed to by numerous political and intellectual leaders, it also succeeded in collapsing the very theological nature of Augustine's vision. Paul Ramsey, therefore, tried to correct Niebuhr's realist excesses and recover some foundation for moral principles using Augustine's

---

175. J. Brian Benestad, "An Introduction to the Work of Ernest Fortin," *Communio* 26 (Spring 1999), 47.
176. Fortin, "Augustine and the Problem of Modernity," 149.

concept of *caritas*. Augustine would also be essential for Ramsey's discussion of the just war and its implication for the twentieth century. We have observed how a more pessimistic tone was present in Herbert Deane's interpretation of Augustine. Deane saw in the Bishop of Hippo a main source of political realism in Western thought. However, one is left to consider to what extent a Hobbesian and Calvinist lens shades Deane's interpretation and evaluation of Augustine.

The continuity with modernity advocated by Deane and Niebuhr's realism would be contested by Ernest Fortin, who argued that Augustine's vision is centered on the pre-modern discussion of virtue. Fortin's discussion of virtue would be a key trend in subsequent contemporary commentaries on Augustine's thought, and his divorce of Augustine from the political thought of modernity remains a stark contrast to many mid and late twentieth century interpreters. As it will become evident, many of the arguments put forward in this period of Augustinian interpretation are taken up again by later commentators, who find in the realism popular in this period either a foundation to build upon or an interpretation to be rejected and replaced. It is now necessary, therefore, to turn to the late twentieth century and see how Augustinian interpretation evolved once again.

3

Disputing the Saeculum

Robert Markus, John Milbank, and Contemporary
Augustinian Interpretations

Most notably with the work of Robert Markus and his "secularist" school of Augustinian interpretation, numerous theologians and philosophers have emerged to debate the nature of Augustine's political vision, and to apply his principles to our contemporary social and political context. Markus's project has also inspired a number of critics, who have sought to redirect Augustinian interpretation from his approach. Chief among these critics is John Milbank and the Radical Orthodoxy movement. In the present chapter, I shall lay out, as synthetically as possible, the major interpretations of contemporary Augustinian scholarship, especially the contributions of influential thinkers such as Joseph Ratzinger and Rowan Williams. It is my hope that by displaying the array of interpretations their connections and disagreements will become apparent and further comparative analysis will be facilitated. The authors will, therefore, be discussed based upon their chronological entrance into the debate.

Joseph Ratzinger and James Schall, S. J., both reflect upon Augustine's political and social vision within the wider context of his theology, especially his Trinitarian theology and his ecclesiology. In the discussion of Augustine's ethics, Ratzinger and Schall maintain the connection of Augustine to a metaphysical realism and a natural law tradition, which are often derided in modern and post-modern interpretation. Such a modern deconstructionist approach is embraced by William Connolly, and his call for a more ambiguous and complex ethical reading of Augustine and his influence in the West. Robert Markus promoted a "secularist" reading of Augustine's political and social thought, where a secular public life is promoted from his reading of the Augustinian tradition. This secularist reading has produced both adherents and critics, and remains an important turning point in the line of Augustinian interpretation. Indeed, John Milbank has responded consistently against the secularist project, and puts into question the hermeneutical foundations of a secular public sphere. Peter Iver Kaufman calls for a more historical reading of Augustine, arguing that a more subdued even pessimistic tone must be recovered in reading the work of Augustine of Hippo. Kaufman insists upon the necessity for deeper reflection in considering what positions should truly be described as "Augustinian."

On a different note is the existentialist reading of Augustine introduced by Gaetano Lettieri, whose work remains focused on the categories of alienation and human sociality. Indeed, all of the interpretations after the Second World War build upon the French speaking authors we have already discussed, and many dialogue with Niebuhr's school of realism, but they remain varied and at times in deep disagreement. However, the emergence of the hermeneutical debate, which we will enter into more deeply later, can be observed in the varied interpretations offered in this chapter, and presents a new set of questions to be answered by subsequent generations.

Joseph Ratzinger

Ratzinger's Interpretation of Augustine's Innovation

In his address to the Federal Parliament of Germany, during his 2011 visit to the Bundestag, Pope Benedict XVI, as we have previously cited, spoke on the role and duty of the politician in the contemporary world. In his address, Pope Benedict cited Augustine's metaphor of a "band of pirates" to describe the Nazi regime and its political aftermath. He stated:

> We have seen how power became divorced from right, how power opposed right and crushed it, so that the State became an instrument for destroying right—a highly organized band of robbers, capable of threatening the whole world and driving it to the edge of the abyss. To serve right and to fight against the dominion of wrong is and remains the fundamental task of the politician. [1]

The fact that Pope Benedict, however, would make such a reference in the context of a speech on the role and duty of the politician is no surprise. Prior to his pontificate, Joseph Ratzinger reflected as a theologian upon the question of Augustine's political vision and attempted to apply Augustinian principles to the contemporary political situation of the West. An early example of this came in his 1971 work, *Die Einheit der Nationen. Eine Vision der Kirchenväter*, where he examined the political influence and approach of Origen of Alexandria and Augustine of Hippo. In this work, Ratzinger applies

---

1. Pope Benedict XVI, *Address to Federal Parliament in Berlin's Reichstag Building: Politics at the Service of Rights and Justice*, September 24, 2011. Original German text in *AAS* 103 (2011): 663-669. Official English translation in *L'Osservatore Romano Weekly Edition in English* 44, no. 39, September 28, 2011.

both negative and positive theological contributions of Augustine to the question of the state and its relationship to Christianity. From a negative theological position, Ratzinger believes that Augustine rejected the political theology of ancient Rome, reversing the role of the divine and political order.

Ratzinger asserts that Augustine's Christian theology, both within the Church and outside of it, changes the role and vision of religion. Within the Church, Augustine rejects the Platonic tendency towards an extreme transcendental faith, which excluded the concern of all natural and human aspects of life from the divine order. Ratzinger states:

> In this excessive emphasis on the transcendence of God, which meant segregating God from the world, excluding God from the concrete processes of life, Augustine rightly saw the true core of the resistance against the totality of the claim of the Christian faith, which could never tolerate the marginalization of the political order from the order of the one God.[2]

Outside of the confines of the Church, however, Augustine also challenged the political religion of Ancient Rome, which lacked any sense of truth. For the Romans, religion was an imperial institution and its practice was governed by civil society, whose good and survival were the goal of its religion. Roman religion, therefore, was subservient to the state and not to the truth.[3] Augustine could not tolerate such an absence of truth in religion. He thus rejected any attempt to divinize the state. Ratzinger, therefore, sees this effort by Augustine as allowing for Christianity's engagement with the political reality, while not being dominated by it.

---

2. Joseph Ratzinger, *L'unità delle nazioni: Una visione dei Padri della Chiesa* (Brescia: Morcellina, 2009), 78. The translations will be my own, unless otherwise noted.
3. Ibid., 81.

From a positive theological perspective, Ratzinger sees Augustine as contrasting Christianity with the two popular extremes of his day: Stoic monism and Platonic dualism. Stoic monism is confronted by Augustine for its divinization of the entire creation, especially positions of power and authority. For Augustine, the Absolute is not in the world; in reality, it remains outside of God's creation.[4] Platonic division is also considered problematic for Augustine because of the incarnation of Christ, whose entrance into creation affirms that God is not just the creator of the world, but also the God of history.[5] These two confrontations have a key application in Augustine's theology, as they allow the bishop of Hippo to see political power and greatness as nothing but "facades." As he says, "Man's true mystery and identity lie not in the state or its trappings, but ultimately in the God who is "above and beyond the confines of power."[6]

Ratzinger also addresses the role of the Church in the midst of history and its relationship to the Kingdom of God. In doing so, he interprets Augustine's two cities as a necessary distinction, since the earthly state, whether entirely or partly Christian, remains earthly, and can never be the true homeland of the Christian. While Augustine views the state as a necessity to preserve order and governance, Christians within it are "strangers in exile" who have not yet arrived in their *patria*.[7] While many interpreters of Augustine are unwilling to posit an association between the heavenly city and the Church, Ratzinger shows no fear in affirming a nuanced connection. He notes a similarity between Origen and Augustine in seeing the *civitas caelestis* not only as the heavenly Jerusalem but also as "the people of God on pilgrimage through the desert of earthly time, the Church."[8]

4. Ibid., 88.
5. Ibid.
6. Ibid., 100.
7. Ibid., 104.

Ratzinger identifies in Augustine's work two realities that clarify the Church's role and identity in the world: Christian martyrdom and Pentecost. The Christian martyr is for Augustine the symbol of the Church in its exile, as the martyr "overcomes [popular opinion and imperial power] in faith, in the greater power of God."[9] The martyr's suffering is for Augustine an important testimony to the Church's need to remain oriented to Christ, even in spite of hardship because of its political nonconformity. The second reality remains the Pentecost event, which for Augustine demonstrates that the Church is not limited by national citizenships or even differences of language. "The Church embraces in its extension all nations and languages; the communion in love for the Lord unites those separated by language: in the body of Christ the Pentecost miracle is permanently present."[10] In marking these characteristics, Ratzinger is able to formulate his interpretation of the relationship between the two cities. Noting that Augustine rejects both the "ecclesiation" (*Verkirchlichung*) of the state and the "nationalization" (*Verstaatlichung*) of the Church, Ratzinger affirms Augustine's respect for the state and its necessary presence in the world, but sees man's unity and transformation only in the Body of Christ. This transformation is accomplished by God as the Church journeys in human history to its completion.

Ratzinger's Application of Augustine's Ideas

The discussions around the formation of the European Union at the beginning of the twenty-first century provided the opportunity

8. Ibid., 104. Ratzinger here expands upon ecclesiological themes, especially the relationship between the Church and the City of God, which he first explored in his 1954 doctoral thesis. See Joseph Ratzinger, *Volk und Haus Gottes in Augustine Lehre von der Kirche*, (München: K. Zink, 1954). In both works, Ratzinger asserts that Augustine maintains a nuanced identification of the pilgrim Church and the heavenly city.

9. Ibid.

10. Ibid., 108.

for then Cardinal Ratzinger to return to the theme of the Church's relationship to the state. In this context, almost thirty years after his initial study of Augustine and Origen, Ratzinger applied the principles he discovered to the contemporary political situation of Europe. Three themes emerge in his work, themes which are particularly relevant to our discussion: the secular nature of the state, the ontological void of postmodern Western society, and the proper relationship between Christianity and Western democracy.

Ratzinger sees no contradiction between the secular state and Christian thought. He clearly rejects any possibility of political theocracy: "To put it in modern language, [Christianity] promoted the secular character of the State, in which Christians live together in freedom with those who hold other beliefs, united by the common moral responsibility founded on human nature, on the nature of justice."[11] For Ratzinger, the Catholic openness to the concept of a "secular, non-messianic state" is in stark contrast to the vision of Martin Luther. This openness derives from an Aristotelian influence on Catholic theology, and more specifically from Catholicism's consistent affirmation of a natural law theory.[12] Since the *civitas Dei* cannot become an "empirical political entity," Ratzinger perceives an acceptance in Augustine of the presence of an imperfect earthly state, a *civitas terrena*. However, Ratzinger does admit that excesses and misinterpretations have occurred and that Augustine himself has at times been misinterpreted. Ratzinger argues:

> [Catholic theology] frequently loaded up the idea of natural law with so much Christian content that the necessary ability to compromise was lost and the state could not be accepted within the essential limits of its

11. Joseph Ratzinger, *Europe Today and Tomorrow*, trans. Michael Miller (San Francisco: Ignatius Press, 2007), 98.
12. Joseph Ratzinger, *Ecumenism, and Politics: New Endeavors in Ecclesiology*, trans. Michael Miller et al. (San Francisco: Ignatius Press, 2008), 201.

secularity. They fought for too much and in doing so cut themselves off from the path to what is possible and necessary.[13]

Ratzinger's embrace of the "secular," however, comes with a caution against the nihilistic and postmodern void which has plagued contemporary Western society. While the secular is an important concept and a lived reality in the West, Ratzinger, like other authors, has noted the ontological void that plagues our culture. "Ethics alone cannot supply its own rational basis. Even Enlightenment ethics, which still holds our states together, is vitally dependent on the ongoing effects of Christianity, which gave it the foundations of its reasonableness and its inner coherence."[14]

For Ratzinger, the concept of an "ahistorical state" based in abstract reason, while pined for by numerous ethicists and philosophers, is an untenable proposition with nothing to ground its ethical collaboration, political organization, or union of its people.[15] To demonstrate the results of a lack of ontology and the problem with such "ahistorical" theories, Ratzinger questions the very foundation of human rights. Such rights, "are incomprehensible without the presupposition that man *qua* man, thanks simply to his membership in the species 'man,' is the subject of rights and that his being bears with itself values and norms that must be discovered—but not invented."[16] Without such a philosophical recognition, rights are merely invented and social ethics are based in nothing more than subjective and relativistic principles.

13. Ibid., 201. Ratzinger goes further in another article, admitting that Christianity's claim to truth can be exaggerated into political intolerance, and that such a situation has precedence in Church history. See *Church, Ecumenism, and Politics*, 202.
14. Ibid.
15. Ratzinger, *Europe Today and Tomorrow*, 99. One can see here an implicit rejection of the Rawlsian project, as well as other philosophical projects to ground the state in mere abstract theory. Ratzinger is quite clear on this point plainly stating: "There is no such thing as an 'ahistorical state' based in abstract reason."
16. Ratzinger, *Church, Ecumenism, and Politics*, 77.

Ratzinger posits that for the West to resolve such a fate and remedy its cultural crisis, it must return to its Christian roots and begin to dialogue again with the Christian tradition from which it was born. He affirms that the state "requires another city that is capable of completing it and revealing to it the moral forces that it cannot draw up from its own depths."[17] The Western democratic tradition arises from its Ancient Greek and Christian heritage. Thus, an attempt to ignore or even to cut off that Christian heritage would mean risking its very democratic identity. Without such a return to its Christian roots, only limited alternatives present themselves, namely attempting to recover a pre-Christian Aristotelianism or looking to Islam. The former, he believes, would simply be another abstraction unable to support society, and the latter would call into question the identity of Western culture.[18] He concludes, therefore, "The reference of the state to the Christian foundation is indispensable for its continuance as a state, especially if it is supposed to be pluralistic."[19]

Robert Markus

Robert Markus's interpretation of Augustine's political and social thought remains among the most debated and discussed commentaries in contemporary Augustinian scholarship. In order to present Markus's work in the limited space provided, and because his basic position is already present in his work *Saeculum*, I will be presenting his position synchronically. As the innovator and proponent of a "secularist" reading of St. Augustine, Markus summarized his fundamental thesis in an article three years before his death. He wrote, "I have myself argued over many years and

17. Ibid., 202.
18. Ibid.
19. Ibid., 206.

at tedious length that a positive valuation of the secular realm and its independence from religion is deeply rooted in the Christian tradition, especially as formulated by Augustine of Hippo, and that it is rooted in the New Testament."[20]

The Origins of Markus's Approach

As a young man, Markus found himself deeply influenced by the shift that occurred in Augustinian and patristic scholarship in general during the 1950s. Before this time, analysis consisted of a scientific, philosophical, and theological study of the content, language, and nature of texts. In the 1950s, there began a movement of "recontextualizing" Augustine's work that employed "overlapping" approaches and interpretations to probe its meaning. Markus and others saw this shift as a "liberation" from the Modernist influenced, decontextualized "scientific" study of Augustine. They proceeded to embrace a method in which Augustine was read in light of the history and culture of Late Antiquity, a field of study that gained wider recognition and clearer definition in this era.[21] Markus credits this shift to the work of Henri-Irénée Marrou, most especially his *Saint Augustin et la fin de la culture antique*. Markus recalls:

> Suddenly, in the 1950s, Augustinian scholarship entered its postmodern phase: Marrou's *Saint Augustin et la fin de la culture antique* and the conference held in 1954 to celebrate the sixteenth century of Augustine's birth . . . are the landmarks of a profound and multiple recontextualisation of Augustine. His oeuvre . . . moved to the focus of intersecting, overlapping interests.[22]

20. Robert Markus, "Political Order as Response to the Church's Mission," *Political Theology* 9, no.3 (July 2008), 321.
21. Robert Markus, "Evolving Disciplinary Contexts for the Study of Augustine, 1950-2000: Some Personal Reflections," *Augustinian Studies* 32, no. 2 (2001), 192.
22. Ibid., 191.

The influence of Marrou's work on Markus, however, would be more than methodological, as much of his intellectual career was spent responding to Marrou's assertion of a *tertium quid* in St. Augustine's *City of God*. For Markus, Augustine points to a Christian presence in society, and not a Christian domination of it. He rejects any situation in which the Church manipulates or influences society's institutions or arrangements. This interpretation leads Markus to expand his Augustinian concept of *saeculum*:

> It offers a way of reconciling Christian secularism with the claim of the Gospel's relevance to social and political life. So conceived, the Church makes no claim to dominating or exerting power over civil society; indeed it can repudiate such claims as incompatible with the nature of its relationship to earthly powers. The Gospel is to be mediated through preaching its message and sustained public debate, without threatening the autonomy of the secular order.[23]

Markus's "Secularist" Interpretation of Augustine

Markus's conception of Augustine's approach to the relationship between a nation and its faith is based first and foremost upon the need for consensus. He argues that "[Augustine] clearly thought consensus, a shared culture and common purpose, so important that we have grounds for expecting him to have wanted to maximize these in his conception of society."[24] This need of a "shared culture" shapes the Augustinian interpretation of a *res publica*, which for Markus is a pluralistic reality. "The people constituting a *res publica* are agreed on valuing certain things; they need not be agreed in valuing them on identical scales of value . . . the *res publica* will inevitably embrace among its members people with a variety of different ultimate allegiances."[25] Such pluralism allows Christians and

---

23. Markus, "Political Order," 322.
24. Robert Markus, *Christianity and the Secular* (Notre Dame, IN: University of Notre Dame Press, 2006), 61–62.

pagans to coexist in a single society, an arrangement based upon a "shared moral basis" and "common objects of love."[26] Attempting to set parameters for his interpretation, he clarifies:

> Any reading of Augustine that denies the legitimacy or value of secular political or social structures and of the established practices of a secular culture in a Christian perspective is a misreading. This conclusion, however, should not be taken to justify the opposite type of claim to Augustinian support, that of secular liberalism that severs any relation between religion and public authority and upholds an open, pluralistic, and religiously neutral civic community.[27]

Markus, in effect, renders the state and its affairs autonomous from the realm of the sacred. Seeking to assure the autonomy of the two and prevent the tensions that arise from a Constantinian imperial Christianity. Moreover, he limits the Church's influence upon public institutions to that which it can accomplish from the pulpit. The Church has no place in Markus's idea of the public sphere outside of exercising its own mission of preaching the Gospel.

> So conceived, the Church makes no claim to dominating or exerting power over civil society; indeed it can repudiate such claims as incompatible with the nature of its relationship to earthly powers. The Gospel is to be mediated through preaching its message and sustained public debate, without threatening the autonomy of the secular order.[28]

The *saeculum*, Markus notes, was assigned great importance by Augustine. He regarded it to be "the historical, empirical, perplexed, and interwoven life of the two eschatological cities."[29] However, the Church, in Markus's interpretation, is to remain distinct from any

---

25. Robert Markus, *Saeculum: History and Society in the Theology of Saint Augustine*, 2nd ed. (Cambridge: Cambridge University Press, 1989), 69.
26. Markus, *Christianity*, 63-64.
27. Ibid., 45.
28. Markus, "Political Order," 322.
29. Markus, *Saeculum*, 101.

political reality. Markus summarizes his view of the relationship of the Church to the *saeculum*:

> Christianity is committed . . . to a belief in a Church-that is, a visible community of believers distinct from a political society. The two will always overlap but never coincide. The inner circle, the Church, is the sacramental anticipation of the future Kingdom which it is charged to proclaim to the world. The outer circle is the secular, the realm which is still in a state of waiting for the proclamation to be heard and received.[30]

A religiously pluralistic society emerges from Markus's Augustine precisely because the authority of the *saeculum* is based upon consensus alone. However, Markus must confront the fundamental problem of grounding this consensus in a lasting foundation, since the members of a society will inevitably not agree on everything. Therefore, Markus enters the discussion of social consensus. To ground his concept of consensus, Markus draws upon a Rawlsian concept of "justice as fairness," where there is a reasonable "conception for the basic structure [of society] alone . . . and no wider commitment to any other doctrine."[31] While the Church may assist in building consensus, Markus affirms that it may not monopolize that consent in itself.

> Consensus, convergence of purposes within a limited sphere, is the essential foundation of civil society and is to be valued as such by the Christian community. The Church's message and Christian influence within a society will always seek to foster consensus, and if possible widen its area, raising the moral level of the society around it, while accepting the limits and the pragmatic possibilities of the given situation. Something like this seems central to Augustine's conception of the co-existence of the two 'cities' in the saeculum.[32]

---

30. Markus, *Christianity*, 15.
31. Ibid., 66, citing J. Rawls, *Political Liberalism* (New York, 1996), 134.
32. Markus, "Political Order," 325.

There is, therefore, for Markus a distance that must be preserved between the Church and the political order. He places the uniqueness of the Christian's identity in society solely in personal motivation, as the Christian seeking heavenly fulfillment necessarily bears some respect towards the *saeculum*. The Christian, unlike the pagan, acts in the *saeculum* fundamentally directed towards the ultimate goal of faith, namely citizenship in the heavenly kingdom. This heavenly goal which motivates the Christian is to be pursued privately in the *saeculum* and not collectively by the society as a whole. For Markus, Christians themselves must be concerned with their salvation. They must not pursue it within the *saeculum*.

> Only the two 'cities' are in the relevant sense 'unmixed'—but in their historical existence they can never be discerned in their unmixed state. This invisibility of the presence of eschatological categories in historical realities is the foundation of Augustine's theology of the *saeculum*.[33]

It must be admitted that while Markus advocates for a *saeculum* where eschatology is "invisible," he fully recognizes the presence of an Augustinian *distensio* in the world. In this way, Markus sees in Augustine's later works a rejection of the Constantinian effort of sacralizing the state. The difference in the Christian's membership in the state, he insists, is not based upon the worldly status of man, but rather upon his citizenship in the *civitas Dei*. Indeed, Christian hope points to a tension between the Gospel and the world. Markus asserts that this tension is not a negative hostility, but rather a "fruitful" challenging of the world and its institutions.[34] The Christian's "homelessness in the world" is a reality, but it does not lead to his removal from the *saeculum*. Rather, the tension it creates is an "eschatological one," lying in the discussion of man's ultimate ends.

---

33. Markus, *Saeculum*, 151.
34. Ibid., 169.

Hence, the individual is responsible for both seeking ultimate fulfillment in the heavenly city and for undertaking necessary efforts to shape positively the earthly city.

> There was no need for Christians to be set apart sociologically, as a community separated from the 'world,' hated and persecuted, uncontaminated by it and visibly 'over against the world' . . . What prevented the Christian from being at home in his world was not that he had an alternative home in the Church, but his faith in the transformation of the world through Christ's victory over sin and death and his hope in the final sharing of this victory in His kingdom.[35]

Another question which Markus addresses in his interpretation of Augustine is the natural virtue exhibited by the Romans, and its distinction from the virtue that flows from Christ's grace. The Romans, Markus believes, were seen by Augustine to have sufficient virtue for their imperial pursuits. Citing *City of God* 5.19, Markus recalls Augustine's introduction of an "imperfect kind of virtue" useful to the earthly city.[36] However, as Robert Dodaro points out, Augustine insists in Letter 138 to Marcellinus that such virtue is transient because it is "devoid of true piety." Without true *pietas*, natural virtue cannot and will not endure in the statesman.[37] Indeed, while Markus correctly notes that natural virtue, though limited by original sin, can exist, he does not add Augustine's emphasis upon the necessity of the mediated virtue of Christ cultivated by a life of faith, hope, and love. Dodaro argues that this understatement leads to a potentially different interpretation of whether a "secular" moral consensus is even truly possible for Augustine.

---

35. Ibid., 168.
36. Markus, *Christianity* , 43, n.28.
37. Robert Dodaro, "Ecclesia and Res Publica: How Augustinian are Neo-Augustinian Politics?" in *Augustine and PostModern Thought: A New Alliance Against Modernity?,* ed. Lieven Boeve, Mathijs Lamberigts, Maarten Wisse (Leuven: Peeters Press, 2008), 252.

Markus undoubtedly recognizes the inability of the *saeculum* to provide man's ultimate good and his eschatological fulfillment, but he recognizes the need of the state and its institutions as a "means to turn human ferocity itself to the fostering of a precarious order, some basic cohesion which Augustine called 'the earthly peace.'"[38] Human beings, for Augustine, remain social beings, and as such the securing of earthly peace, while distinct from the lasting peace of the *civitas Dei*, is a necessary responsibility of the *saeculum* and a good for both cities. However, Markus notes that it is in the family that man's virtue is clearly exhibited and his sociality is peacefully manifested. He writes, "The household, or extended family, is the community in which domination has no place; the hierarchy of command and obedience exists for the mutual good. Here, rule is truly service, and obedience is learning or practicing virtue.'[39]

Indeed, Markus makes clear in concluding his interpretation that Christendom is not the Augustinian solution to all ills. This fundamental fear is the cause of his insistence upon a secularist vision, and makes the risks that necessarily arise, as a result of this interpretation, worth taking.

> To endorse a shared loyalty which falls short of a Christian's loyalty to the gospel is not a betrayal and does not imply thinking of society in amoral, quasi-mechanical, terms as being driven purely by 'internal' dynamics rather than led by moral purposes.' It is to deny only the kind of claims made by upholders of the ideal of 'Christendom,' implicitly affirming a Christian duty to seek to shape society and political forms.[40]

38. Markus, *Christianity*, 58.
39. Ibid.
40. Ibid., 68.

James Schall, S. J.

Schall's "Orthodox Approach" to Augustinian Interpretation

James Schall, S. J., approaches the question of politics in Augustine from a political-philosophical perspective, all the while maintaining a sensitivity to the larger theological context and implications of Augustine's argument. In his 1981 work *Christianity and Politics*, Schall puts forward what he calls an "orthodox view," which contests the absolute nature of politics proposed in Marxist and "liberal based" projects.[41] Confronting the "secular apocalyptic" view, which he sees as a rejection of natural and Christian values in search for a secular ideal, Schall argues that an "orthodox" Christian approach can retain doctrinal essentials without confusing good and evil. He argues:

> There is within the Christian analysis a case to be made for a better world order, one more international, yet more local too, one that does respond to the exigencies of poverty, to the need for good institutional systems. Nevertheless, such an intellectual system must also account for man's sins and his weaknesses. Likewise, it must not confuse politics and salvation. States are not saved. Persons are.[42]

Augustine is the model of such an approach, since the origins of Augustine's views on the state and statesman emerge from the life of the Trinity itself. Schall notes, "Augustine suggested how it might be possible for there to be three persons, yet one God with one intellect and one will. Intellection and volition, he pointed out, are aspects of the human life to man. That are not outside him."[43] These faculties cause man to move beyond self-isolation, and "imply that man's destiny is to be open to the knowledge and love of all things."[44]

41. James V. Schall, *Christianity and Politics* (Boston: St. Paul's Editions, 1981), 2.
42. Ibid., 8-9.
43. James V. Schall, *Redeeming the Time* (New York: Sheed & Ward, 1968), 63-96 in James Schall, *The Mind That is Catholic: Philosophical and Political Essays* (Washington D. C.: Catholic University of America Press, 2008), 137.

Indeed, humanity is called to respond to the divine invitation to participate in "the personal life of love and freedom," which is the life of the Trinity.[45] For Schall, building on Augustine, the mysteries of the Trinity and Incarnation, which expose the truth of God's inner life, also form the foundation of all society, namely "the total material and historical life of man with God in Christ."[46] This invitation is made in the midst of human finitude and sinful will, or as Schall calls it, "the context of his temporal life and task." The ultimate goal of the transformation is human life lived in "mutual openness and friendship."[47]

Schall identifies readily the ontological deficiency in the post-modern nihilistic and post-Marxist political projects as being a complete lack of the notion of community that bears "both diverse personalities and their common relationship to one another."[48] Such an absence, however, cannot be considered a surprise, as these systems lack metaphysics or have rejected them outright. In doing so, they have abandoned the ethical principle of a natural law. "The natural law presumes ethics. Ethics presumes metaphysics. Metaphysics does not presume, but it does not exclude revelation."[49] Only in the truths of the Trinity and Incarnation can the ontological void from which contemporary political systems suffer be filled and a notion of community find a philosophical foundation.

> No effort to foster value is, in itself, apart from the divine purposes for men. This divine purpose, ultimately, is the intention of associating man with God in realizing the destiny of the terrestrial world and through

44. Ibid., 137.
45. Ibid., 146.
46. Ibid., 147.
47. James Schall, "On the Death of Plato: Some Philosophical Thoughts on Thracian Maidens," *American Scholar* 66 (Summer 1996): 401-15 in Schall, *Christianity and Politics*, 90; Schall, *Redeeming Time*, in *The Mind that is Catholic*, 146.
48. Schall, *Christianity and Politics*, 107.
49. Ibid., 240.

that destiny to realize the relation of men to one another and to God. Christianity has never believed that men could give themselves their ultimate destiny . . . in the acceptance of the gift that has been offered, there would be a renewed vitality even in the temporal order.[50]

To demonstrate synthetically the contrast between his proposed "orthodox" approach and the position of numerous contemporary political systems, Schall, departing from Herbert Deane's claim of continuity, employs a comparison between Augustine and Machiavelli. This comparison illustrates the differences between Augustine and many of his self proclaimed "disciples." The most essential difference that Schall analyzes is their varying conceptions of freedom. Modernity holds that freedom should be defined "not by nature or by nature's God, but by a freedom itself subject to nothing further than the self."[51] Contemporary political theories, influenced by Marx and Nietzsche, hold a fundamentally subjective foundation of human freedom, which inevitably intertwines it with the concept of choice. Machiavelli's vision of the prince's freedom is one embraced by the majority, which like him believes that "every man is a king."[52] Such a perverted view of freedom, however, influences also the concept of virtue, which, in accord with Machiavelli's vision, is seen as the preference of "good arms to good laws."[53] Furthermore, human actions cease to be evaluated morally, and the question of "means" is reduced to a pragmatic evaluation. Schall summarizes these modern trends. "What modernity has provided is a way out of the Augustinian caveats about the location of the City of God and the weakness of human virtue and resolve . . .

---

50. Ibid., 91.
51. Schall, "The 'Realism' of St. Augustine's 'Political Realism,'" *Perspectives on Political Science* 25 (Summer 1996): 117–123 in The *Mind That is Catholic*, 194.
52. Ibid., 194.
53. Ibid., 196.

all the objections to the exclusively heavenly location of the perfect city disappear."[54]

The Uniqueness of Augustine

In the face of such trends, Augustine's thought presents a different path that is based in both Christian doctrine and a theologically grounded anthropology. The first evident difference in Augustine's vision is the introduction and insistence upon the transcendence of human fulfillment and a "perfect" order. The classical political religion is rejected by Augustine, as he separates the question of politics from the question of salvation. He disassociates the human search for fulfillment, his ultimate happiness, from the political and earthly order.

> The meaning of Christianity in politics, then, came to be that it enabled politics to disassociate itself from man's quest for ultimate happiness, while at the same time giving him something valid to do during his life. Politics was only politics. Salvation was to be found elsewhere . . . Politics was not holiness but its end was not salvation either, since salvation is a gift that transcends all worldly orders. Thus, the world could have a purpose, and man within it, neither of which need be identified with the ultimate kind of goal for which man was created.[55]

However, while insisting on such transcendence, Schall argues, Augustine also maintains in his vision a true "realism." In a manner similar to Jean Bethke Elshtain, whose work we will discuss later, Schall affirms that Augustine was aware of the evils present in politics and society, as he records them in the first books of *City of God*. Therefore, as Schall notes, Augustine rightfully harbored a "pessimism" towards human actions, a pessimism not simply based in

54. Ibid., 197.
55. Schall, *Christianity and Politics*, 320–321.

his interpretation of history, but also "because he could see himself, could see the reality and power of his own choices."[56] Augustine was aware of the disorder present in the human city, even under Christian rule, and saw such disorder based not in external desires but internal desires from the human heart after the Fall. The state, Schall argues, is a postlapsarian necessity for Augustine, a remedy for sin that emerges because "men in all societies would be proud, spiteful, greedy, and grasping."[57] Yet, the earthly state in Augustine is by its nature incapable of offering people the peace and salvation they seek. "When Augustine said that 'There is no peace in this life,' he was speaking for the life in the best *and* worst regimes, both . . . He was saying that human persons transcend every political regime, that their main task and dignity in this world were precisely that they were not limited to or exhausted by an earthly task or time."[58]

Augustine's solution, therefore, is the "City of God," which does exist and is humanity's final destiny. "It is an 'actual' city, though one unlike any existing political city . . . [it] does not come about through man's own efforts alone . . . The City of God does not by itself denigrate the dignity of politics, but it does imply that politics is limited and circumscribed."[59] The earthly state, while divinely designed, is not the location of perfection or grace, but rather it is a remedy for man's sinfulness and his rejection of grace. Original sin, Schall notes, assures in people that their condition will always signal an incompleteness and void, a void that will be filled only through the response to God's invitation, acceptance of His grace, and entrance into the City of God. "The state is an institution that must deal with disordered souls as they manifest their desires and degeneracy in public. It is a necessary evil."[60]

56. Schall, *The Mind that is Catholic*, 200.
57. Schall, *Christianity and Politics*, 201.
58. Ibid., 324.
59. Schall, "The 'Realism'," in *The Mind that is Catholic*, 202.

However, Schall contends that Augustine is not apathetic to the fate of the earthly city. Augustine's "pessimism" is tempered by his faith in the workings of grace in the hearts of real men and women, and his realism is shaped by the eschatological hope of man's salvation in Christ. Indeed, Augustine sees "two loves" active in the world: love of self and love of God. Both of these loves continue to build their respective cities. While Platonism spoke of the ideal city, which Schall calls the "city in speech," Augustine's discussion of *civitas* exhibits a realism that tends more towards Aristotle than Plato. "The mystery was more in our wonderment about why we did not do what we knew we ought to do. This perplexity brought him to the Christian context of grace and redemption."[61] This Christian context, by "removing from politics what it cannot deliver," frees man from a state of perdition and simultaneously gives value to human endeavors and history. For Schall, this is the fundamental mystery which is often misunderstood in interpretations of Augustine. Schall believes that Augustine remains so relevant for the contemporary world precisely because of this fundamental mystery. "We seek in this world and we do not find. It is for this that Christianity was finally given to us."[62]

John Milbank and the Radical Orthodoxy Movement

Milbank in Light of Radical Orthodoxy

To understand John Milbank's interpretation of Augustine, it is helpful first to understand the movement from which his interpretation arises. The Radical Orthodoxy movement is an ecumenical theological movement that has attempted to respond to

60. Schall, *The Mind that is Catholic*, 204.
61. James Schall, "Mysticism, Political Philosophy, and Play," *Modern Age* 48 (Summer 2006): 251-259 in Schall, *The Mind that is Catholic*, 244.
62. Schall, *Christianity and Politics*, 326.

postmodern trends in theology by restoring unity and promoting integrity within theology.[63] As Bernard Mulcahy, O. P., explains, "Radical Orthodoxy considers that faith has given believers a participation in God's knowledge, thus to regard all of reality in its comprehensive theological unity."[64] Markus's secularist approach is a natural contrast to the movement's project, which seeks to include all realms of human life within theological study and the "narrative" of Christ.[65] For this reason, Milbank opens his work *Theology and Social Theory* with the statement: "Once there was no 'secular'. And the secular was not latent, waiting to fill more space with the steam of the 'purely human,' when the pressure of the sacred was relaxed."[66]

Radical Orthodoxy seeks to respond to a fractured postmodern intellectual project by reclaiming "the world" and the "secular realm" theologically with the "ceaseless re-narrating and 'explaining' of human history under the sign of the cross."[67] Indeed, all human life and elements of human knowledge are seen as theological, whether one discusses political science, philosophical theory, or historical narrative.[68] For this reason, Milbank and Markus propose opposing Augustinian interpretations. Their respective readings of Augustine bear the traces of their respective philosophical movements. Milbank summarizes his goal thus:

> I sought to show why, for reasons quite exceeding the political, a Catholic Christian account of reality might be entertained as the most finally persuasive one. But then, for both theological and historico-

---

63. John Milbank, *Theology and Social Theory: Beyond Secular Reason*, 2nd ed. (Oxford: Blackwell, 2006), 390.

64. Bernard Mulcahy, O. P., *Aquinas's Notion of Pure Nature and the Christian Integralism of Henri de Lubac: Not Everything is Grace*, (New York: Peter Lang Publishing, 2011), 182. Mulcahy's work examines John Milbank's work and Radical Orthodoxy in light of the theology of Henri de Lubac and the question of "pure nature."

65. Milbank, *Theology and Social Theory*, 390.

66. Ibid., 9.

67. Ibid., 263.

68. Ibid., 12.

philosophical reasons, I sought also to argue that only a new embracing of such an account could free us from our contemporary historical deadlock.[69]

John Milbank's Interpretation

Milbank's starting point in reading Augustine is similar to the goal of Radical Orthodoxy, namely, to break down the "barriers" between the sacred and the secular. Indeed, for Milbank, the Church is not simply a spiritual reality, but a political one as well, a reality which embraces all elements of human society. The Church is not simply a part of human society that ought to be given rights by the state; rather, it is itself a *societas perfecta*, which "has specific roots in one particular culture, and one particular history."[70] The Church does not seek to "overlap" with the *civitas terrena* in the *saeculum*; rather, it remains "an *asylum* from the ravages of the state."[71] While Markus and others have stressed a disassociation between the *civitas Dei* and the Church, Milbank does the opposite. He sees a clear theological rationale for this association in the fact that, for Augustine, soteriology and ecclesiology cannot be separated from one other. "For Augustine, it is the *Church* that is the adequate sacrifice to God; in other words the realisation of perfect community. The centrality of incarnation and the cross in no way contradicts the truth that the central aspect of salvation is the creation of perfect community."[72]

Milbank also criticizes the "secularist school" for rendering the Church irrelevant in social and political affairs.

---

69. Ibid., xi.
70. John Milbank, "An Essay Against Secular Order," *Journal of Religious Ethics* 15, no. 2 (1987): 208.
71. Ibid., 209.
72. John Milbank, "'Postmodern Critical Augustinianism': A Short Summa in Forty Two Responses to Unasked Questions," *Modern Theology* 7, no. 3 (April 1991): 232.

All 'political' theory, in the antique sense, is relocated by Christianity as thought about the Church . . . In Augustine, there is, disconcertingly, nothing recognizable as a 'theory of Church and state,' no delineation of their respective natural spheres of operation . . . There is no set of positive objectives that are its own peculiar business, and the city of God makes a *usus* of exactly the same range of finite goods, although for different ends, with 'a different faith, a different hope, a different love'.[73]

Milbank interprets in Augustine a negative evaluation of the *civitas terrena*, whose ends are not simply "limited, finite goods," but in fact stray from the eternal good and, as a result, are "unconditionally bad ends."[74] While Markus and other secularist interpreters view the *saeculum* as a point of "overlap" between the two cities, for Milbank, such a realm "is quite simply a realm of sin."[75] Indeed, the political order is not an aid to humanity in its fallen condition. Since the dominion of the "political order" results from humanity's fall, humanity must be saved from the political order itself. Milbank, therefore, argues that the Church, the *societas perfecta*, stands in contrast to that sinful realm and must necessarily act in human society in contrast to the political order.

The Church, for Augustine, is the society whose goal is peace, and whose means are non-coercive. This 'city of God' exists in its full perfection in heaven, but nevertheless it is also a social reality here on earth where it is 'on pilgrimage.' The Church on earth is part of *societas perfecta*, a properly self-sufficient society with its own means of establishing and maintaining norms, its own mode of social organisation. Outside the real, historical fact of the impingement of this new sort of society upon the antique political order there would, for Augustine, be no such thing as 'salvation.'[76]

73. Milbank, *Theology*, 406.
74. Ibid.
75. Ibid.
76. Milbank, "An Essay Against Secular Order," 207.

While some argue that the earthly city allows for a necessary peace, Milbank makes clear that such efforts are simply the "curbing of sin, by sin," which is prone to falling into pride and the mirage of "self sufficiency."[77] Milbank's interpretation of Augustine holds much more skepticism towards natural virtue and its presence in the Roman Empire. Indeed, Milbank sees the fantasy of self-sufficiency present in many polities as the downfall of any trace of "pagan virtue," and reinforcing a circle of violence that simply becomes legalized by the corrupt polity itself. He argues, "Roman virtue is a merely relative matter because it is only possible within a circle bounded by arbitrary violence: a circle, however, which more and more recedes from view as time goes on and political coercion assumes more and more 'commuted' and legally regular forms."[78]

Milbank insists, therefore, that the nature of political rule is itself not excluded from the ecclesial realm. His main source, *City of God* 19.14-17, speaks of the heavenly city utilizing earthly peace in its pilgrimage and "directs that earthly peace towards heavenly peace . . ."[79] From this, Milbank sees an inevitable relationship between the faith of converted citizens and rulers and their political governance, or public life. Indeed, such an exercise of power, he argues, is to be placed within "the scope of the ecclesial rule."[80] This applies, therefore, to magistrates, public officials, and emperors. "The 'Christian emperor,' therefore, is a just ruler exactly to the extent that he treats his political function as an inner-ecclesial one, or as an exercise of pastoral care."[81] For Milbank, Augustine's ecclesiology bears necessary political consequences. As such, the later Thomistic

---

77. Ibid.
78. Ibid.
79. *City of God* 19. 17. Robert W. Dyson, ed. *St Augustine of Hippo: The City of God Against the Pagans* (Cambridge: Cambridge University Press, 1998), 947.
80. Milbank, *Theology*, 400.
81. Ibid., 407.

movement towards a "natural sphere" of political activity stands in contrast to the true Augustinian vision. Indeed, activities once considered "ecclesial" are removed from the Church's domain and become "political." In this way, Milbank laments that the Church began to "mimic the procedures of political sovereignty, and invent a kind of bureaucratic management of believers."[82] The Church, for Milbank, is relegated to a parochial existence as a result of such an interpretation. He notes that its proper role is the only place of true consensus, the true *societas*. A direct rejection can be found here of the secularist "distance" between the Church and the *saeculum*. The affirmation of the Church as the true *societas* directly inverts the secularist interpretation.

Where Markus and others see the need for the *res publica* to secure the rights and practice of the Christian religion, Milbank argues that such authority within the *res publica* belongs to the Church itself. If, as Markus contends, "consensus" is the necessary principle of society, then the Church must be seen as the "only true society" in human history. "True society implies absolute consensus, agreement in desire, and entire harmony amongst its members, and this is exactly . . . what the Church provides, and that in which salvation, the restoration of being, consists."[83] The Rawlsian project of a consensus without reference to doctrine is for Milbank, therefore, a misguided and impossible endeavor. Milbank sees the consensus and harmony of the Church as recognized by Augustine in his *De Musica*, which bears relevance to his ecclesiology:

> Christianity is peculiar, because while it is open to difference—to a series of infinitely new additions, insights, and progressions towards God, it also strives to make of all these differential additions a harmony, 'in the

82. Ibid., 408.
83. Milbank, *Theology*, 402.

body of Christ,' and claims that if the reality of God is properly attended to, there can be such a harmony.[84]

The earthly city and its inherent sinfulness and division are contrasted by the Church, which Milbank unhesitatingly associates with the heavenly city and the *"telos* of the salvific process."[85] The unity of the Church, according to Augustine, relates not to the earthly city, but in fact to the *oikos*, or household. As each Christian household is in itself a "little republic," it is analogous to the relationship of the soul and the community and ultimately the body governed by Christ the head.[86] Therefore, while some see in Augustine the source of an individualist, secular liberalism, Milbank sees Augustine as advocating a harmony between souls, households, and the city, a harmony that can only be secured by the Church and the salvific action of Christ, its head. Therefore, the human pride and private dominion so prevalent in the earthly city are, for Augustine, a result of the Fall. They remain contrary to Christian ontology, which tends towards the recreation of harmony within a community journeying towards true peace. Here again, Milbank makes plain the contrast between the earthly city and the heavenly city.

> Augustine already put the idea of the peaceful community at the centre of his theology; thought of God, of revelation from God, was for him inseparable from the thought of heaven, of words and 'musical laws' coming down from heaven. The heavenly city meant for Augustine a substantial peace; but this peace could also be imperfectly present in the fallen world, in the sequences of time, and time redeemed through memory.[87]

84. Milbank, "Postmodern Critical Augustinianism," 228.
85. Milbank, *Theology*, 403.
86. This relationship and concept in Milbank is summarized by Robert Dodaro in his article "Ecclesia and Res Pubblica: How Augustinian are Neo-Augustinian Politics?" in *Bibliotheca Ephemeridum Theologicarum Lovaniensium* 219, edited by Lieven Boeve, Mathijs Lamberigts and Maarten Wisse (Leuven: Peeters Press, 2008), 259.
87. Milbank, "Postmodern Critical Augustinianism," 229.

While Augustine regards the Church as the truly "peaceful community," Milbank sees Augustine's use of coercion as a clear exception to this reality. And here we find a singular point of convergence between Markus and Milbank. Since true peace is to be promoted by forgiveness, Augustine's use of coercion in the Donatist controversy is a cause of great concern for Milbank. It is a use of earthly peace, rather than the true divine peace which ought to resound in the Church. In the suppression of Donatism, Augustine can be seen as using the methods of the earthly city, the coercion of the secular city within the Church itself. As a result, he opens the door to "a new sacrilization of a sovereign, coercive, and legally defined authority."[88] This authoritative shift is essential to the "Political Augustinian" movement, which both Markus and Milbank decry. For Milbank, it is an aberration from Augustine's vision and is inconsistent "in the realm of ontology."[89] Indeed, Milbank asserts that the Christian ruler is to make use of earthly peace and exercise earthly authority not in a coercive manner, but in a manner that is both "inner-ecclesial" and even "pastoral."[90] Unlike Markus, Milbank argues that the Christian's exercise of power is to be rendered unique not because of the needs of the earthly city, but because of the Christian ruler's membership in the Church of Christ. As a result, while Markus and Milbank both see a common foe in "Political Augustinianism" and its degenerative movement away from Augustine's true vision, their interpretations of Augustine remain very different.

88. Milbank, *Theology*, 419.
89. Ibid., 419.
90. Ibid., 407.

Rowan Williams

Williams's Interpretation of Augustine

Rowan Williams's study of Augustine and his influence on political and social life is one that seeks to defend the Bishop of Hippo from claims that he and his theology have "subverted public life." Citing the criticisms of Hannah Arendt and other political theorists, Williams notes that Augustine and "Augustinian Christianity" have been charged with rendering society "incapable of intelligent speech, common imagination, increasingly enslaved to idolatrous objectifications, fetishes and slogans."[91] Williams, like Ratzinger, however, sees in Augustine not a subversion of public life, but rather a shift from "the values of the classical public and political realm" of ancient Rome.[92] For Williams, Augustine's *City of God* is not a division of human association into two realms, the secular and the sacred, but rather an examination of "corporate human life in light of what is understood to be its last end."[93] Augustine, therefore, is credited by Williams as affirming the Christian's political identity, while applying a gradation of loyalty which places the Christian's heavenly citizenship above the true allegiance he must have to the state.

> What was virtually impossible for the Imperial administration to comprehend was the idea that there were graded levels of loyalty: that the level of acceptance of legitimate authority which made you pay taxes or drive your chariot on the right side of the road was something different from the loyalty that dictated your most fundamental moral

91. Rowan Williams, "Politics and the Soul: A Reading of the City of God," *Milltown Studies* 19/20 (1987): 56. Arendt's study of Augustine, *Love and Saint Augustine*, has been translated recently and published by University of Chicago Press. See Hannah Arendt, *Love and Saint Augustine*, ed. & trans. Joanna Vecchiarelli Scott and Judith Chelius Stark (Chicago: University of Chicago Press, 1996).
92. Ibid., 57.
93. Ibid., 58.

options on the basis of convictions about the relationships between the world and humans—in particular to their creator. For practical purposes, most of the time, ordinary legality would be uncontroversial; the disturbing thing was that Christians believed that there were circumstances in which loyalty to God trumped the demands of the civitas. The state's power was not the ultimate and sacred sanction.[94]

While Williams admits that medieval excesses caused the Church's administration to appear like a rival state, he notes that Christianity never lost sight of the fact that the state's demands on a Christian were limited by responsibilities and obligations beyond its own jurisdiction. Those responsibilities and obligations beyond the state are derived from the Creator and are essential for the maintenance of a society. "Where there is no *ius* toward God, there is no common sense of what is due to human beings, no *iuris consensus*."[95] For this reason, Williams argues that Augustine saw the state, on its own, as doomed, since it lacked any access to the true "abiding values" which respond to man's "truest needs."[96] The *res publica* is itself insufficient in the building of a commonwealth precisely because it lacks a true sense of public virtue. This, for Augustine, was evident in the unbridled *libido dominandi* of ancient systems, which seeks misguided ends often in less than virtuous ways.[97]

Augustine, therefore, regarded the divine source of man's truest ends as being outside the earthly city. Indeed, humanity's ultimate security and fulfillment rests in the *civitas Dei*. Williams demonstrates this in his discussion of Augustine's view of the ideal leader.

> The only reliable political leader, the only ruler who can be guaranteed to safeguard authentically *political* values (order, equity, and the nurture

94. Rowan Williams, "Secularism, Faith and Freedom: Address to the Pontifical Academy of Social Sciences," in *Faith in the Public Square* (London: Bloomsbury, 2012), 29.
95. Williams, "Politics and the Soul," 59.
96. Ibid., 60.
97. Ibid., 61.

of souls in these things) is the man who is, at the end of the day, indifferent to their survival in the relative shapes of the existing order, because he knows them to be safeguarded at the level of God's eternal and immutable providence, vindicated in the eternal *civitas dei*.[98]

Augustine and Williams's "Procedural Secularism"

Rowan Williams, like other commentators, sees in the current "secular ideal" a limitation on reason, as no exchange is deemed possible between basic commitments about God, humanity, the universe, and "public" secular reason. "There is public reason and there is private prejudice—and thus no way of negotiating or reasonably exploring real difference."[99] However, with the insistence upon public neutrality and exclusion of any discussion of religion and religious values, Williams sees an inability in society to create cohesion and to ground man's common nature and responsibilities. In fact, he notes that the prevailing view today is that the secular state is threatened by "the public or communal expression of religious loyalty."[100] Williams recognizes that such a crisis emerges from a concept of "secular" freedom that on its own is insufficient to answer and resolve the fundamental questions of the human person.

> The tempting idea that there is always an adequate definition of what everyone will recognise as public and reasonable argument needs to be looked at hard—not in order to re-establish the dominance of some unchallengeable ruling discourse, religious or ideological, but to focus the question of how a society deals with the actual variety and potential collision of understandings of what is properly human.[101]

---

98. Ibid., 67.

99. Williams, "Secularism, Faith and Freedom," 27.

100. Rowan Williams, "Convictions, Loyalties, and the Secular State: Chatham Lecture at Trinity College, Oxford" in *Faith and the Public Square*, 37.

101. Ibid., 24.

Williams, therefore, calls for an alternative to the current state of affairs by recovering a "procedural secularism," in which religious convictions are granted a public hearing. This hearing is not necessarily a privileged one, but rather one in which religious convictions can represent "the considered moral foundation of the choices and priorities of citizens."[102] Williams contends that such a proposal will not end in cacophony or confusion; rather, civility is guaranteed by a "shared recognition of law," which ensures that all groups in society will renounce violent struggle and will work towards harmony. Admitting the risk of his proposal, Williams clearly sees it as a better alternative to an absolute secular ideology that privatizes any ethical or religiously-influenced position: "In a society where there were rigidly fixed standards of what could rationally or properly be legislated, there would be the danger of such legal decisions becoming effectively irreformable . . . but if the alternative is a view that absolutises one and only one sort of public rationality, the risks are higher."[103]

Williams, relying on Augustine, recognizes that faith is the root of freedom and that it guarantees collaboration or "solidarities" beyond the confines of the state. For this reason, he affirms the Christian origins of a "secular" ideal, an ideal formulated eloquently at the end of the eighteenth century by men such as Carl Theodor von Dalberg. Dalberg was the Archbishop of Mainz, a friend of Goethe, and the great uncle of Lord Acton. He called for "the interpenetration of two sorts of political action . . . on the one hand the routine business of a law-governed society, on the other the relations and obligations that exist in virtue of something other than pragmatic or self-interested human decisions . . . solidarities that do not depend on human organisation."[104] These solidarities, therefore, provide a

102. Williams, "Secularism, Faith and Freedom, 27.
103. Ibid., 28.

necessary perspective and moral importance to public life that goes beyond economic interest and pragmatism. Such a perspective, however, is built upon human dignity, which is not assigned by the marketplace and cannot be provided by citizenship in any particular state. Such dignity is only endowed by a "Creator who addresses us and engages us before ever we embark on social negotiation."[105]

Williams recognizes the criticism of what he calls the "liberal Christian approach," which has been advocated by Niebuhr and others. This approach to such a social negotiation consists of a "Christian commitment" that seeks not the "holiness of Christ so much as lives that can be lived with a fairly easy conscience within the arrangements of the modern state, motivated by a rather unspecific inspiration."[106] Citing William Cavanaugh and Stanley Hauerwas, this liberal approach proves, however, inadequate for the Christian community, which must testify to a narrative different from that at the basis of the liberal state.[107] Here Williams demonstrates the importance of Augustine's two cities, as the basis of human "solidarities" and the assurance of a dignity beyond one's earthly status or citizenship were assured by Augustine's rejection of the ancient Roman political order. As a result, Augustine affirmed that the Church's presence in the world did not depend on the earthly city. Indeed, the Church exists by the design of the Creator and bears a positive identity, while Williams argues the state bore a negative role, namely to quell the violence and disorder prevalent in human society.

> To the end of time, there will always be two kinds of human love, human motivation, creating two kinds of society—the commonwealth of God, in which everything is done for the sake of God and the

104. Ibid., 31.
105. Ibid., 36.
106. Williams, "Convictions, loyalty, and the secular state," 42.
107. Ibid., 43.

neighbour, and the commonwealth of this world, whose best hope is only to limit the excess of competitive, acquisitive violence by artificial and external means.[108]

Like Ratzinger, Williams looks at potential alternatives, most especially Islamic political thought. However, in Islam, he sees a problematic absence of the "secular." He asks what citizenship looks like for a non-Muslim in a Muslim society and how an Islamic state that acknowledges the sovereignty of Islamic law, can maintain loyalties outside the community of Muslim believers. While there is Quranic prohibition of compulsory religion, converts are vulnerable to penalties and violence. Williams admits that future Christian-Muslim dialogue must examine "whether the idea of a 'secular' level of citizenship—with all that this implies about liberties of conscience—is indeed compatible with a basically Islamic commitment in the shape of society at large."[109] The only way to assure that a "concept of the personal" can withstand the functionalist and reductionist climate present today remains the need for secularism to allow faith into the public square and moral discussions. As Williams states quite directly, "We need a theology to arrest this degeneration."[110] This theological appeal is necessary in light of the consequences of the neutrality imposed by a secular public square, which has reduced public life to a "negotiation of practical goods and balances."[111] This appeal alone, therefore, will allow for the "broadening of the moral sources from which the motivation for social action and political self-determination can be drawn."[112]

108. Rowan Williams, *Why Study the Past?: The Quest for the Historical Church* (Grand Rapids, MI: Wm. B. Eerdman's Publishing, 2005), 16.
109. Williams, "Secularism, Faith and Freedom," 34.
110. Ibid., 36.
111. Ibid., 35.
112. Ibid.

Gaetano Lettieri

Lettieri's Approach to Augustine's "Sense of History"

Humanity's search for the "*unum*," the divine, defines the nature of history and is the starting point of Gaetano Lettieri's interpretation of Augustine's political and social vision in *Il senso della storia in Agostino d'Ippona*. The search is essential to the *saeculum*, which is the time of the Fall and hence a time in which man is alienated from God. Lettieri's existential reading of *City of God* equates the two cities with two *relations of being*, namely, the earthly and the divine.[113] The former is a journey towards an "*unum*," which is immanent. While it is above creation, it is the origin and completion of creation. The latter is a human acceptance of humility, a transcendent sense that causes "inquietude" and confronts the saeculum, history and even death.[114]

Augustine identifies the *civitas Dei* with the unity of the Triune God, for it is "this eschatological participation of man to the perfection of the Trinity, full unity of perfected image with its model: the Trinity."[115] These two cities, Lettieri notes, have two corresponding loves: love of world (*amor saeculi*) and love of God (*amor Dei*), which is the relationship with God that is bonded in His grace, revealed in Christ, and centered in his *civitas*. This love of God is characterized, therefore, by *humilitas*, which is opposed to the pride (*superbia*) of the earthly city. "Now, for Augustine, every creature, as we have shown, moves toward the realization of his nature, but while the humble creature invokes the Other and accepts from him, in Christ, this realization, the prideful creature conceives the existence

---

113. Gaetano Lettieri, *Il senso della storia in Agostino d'Ippona* (Roma: Borla, 1988), 11.
114. Ibid., 11.
115. Lettieri, *Il senso della storia*, 34.

as autonomous."[116] Lettieri affirms, therefore, that the celestial city, which holds humanity's realization, is manifested "mystically" in the *sacramentum*, the Eucharist.

After discussing the two cities in Augustine, Lettieri turns to the *saeculum*. Humanity, which in Adam has an intermediary nature between angels and beasts, is called to a spiritual end, namely the *consortium angelicum*, the true *civitas Dei*. This beatitude for Augustine is the end of humanity, the participation in the Trinity and the recovery of the unity lost by human pride. This pride causes three alienations: from God, from self, and from society. The alienation from God is the replacement of the love of God with the love of self. The alienation from self is the person in discord internally, as the soul no longer governs the body and the person is racked by *pertubationes*, *passiones*, and *motus*. Social alienation is the perversion of human natural sociality and is manifested in our *libido*, which renders society victim to rivalries and creeping suspicion.[117] Lettieri, like other commentators, examines human sociality, which he sees as pining towards the reconstruction of the fallen world. It is a fundamental ontological force seeking to maintain the peace of society in which it is realized.

Lettieri sees human sociality as a neutral force, in that it requires a "choice of existence." Using Augustine's concept of *amor*, Lettieri notes that such love needs an object; hence, the will provides the direction of human love. For the Christian, no earthly, finite good can truly satisfy him, as he is created for participation in eternity. Hence, on earth there is a choice between love of self and love of God, a society of pride and a society of humility, and, in Augustinian terms, the example of Abel and the example of Cain.[118] For Augustine, this is the cause of the state's ontological function. As a

116. Ibid., 48.
117. Ibid., 79.

prolongation of the family, the state is a necessary good providing "order, hierarchy of responsibilities, of powers, and assures social peace, order, and human community."[119] However, while the *civitas* has a clear role in light of human nature, the *saeculum* is but a period of transition in which any certainty about man's participation in either of the two cities is impossible to comprehend. Building upon Marrou's analysis, Lettieri sees the *saeculum* as a "mixed" time with empirical historical good and also evil.[120]

Lettieri on the *Saeculum*

While recognizing the importance of Robert Markus's work, Lettieri also clarifies his understanding of the *saeculum* by dissenting from a number of Markus's conclusions. Lettieri does not agree with Markus's interpretation of the *saeculum* as neutral in its historical-objective dimension, arguing that such an interpretation loses Augustine's mystical sense. For Lettieri, Markus's neutrality contributes instead to a secularization of the relationship between the state and the Church, a secularization that creates barriers between the secular and any "ultimate significance"[121] Markus empties Augustine's vision of any eschatological meaning and ignores the eschatological nature of his concept of *permixtio*. A neutral saeculum "risks cutting off all value of the 'visible' dimension and concreteness of history."[122]

In response, Lettieri puts forward his own interpretation of the Augustinian term *saeculum,* seeing this period as having three

---

118. It is this focus on human choice and the role of the human subject which causes me to call Lettieri's approach existential.
119. Lettieri, *Il senso*, 102.
120. Ibid., 113.
121. Ibid., 116.
122. Ibid., 117.

fundamental levels. The first level of *saeculum* is "concealment," the moment in which each person encounters the punishment of sin and confronts his humanity and its mortality. This is the period in which man's alienation due to sin is manifested and in which it appears that each person stands in front of a "profound, obscure abyss."[123] The second level is recognition, in which the *saeculum* is recognized as a sinful or "evil" time. The pagan *saeculum* would fall into this category, since it is a sterile moment in which human perdition is inevitable for it is nature without grace.[124] Here, the response to death is completely human. Man flees from the void of his existence and responds to his mortality by a love of self, making his image without God absolute. Fame and glory are sought for this reason and *claritas*, which is the divine prerogative, is imitated in the earthly city. Lettieri notes that such human recognition is the "perverse imitation of the glorious splendor of God."[125] This perversion, which is demonic for its idolatrous nature, is the root of man's *libido dominandi*, as love of self, *amor sui*, becomes the dominant element of the individual person and human participation in community.

The third level is "awareness," which is defined by the incarnation of Christ and the interruption of human history which it causes.[126] This event alone breaks humanity's imprisonment in the *saeculum* and its pagan recognition of self-transformation to a time of grace and mercy. What was a sterile age for man has now become fertile and the source of renewal.[127] This awareness, or awakening of humanity's sense of being, is found in the *novum saeculum*, which for Augustine is

123. Ibid., 123.
124. Ibid., 128.
125. Ibid., 134.
126. The term used here is "riconoscibilità," which is difficult to separate in English from the term describing the second level of "riconoscimento." Hence, I have used "recognition" for the former and "awareness" for the latter. Also, here again an existentialist influence must be seen, as man's sense in front of the *saeculum* is a central concern of Lettieri's analysis.
127. Lettieri, *Il senso*, 142.

the time of the Church, as the Church gives witness to this openness of man's reality to his fulfillment through Christ's grace. For Lettieri, Augustine's sense of history is completely changed in the incarnation, as the *saeculum* is now a time in which the hour has been revealed and human history has been rendered a "sacred sign," a sacrament. The *saeculum*, once a culture of death and sin in Christ, becomes the sign of God's revelation and proof of faith's credibility.[128] The *saeculum* is always in time and incommensurable to eternity. Instead of being neutral, however, it becomes a place of tension. Though death and sin are still present, salvation is not recognizable. Salvation for Lettieri is not fully knowable in the earthly city. While *claritas* is no longer seen as a human achievement, it is evident in the manifestation of God in Christ and in the history of the Church. For Augustine, this tension is embodied for all time in the "scandalous obscurity" of the cross of Christ, in which the dialectic of the *saeculum* is manifested by Christ Himself, embodying both the obscurity of this age and the awareness of man's final destiny. Lettieri writes that "all of his existence is not dominated by men, but man searches for God, not possessing Him but dependent on His salvation, the grace of God, and this is not possession either, but the mysterious action of God with the most hidden realms of the human soul."[129]

Another problem in Markus's concept of *saeculum* to which Lettieri responds is the invisibility of the sacred, which is completely absorbed in the *permixtio* of this "hidden" period. Augustine's *permixtio*, Lettieri notes, is only conceivable in relation to the possibility of grace. Augustine's concept of a mixed city is connected to the reality of Christian time and its "sacramental" sense of history. The visible Church, therefore, is where the grace and love of God can be made interiorly fruitful. However, Lettieri notes that, for Augustine,

128. Ibid., 151.
129. Ibid., 177.

salvation is not just the fruit of interior "subjective" adhesion to Christ, but also it is realized in and through the "objective" mediation of the Church.[130] The human choice directing *amor* is concretely manifested in the sacraments and the practice of *caritas*. Hence, Lettieri argues that Augustine's "ecclesiological secret" is a complex relationship between subjectivity (in faith) and objectivity (in discipline and charity).[131] This is why Markus's distinction of the sacred and the *saeculum* is problematic, as it renders *caritas* as something purely eschatological. Also, Lettieri argues this eschatological shift ignores Augustine's ecclesiology, in which the Church "cannot be compared to any secular society, no other secular society is the place of the 'holy,' no other has in itself the power to lead to the Eternal."[132]

Augustine, Lettieri argues, insists that the Christian does not live in "obscurity" while he is in the *saeculum*. Rather, he already participates in the salvific design and redemption actualized and realized by God through and in the visible Church. Admittedly, this salvation, the work of grace, will only be manifested in eschatological judgment. However, the work of the Church allows the Christian to know his redemption, which cannot be recognized or possessed in this *saeculum*. As Lettieri concludes:

> In the Church, therefore, the *obscurity* is maintained, but it is forever an obscurity that participates in a mystery of grace witnessed to by the visible and pilgrim Church: *recognition*: an anticipation that has sense only in as much as it is an allusion to that which is already hidden, to a full realization that will be only eschatological, but that is on the other hand recognizable and attainable only through the grace of its "sign," of its partial realization *in hoc saeculo*.[133]

130. Ibid., 183.
131. Ibid., 188.
132. Ibid., 192.
133. Ibid., 193.

Peter Iver Kaufman

Kaufman's Recovery of Augustinian Caution

Dissenting from the secularist and Radical Orthodox interpretations of Augustine, Peter Iver Kaufman interprets Augustine's position towards social and political life in a tempered and more pessimistic manner. Indeed, Kaufman doubts the authenticity of interpretations of Augustine that see Christianity as having a positive impact on public life. As a result, he puts forward a more pessimistic Augustine on such issues.[134] While Markus and other liberal interpreters are scandalized by Augustine's use of coercion against the Donatists, seeing it as an exception to Augustine's wider thought, Kaufman notes that "Donatist causalities have become the chief witnesses against Augustine's Augustinian liberalism . . . Augustine embarrasses liberals."[135] Therefore, Kaufman argues that the Augustinian condemnation of both Pelagians and Donatists was also a rejection of "naive idealist perfectionism," against which Augustine posited confidence not in institutional impact, but in "personal sentiments." "With help, good could come from evil, not in the form of political sentiments, Augustine surmised, but as personal sentiments, that is as promising shoots sprouting from the ruins of a fallen nature. We grow compassion."[136]

Augustinian confidence, Kaufman argues, must be seen not in wider change by Christianity, but in the "personal" contributions and dispositions of Christians themselves. To demonstrate this, Kaufman focuses on Augustine's letters to public officials, which were "more concerned to improve magistrates' dispositions than to change the

---

134. Peter Iver Kaufman, *Incorrectly Political: Augustine and Thomas More* (South Bend, IN: University of Notre Dame Press, 2007), 227.
135. Peter Iver Kaufman, "Christian Realism and Augustinian (?) Liberalism," *Journal of Religious Ethics* 38, no. 4 (2010): 712.
136. Ibid., 700.

policies and structures over which they presided."[137] Indeed, the accomplishment of the latter was doubtful, Kaufman believes, in the mind of a skeptical Augustine struggling with the Donatists and the entrance of Pelagianism into Africa. While addressing magistrates, he reminds them that they "could only hope to make bad situations and corrupt systems a little less dreadful."[138] This is far from the consensus-building hopes of Markus. In fact, this perspective finds Augustine moving closer to Niebuhr's "anti-utopian imperatives."[139] While Markus and Gregory see Augustine consumed with a desire to positively impact his social and political context, Kaufman disagrees and sees no political program in Augustine's work, especially his letters.

> Consumed? Augustine more often seems composed than consumed. He as much as conceded some incompatibility between that "true" theology and politics when he explained that the virtues prescribed by Christianity's sacred texts, "forbearance and benevolence, should be kept secretly in one's own mind" as one—say a Christian who acquiesces to become a magistrate—upholds a judgment that requires retribution as well as reparations.[140]

Kaufman also expresses skepticism regarding Augustine's treatment of Christian martyrdom, which he believes exposes the limited expectations of the Bishop of Hippo for wider change in the earthly city. Christian martyrs manifested to their fellow believers the grim nature of the earthly city itself and the eschatological hope necessary in Christian life.

> On earth, the pilgrim city was austere, alien; its journey through time, troubled and wretched (aerumnosa). However, settled they may seem, genuine Christians were citizens of this other, transcendent realm. They

---

137. Kaufman, Incorrectly Political, 108.
138. Ibid., 229.
139. Kaufman, "Christian Realism," 700.
140. Ibid., 706.

must expect only hardship here but may expect reward hereafter . . . No better reminder that the genuine Christian was not at home here, that Christ's kingdom was not of this world, could have been set before the faithful, save perhaps the Christian martyr.[141]

In light of such Augustinian skepticism, Kaufman rejects the Augustinian liberal project, or at the very least its appropriation of Augustine as a "patron" and founder. For example, in response to Eric Gregory's "ethic of democratic citizenship," Kaufman notes: "To my mind, the results are more liberal than Augustinian, more liberal than Augustine's results."[142] He considers the attempt of Rawlsian liberals to build social consensus in the *res publica* without doctrine to be a self-defeating impossibility. He notes that lacking religious conviction, such theorists "close an artery" from which compassion enters public deliberation. Like Paul Ramsey and Eric Gregory, Kaufman freely admits that love is central to the Augustinian liberal project. However, he notes that because "love empowers justice," the restriction of religion in public life renders love unsustainable and justice unlikely.[143]

Recovering Augustine's Eschatology

For Kaufman, the essential and often misunderstood element in this discussion remains the eschatological character of Augustine's *City of God*, meaning the concern for man's final goal and the fulfillment of creation itself. Augustine repeatedly sought to move Christians to "rejoice in expectation" and recognize their true home as the heavenly kingdom. Recognizing the fleeting nature of civic virtue, the driving force of private interest, and indeed the spiraling force of

---

141. Peter Iver Kaufman, "Augustine, Martyrs, and Misery," *Church History* 63, no.1 (March 1994): 6.
142. Kaufman, "Christian Realism," 712.
143. Ibid., 707.

pride, Augustine wanted to ensure that Christians would not mistake politics for piety.

> Even if civic virtues were diligently practiced en route and self interest (*privates res*) was sacrificed for the common good (*pro re communi...contempserunt*), *vera via* ought not to be mistaken for piety. It was politics. Augustine's *City*, marking the contrasts, as noted, strives to tidy up those two categories...Politics and truth had gone their separate ways.[144]

While Milbank and others argue that imperial rule was seen as a "pastoral reality," Kaufman cautions that Augustine held no dream of a "lasting peace" being provided by any emperor or empire, whether Christian or pagan. In fact, Kaufman believes, Augustine much preferred public officials seeking vainglory to be amongst scoundrels than amongst true Christians seeking God.[145] Kaufman raises another problematic issue with Milbank's position. It is, he argues, difficult to reconcile Milbank's view of the Church as *societas perfecta* associated directly with the *civitas dei*, and simultaneously maintain Augustine's vision of *ecclesia permixta*. Kaufman seeks to build upon the work of Wilhelm Kamlah in recovering the "eschatological orientation," of this association.[146] Kaufman notes, "The question is one of survival, that is, the survival of Augustine's care for the life and reform of the institutional church, what Kamlah called the 'empirical Catholic church,' in the presence of his pronounced individualistic understanding of righteousness and reform . . . and in the face of his eschatological orientation."[147] The "eschatological orientation" of Augustine is necessary to understanding the pilgrimage the Church has to undergo, especially in light of its mixed nature on earth.

---

144. Ibid., 720.
145. Kaufman, "Augustine, Martyrs, Misery," 13.
146. Peter Iver Kaufman, *Augustinian Piety and Catholic Reform* (Macon, GA: Mercer University Press, 1983), 25.
147. Ibid.

On earth, [the churches] would always encompass capricious and wayward Christians. On earth, they would forever be mixed congregations of the reprobate, the rogues, and the righteous. The reprobate were lost. The bishops' pastoral responsibility was to make the rogue (*adhuc carnales*) righteous and the righteous more so.[148]

Kaufman notes that although the intersection of politics and piety is not a new reality, the translation of Augustine into specific ideological schools within social and political life is a dangerous project. "The realists' restrained hopes for progressive justice and the liberals' search for a consensus or conversation that encompasses respect for difference . . . take Augustine's hopes for souls as hopes for society."[149] Indeed, Augustine's evaluation of political life in his letters and in the *City of God* was not to offer systematic reform, but to offer caution to the Christian completing his earthly pilgrimage and assuring that his final destination was his eternal home. He concludes:

Augustine turned to Rome to extract a very different lesson. Any earthly triumph or happiness, if it obscures the expectation for the pilgrim city's celestial victory and beatitude, promptly occasions fresh misery and the increase of misery which was always there (*quae inerat augeatur*). Each 'fall' or failure deflates the wrong kind of hope and gives the Christian ministry a chance to retrain perfectionists, reaffirm paradox, reorient expectations, and people the pilgrim city of God.[150]

---

148. Ibid., 13.
149. Kaufman, "Christian Realism," 721.
150. Kaufman, "Augustine, Martyrs, Misery," 14. We will be returning to Kaufman's interpretation of Augustine and its important hermeneutical implications, as this more pessimistic and cautious understanding of Augustine is central to the efforts at recovering a more "authentic" Augustinian vision.

William Connolly

Connolly's "Augustinian Imperative"

William Connolly takes a deconstructionist approach towards the Augustinian tradition in Western political thought, most especially in his work *The Augustinian Imperative: A Reflection on the Politics of Morality*.[151] Connolly's work, influenced most notably by Nietzsche and Foucault, attempts to identify and deconstruct what he observes as subtle and often unnoticed influences in our political and ethical systems, in order to create "an ethical sensibility appropriate to the complexity and ambiguity of cultural life."[152] K. Roberts Skerrett summarizes Connolly's task as "how to envision human freedom without overplaying responsibility while still seeking to generate sufficient responsibility that one can oppose crushing constraints on human freedom."[153] His treatment of Augustine's influence, therefore, is based on what he calls "the Augustinian imperative."[154] He describes this imperative as "the insistence that there is an intrinsic moral order susceptible to authoritative representation. This imperative in turn, is linked to an obligatory pursuit: the quest to move closer to one's truest self by exploring its inner geography."[155]

---

151. The role of Connolly in introducing deconstructionist methods into the discipline of political science has been reaffirmed by Jonathan Culler in the most recent edition of his work *On Deconstruction*. See Jonathan D. Culler, *On Deconstruction: Theory and Criticism after Structuralism* (Ithaca, NY: Cornell University Press, 2007), 4.

152. William E. Connolly, *Why I Am Not a Secularist* (Minneapolis: University of Minnesota Press, 2002), 11.

153. K. Roberts Skerrett, "The Indispensable Rival: William Connolly's Engagement with Augustine of Hippo," *Journal of American Academy of Religion* 72, no. 2 (June 2004): 490.

154. However, Connolly openly admits at the outset of his work that Augustine is "neither the first nor last bearer" of this concept. See William Connolly, *The Augustinian Imperative: A Reflection on the Politics of Morality* (Newbury Park, CA: SAGE Publications, 1993), xvii.

155. Connolly, *Augustinian Imperative*, xvii. For Connolly, both the imperative and the pursuit cannot be realized, but are both essential to understanding Augustine's worldview and the subsequent Augustinian tradition.

Citing as an example Book XVI of *City of God,* Connolly argues that this imperative, especially its sense of intrinsic moral order, derives from faith in an omnipotent God who has endowed his creation with a specific order. "A Christian god is the single moral source for Augustine. This god is both a commander and a designer . . . We receive glimpses of its *design* through scripture and through a common experience of harmonies in the world."[156] In Connolly's view, however, Augustine has both shielded this imperative from opposition and transmitted it to the West by his concept of a divided human will and the subsequent necessity of the practice of confession of one's sinfulness.[157] He argues:

> The royal road to morality is also the rocky road to salvation. The route that takes you through the interior of the self to a closer relation to god, the fundamental source of creation, morality, and salvation. The vehicle capable of carrying you along this route is confession. Through confession you call on him by calling into yourself. Confession serves as a vehicle of purification and moralization.[158]

Thus, Connolly sees the practice of confession as based in a narcissistic search for "conversion." He notes that it simultaneously excludes any other form of religiosity from attaining the same experience. In this way, Connolly implicates Augustine in the institutionalization of a personal mode of confession which spreads into the wider Church and empire. To demonstrate how the Augustinian imperative was applied and transmitted, Connolly turns to Augustine's monastic regulations, especially focusing on Epistle 211, which is addressed to a monastery of nuns in Hippo.

---

156. Connolly, *Augustinian Imperative,* 39.
157. See Connolly, *Why I Am Not a Secularist,* 116-7. In this section, Connolly argues that the Augustinian concept of will appears after Adam's fall and that it is necessarily divided in order "to protect divinity from responsibility for evil in the world" and to reject opponents who point to alternate ways of interpretation.
158. Ibid., 43.

A system of graded authority, the imperative to moral unity, a meticulous specification of rules, the production of sinful desires, the obligation to confess, a network of mutual surveillance among equals, a system of punishments, the manufacture of the inward self, the confession of a divine source hovering over the entire complex. These . . . form the confessional complex. They constitute the authoritative network of confessional morality.[159]

Citing the clash at Calama between Christians and pagans, Connolly goes on to argue that Augustine not only spread this imperative interiorly within the Church, but also sought its spread into wider society.[160] Here, drawing primarily from Augustine's treatment of the Manicheans and Pelagians, Connolly contends that while a "politics of identity," or relative flexibility, was present within the Church, a "politics of difference," or coercion and exclusion, governed relations with those outside of it.[161] He notes, "Within the circle of his faith, Augustine evinces a measure of appreciation for plurality . . . But stringent lines are drawn around this zone of tolerance, beyond which diversity is intolerable."[162] Finally, Connolly claims that this insistence upon the superiority of the Christian moral order would carry over even into the soteriological and eschatological responses to the anxiety of death, where again Augustine would enforce a system of reward and punishments.[163]

Connolly's dissent from Augustine, therefore, centers on the invocation of an intrinsic moral order, which he believes is reinforced through a cycle of guilt and confession. Connolly believes that this

159. Connolly, *Augustinian Imperative*, 71.
160. Ibid., 76-7.
161. Connolly applies here a model proposed in his previous work *Identity and Difference* to his understanding of Augustine's ecclesial context. See *Identity\Difference: Democratic Negotiations of Political Paradox* (Minneapolis: University of Minnesota Press, 1991).
162. Connolly, *Augustinian Imperative*, 77.
163. Ibid., 82-3. Like Kaufman, Connolly's arguments will be returned to in the hermeneutical discussion of Augustine's political and social vision. Connolly's dissent from Augustine offers another side of Augustinian interpretation, namely critique of Augustine's influence in Western society and culture.

trend in Western ethics must be identified and surpassed, and in order to accomplish this he invokes the philosophy of Nietzsche and Foucalt. Connolly's project, therefore, is emblematic to the efforts of numerous contemporary political thinkers and ethicists, who seek a post-Christian ethics, which lacks intrinsic values and any element of natural law theory. Connolly, therefore, in light of the diversity of Western society and the concrete reality of a globalized world calls for an ethics built upon tolerance and inclusion. However, like other thinkers he recognizes the difficulty in grounding such ethics philosophically. Connolly's dissent from Augustine's ethics and his part in the larger movement to refute Augustine's social influence, will be discussed later. His work engages larger hermeneutical questions that we will also address later.

Conclusion

The authors we have discussed in this chapter, from Markus to Connolly, have laid the groundwork for the contemporary post-Niebuhrian discussion of Augustine's political and social vision. While after World War II, Niebuhr's realism dominated many ethical circles, the authors we have discussed here represent movement forward in the interpretation of Augustine's political and social implications. While Niebuhr's influence and significance remain strong, this era of Augustinian interpretation sought a recovery of the historical and contextual questions surrounding Augustine's *City of God*. Chief among these works remains Robert Markus's *Saeculum*, which remains an important analysis of Augustine's political thought and the context from which it emerged. Indeed, Markus's commentary largely overshadows the entire contemporary debate. However, as we have also observed, Markus's work has also inspired dissenting opinions. Here, we can observe the work of John Milbank, who has also greatly influenced the contemporary discussion of Augustine's political thought. The Radical Orthodoxy response to Markus and the secularist reading of Augustine's two cities, as we will see, reemerges in the next generation of scholars.

We have also discussed in this chapter other ecclesiastical authors, who have grappled with these questions and have allowed this debate to bear greater ecclesiastical and theological importance. Here the Augustinian foundations of the theology of Joseph Ratzinger and Rowan Williams can be observed, especially as many ideas in their later discourses on politics and public life are shaped by the questions surrounding this discussion. As we will see in the next chapter, many of the ideas discussed here will be advanced or critiqued further in the latter part of the twentieth century, as a new generation has emerged and begun to grapple with these issues in our contemporary political and philosophical context. In this period, as well, new light has been shed upon hermeneutical questions, and a search is undertaken for an "authentic" Augustinian vision.

4

Recovering Augustine's Vision of Public Life and Virtue

The Debate Entering the 21st Century

In the last chapter, we observed the post-Niebuhrian response provided by numerous authors, most especially Robert Markus and John Milbank. As we have already noted, these authors would themselves lead to further commentary and efforts at interpreting Augustine's political and social ideas. However, as the debate neared the end of the twentieth and beginning of the twenty-first century, a theological shift occurred. A new hermeneutical interest emerged in the theological context and influences that shaped Augustine's vision. With schools of interpretation emerging and presuppositions varying widely, this chapter marks the next generation of interpretation, working in the late-twentieth century into the present day. This new hermeneutical interest is present in the work of Peter Iver Kaufman, Robert Dodaro, and others, who sought to "recover" Augustine from the midst of the secularist school of interpretation, which in the late twentieth century had grown in popularity. The struggle of many of the authors discussed in this chapter, therefore, is to recalibrate expectations in light of Augustine's thought. James Wetzel seeks a recovery of Augustine's ambivalence toward the public sphere, and his consummate focus on virtue and its proper ordering. Miikka Ruokanen leads an eschatological rediscovery within Augustinian interpretation, especially focusing on the concepts of *ordo, amor,* and *civitas.* Oliver O'Donovan dissents from many interpretations by rejecting even the very notion of a *tertium quid.* O'Donovan instead imposes a "theo-political framework" present in Augustine, whom he argues calls for an undivided loyalty and commitment towards the heavenly city. In a very different manner, Augustine's theology and its various aspects is cohesively treated by Robert Dodaro, who introduces new sources from Augustine's corpus into the discussion. Dodaro places Augustine's theology of virtue at the core of his interpretation. Charles Mathewes, Eric Gregory, and Graham Ward offer different examples of how Augustine's thought is to be applied to the current social and theological milieu. While the points of debate among these interpretations is at times clear, the question has emerged as to whether the Augustinian interpretations being put forward are themselves consistent with the work and thought of Augustine of Hippo. As a result, a number of the authors we will discuss here will reemerge in the last chapter, where we will foray into contemporary hermeneutical questions and different applications of Augustine's thought.

James Wetzel

Augustine's "Reformulation of Virtue"

In describing James Wetzel's contribution to the Augustinian conversation on the *saeculum*, John Bowlin notes: "Wetzel offers an Augustinian reconstruction of Augustine, one that insists upon the unresolved character of love in time . . . every effort to strip away the virtues of our enemies and expose their vices falls victim to Augustine's 'thick expectation of ambivalence.'"[1] Indeed, Wetzel's work *Augustine and the Limits of Virtue* is dedicated both to examining Augustine's dissatisfaction with pagan virtue and its neglect of inner conflict and to promoting the "reformulation of virtue as the motivational integrity of graced willing."[2] Wetzel argues that while many accuse Augustine of excluding all human activity from virtue, Augustine in reality has invoked God in the reconnection of human power to the perception of order.

> Love of justice, the gift of God's spirit, is nothing other than representing and willing the order of creation. Saints are empowered in will in so far as they can recollect the ordered self that God has created them to be. What Augustine has that Pelagius lacks is appreciation for the blindness in human self-knowledge and the trial of having overcome it . . . Augustine leaves virtue to its temporary vulnerability, but not without revealing the image of eternity in time—the unity of a redeemed memory.[3]

Wetzel's philosophical concerns on the notion of free will and virtue cause him, therefore, to comment on the discussion of Augustine's vision of *civitas* and the debate between Robert Markus and John

---

1. John Bowlin, "Parts, Wholes, and Opposites: John Milbank as *Geisteshistoriker*," *Journal of Religious Ethics* 32, no. 2 (Summer 2004), 266.
2. James Wetzel, *Augustine and the Limits of Virtue* (Cambridge: Cambridge University Press, 1992), 16.
3. Ibid., 218.

Milbank. At the outset, Wetzel agrees with Milbank's interpretation of Augustine, especially the Augustine who wrote *City of God*. Wetzel sees, like Milbank, an absolute separation in Augustine's two cities and recognizes that the impossibility of separating the citizens of the two cities in time, which remains the foundational principle for Robert Markus's interpretation of the *saeculum*. "It is only because Augustine disavows knowledge of who's on what side of history that Markus sees some grounds for moving from *saeculum* to secular history."[4] Therefore, Wetzel and Milbank see the *saeculum*'s ambiguity as misplaced in Markus's analysis. Rather than seeing it as the basis of a proto-modern secularism, they argue that the apparent ambiguity of Augustine in his discussion of the *civitas terrena* is only understood in light of his theology.

> There is nothing about the expectation of ambivalence that prevents us from trying to serve the better angels of our nature. It does, however, mortgage the virtuous life to the powers of faith, hope, and love. The Augustine that would allow me to call those powers 'secular' is the Augustine I wish to honor in this essay. He bears an ambivalent relationship to Milbank's Augustine.[5]

Wetzel sees in Augustine the necessity of two polarized cities, one good and the other evil. The need for the earthly city to navigate between them can be seen as Marrou's *tertium quid*.[6] In the *civitas terrena*, Augustine admits that virtue exists to "wed natural happiness and the higher good of self rule," but any claim of the accomplishment of that union in this life must be rejected. "Augustine will claim that all the virtues that aim at happiness in this life—not just temperance but also prudence, justice, and

---

4. James Wetzel, "Splendid Vices and Secular Virtues: Variations on Milbank's Augustine," *Journal of Religious Ethics* 32 no.2 (Summer 2004), 274.
5. Wetzel, "Splendid Vices," 276.
6. Ibid.

fortitude—bear witness to continuing human misery and wickedness."[7] Indeed, the distinction Milbank and Wetzel focus on is within the Augustinian conception of peace, as there remains both the corrupt and earthly variety and the perfect divine peace. Milbank sees an ontological association of these two varieties of peace, the former with an "ontological antagonism" and the latter with "ontological peace."[8] The ontological distinction here exposes the difference between virtue for its own sake and virtue for divine motives. "In referring to the virtues of God he advocates there a *return* of the virtues to their source—a matter of attribution, but also of surrender . . . He wants to distance himself thoroughly from the view that the virtues belong to those who exercise them."[9]

Milbank's insistence on referencing virtue to God is a mission that Wetzel sees as essential in a postmodern context, in which self-autonomy and choice dominate the discussion. In fact, essential to Wetzel's project is the rejection of the association of free will with freedom under "Augustinian" protection.

> Augustine never identified free will with freedom from constraint . . . Compulsory action (as in involuntary sin), blindly sinful action (as in voluntary sin), and virtuous action (as under grace) all express *liberum arbitrium*. Only the last, however, expresses free will.[10]

Wetzel notes two obstacles to contemporary thinkers that prevent acceptance of Augustine's concept of free will, as associated with virtuous action under grace, namely the disassociation of free will from the concept of multiple alternatives and the inability to disassociate an action's morality from freedom. While many thinkers see the freedom of an action as a separate question from that action's

7. Ibid., 279.
8. Ibid., 280.
9. Ibid., 282.
10. Wetzel, *Augustine and the Limits of Virtue*, 221.

moral value, such a separation is impossible for Augustine, for whom "normative and metaphysical concerns meet in free will."[11] Wetzel makes clear that our attempts at autonomy "are at best way-stations to the knowledge and freedom that we call, often too glibly, love."[12] Any Augustinian discussion of "self" can only occur in reference to God, since referencing the virtues to God necessarily leads to our own dispossession of them.

Wetzel's notion of the secular is defined, therefore, not by neutrality but by "ambivalence." This ambivalence "refers to the struggle in the human soul between broad and narrow conceptions of self love," which, Wetzel notes, cannot be translated easily into categories of good and evil.[13] Wetzel shares Milbank's rejection of a "neutralized" secularity, which is cut off from any eschatological or "redemptive" implication. However, he also avoids what he perceives as Milbank's unnecessary exaggeration of the Augustinian sense that the secular is "evil."[14] Indeed, for Wetzel, ambivalence must dominate any discussion of an Augustinian concept of secular. One must always keep in mind, however, "the necessity of grace's effect, the ability of virtue to define and maintain the boundaries of the self against the intrusive chaos of the world."[15]

Wetzel's work, therefore, seeks to recapture the ambivalence and tension present in Augustine's concept of two cities. Like Dodaro and others in this chapter, he focuses on the question of virtue in Augustine. While imperfect and flawed in history, virtue remains the vehicle by which, with God's grace, humanity's likeness to God and eternal vocation is manifested. Wetzel's commentary on the debate between Markus and Milbank delivers a necessary and significant

11. Ibid., 222.
12. Wetzel, "Splendid Virtues," 299.
13. Ibid.
14. Ibid.
15. Wetzel, *Augustine and the Limits of Virtue*, 218.

reminder, namely the need to explore the question of what is the nature of the *saeculum*. Wetzel recovers Marrou's sense of ambiguity in the *tertium quid;* an ambiguity that, like Milbank, he believes is not a political caveat, but a theological necessity. For Wetzel, the *saeculum* is not to create neutral space, but rather emerges because of the uncertainty as to the citizenry of the two cities. It remains an uncertainty for Augustine, which will only be clarified at the end of time.

Miikka Ruokanen

Finding Augustine's "Inner Logic"

Miikka Ruokanen's work *Theology of Social Life in Augustine's De Civitate Dei* seeks to overturn what the author sees as a "one-sided application of a diachronic or historical method" of interpreting Augustine.[16] To accomplish this, Ruokanen seeks to place Augustine's theology of social life in the context of his theological corpus and an analysis of "the inner logic of his thought."[17] Augustine, according to Ruokanen, sees social life as the "specific characteristic of rational beings in God's creation." Sin's most apparent effect is the deterioration of social life.[18] This social life consists of relationships between rational beings and their creator and between rational beings themselves. However, Ruokanen maintains that such an examination of the concept of social life in the work of the elderly Augustine cannot ignore his focus on sin and sin's overwhelming power and consequences "penetrating all the spheres of human life."[19] For this reason, Ruokanen believes that "[t]he only

---

16. Miikka Ruokanen, *Theology of Social Life in Augustine's De Civitate Dei* (Göttingen: Vandenhoeck and Ruprecht, 1993), 19.
17. Ibid.
18. Ibid., 21.

true counterweight to this aggravating weight or *pondus* of human misery is the eschatological hope of *civitas Dei*."[20] Ruokanen's method combines the philological examination of key terms in Augustine with their wider theological implications. As a result, Ruokanen divides Augustine's work according to the analysis of particular terms: *ordo*, *amor* (and its synonyms *dilectio* and *caritas*), and *civitas*.

Ruokanen's analysis of *ordo* builds upon the insight of Peter Brown, that a positive doctrine of *ordo* is presented throughout Augustine's *City of God*.[21] Turning to Augustine's *De ordine*, as well as to his commentary on the Psalter, Ruokanen affirms the prevalence of a concept of *ordo*, which in *City of God* is referred to as *ordo naturae*. "God created things and beings, those with a higher essence having set above those with an essence of lower grade. There thus exists an ontological hierarchy in the universe . . ."[22] This order allowed for a harmony in creation formed by peace in the human body and soul, amongst human beings, and between man and God through the obedience to God's *lex aeterna*. For Augustine, this eternal law is inscribed on the human soul; despite sin's alienation of humanity from their creator and the rest of creation, access to an expression of the eternal law, which is the "natural law," is not erased. Human deviation from the harmony of this divine order originates in the will and is centered in *superbia*, or pride. It is for this reason, Ruokanen notes, that Augustine employs the idea of *pondus voluntatis et amoris*, "the weight of will and love," since "it is the gravity of distorted will and improper ranking or order of love that break down the harmony and peace in God's creation."[23] The breakdown of this

19. Ibid.
20. Ibid.
21. Ibid., 29.
22. Ibid., 30.
23. Ibid., 35.

harmony leads to another use of the *lex aeternae*, namely, the *lex iustitiae*, which has also been described in the concept of God's double providence: "God both rules the natural order itself and regulates the voluntary maintenance of that order through his punitive measures. In the life of rational beings, there are realities—above all the use of will—which are not subject to the order of nature, but they are subject to the eternal law."[24]

For Ruokanen, it is essential to see the context of the law of justice as the *pondus* of man's existence, as it implies an eschatological fulfillment, allows for the presence of man's *libidines* (especially socially in the *libido dominandi*), and ultimately explains the foundations of human society: "Man lives in a society ruled by coercive social power which makes each man subject to another man . . . coercive social power is both a part of sin, *superbia*, itself and a punishment for sin ordained by the divine law of justice."[25] Ruokanen follows Augustine's concept of *ordo* to a pessimistic interpretation of man's social life, a life which has been perverted after the Fall by human pride. Indeed, the only minute justice possible is that which is arrived at by the citizens of the *civitas dei* maintaining their direction toward their ultimate end.[26]

Augustine's doctrine of love forms the underlying premise of his conception of social life. Unlike Cicero's anthropology, which is centered on man and his pride, Augustine's anthropology is based on humility. On its own, humanity is incapable of attaining its true end. Therefore, what is required is "humble subjection to him who alone is the only true Creator of all."[27] Moving from idealism to an anthropological realism, Augustine posits not "cool reason, but

24. Ibid., 37.
25. Ibid., 41.
26. Ibid., 144.
27. Ibid., 49.

the irrational, overwhelming power of liking, adherence, desire, and inclination—various forms of 'love'—is the fundamental motivation of human attitudes and behavior."[28] Ruokanen believes that love, more than knowledge, is the power of life in Augustine. Indeed, its proper ordering or its perversion determines the orientation of a life's ultimate end, namely towards God or away from Him.

While love itself is always good, it can be perverted by the "incorrect orientation or rank of love, *ordo amoris*."[29] Augustine's use of the term *fruor*, which means "to enjoy," to describe the correct order is seen by Ruokanen as signaling the enjoyment of human beatitude, *summum bonum*. This attainment of beatitude is, for Augustine, the completion of humanity's "eudaemonistic search," since loving God and one's neighbor in God constitutes the harmony and peace of the *ordo* of nature for rational beings.[30] Such harmony, and hence the love that achieves it, has both a transcendental and an eschatological character. *Fruor*, therefore, must be seen as a theological term. Indeed, all of the other terms translated as "love," for Ruokanen, imply the basic idea of *fruor* and *adhaereo* and the role of these concepts in the *ordo amoris*. This makes Augustine distinct from classical writers.

> Augustine's eudaemonism is oriented to the final liberation of creation from the turmoil and bondage of sin. This eudaemonism *in spe* differs considerably from the classical philosophical views of eudaemonism: realization of the good never becomes an immanent reality in the postlapsarian state of mankind but remains an eschatological object of faith.[31]

28. Ibid.
29. Ibid., 51.
30. Ibid., 52.
31. Ibid., 54.

Having established the *ordo amoris* in Augustine, Ruokanen turns to the concepts of *iustitia* and *civitas*. Ruokanen notes that justice is a matter of love's correct ordering, rather than the moral law: "True justice is not a reality of rationality, but a reality which is behind rationality, the premise that conditions the functions of reason. Justice has to do with the deepest essence of the disposition of life."[32] Indeed, unlike Cicero and other classical authors who posit a conception of justice around consensus and *communio*, Augustine places *vera iustitia* directly in a teleological and transcendental light.[33] Augustine does not allow philosophy or consensus to lead to justice, but rather to humility before God.

> There is basically only one idea of *iustitia* which interests Augustine in CD: the concept of transcendental and eschatological ideal justice expressing the original harmony of God's creation . . . the realization of justice or righteousness *in fide et in spe* presented to the sinner by the grace of God.[34]

In turning to the question of the *civitas*, Ruokanen argues that good social life is possible only in "the transcendental society, in *civitas Dei*, not in any human society."[35] Like other authors, Ruokanen observes an Augustinian connection between the two cities in the *duo amores* of man. The life of the citizens of the *civitas terrena* is based on pride and the *terrenum* is the object of their love, which includes themselves . . . [36] On the other hand, the citizens of the *civitas Dei* live based on the principle of humility that sees one's ultimate end as the enjoyment of God, by the love which God himself has inspired in them.[37] While

32. Ibid., 72.
33. Ibid., 127.
34. Ibid., 73.
35. Ibid., 77.
36. Ibid., 80.
37. Ibid., 81.

these two cities are certainly different in Augustine's thought, this division was based on faith and not a "visible sociological reality."

> As an individual believer is a member of the heavenly city and yet suffers from the distorting and penal presence of sin characteristic of the terrestrial city, in an analogous way human society itself is sociologically indivisible, being capable of holding . . . both the reality of *civitas Dei* and of *civitas diaboli*.[38]

In *City of God*, Ruokanen demonstrates how Augustine seeks to show that this *civitas Dei* is a *civitas peregrina*, as the human part of the heavenly city is on pilgrimage towards its celestial fulfillment. Although this *civitas peregrina* is a mixed reality containing true and false citizens, the division will not occur until its eschatological completion is reached: "*Civitas Dei* is, for Augustine, not an external reality, but above all an object of faith and hope on the pilgrimage of God's people toward the true *finis* of life."[39] For Ruokanen, Augustine's ecclesiology is peripheral to this discussion in *City of God*, as the Church is nothing more than the "historical aspect" of Augustine's idea of *civitas Dei* continuing the salvific history begun in the "Old Covenant."[40]

The true Church grounded in the "transcendental-eschatological *civitas*" will be joined to the celestial *civitas* at the end of its earthly historical pilgrimage. In this way, the Church can be identified with the *civitas Dei*. However, while eschatologically this identification is possible, its historical reality for Augustine must be regarded as the *ecclesia peregrina* and *corpus permixtum*. However, while there is an association with the *civitas Dei* and the Church, Ruokanen rejects the notion that the *civitas terrena* is a "neutral sphere" in which the

38. Ibid., 82.
39. Ibid., 86.
40. Ibid., 87.

souls of rational beings are in balance between God and the devil. The terrestrial city is not neutral: its citizenship is not natural: it is not inherited biologically, Rather, "it is a lapse from the created goodness of human existence."[41] While natural virtue is not denied by Augustine, the grace of God is necessary to escape from the *civitas terrena*, which for Augustine is founded on the sin of Cain.[42] Like Cain, the terrestrial city maintains a perverted order of love and is filled with envy caused by pride and expressed in the *dominandi cupiditas*. The *libido dominandi*, the lust for the domination of others, is nothing more than the symptom of the lost harmony and perversion of the order of love in sinful humanity. "All human social history is a history of the dominance of *civitas diaboli Babylon* in human societies, a history of disorder and confusion."[43] Ruokanen believe that the only exception given by Augustine to this rule is the affection of family, which is not coercive and is opposed to the *libido dominandi* of the political structure.

Ruokanen rejects any "idea of a divinely ordained structure of political social order in *City of God*, and insists that true justice is a transcendental-eschatological reality which is an object of faith.[44] There is, therefore, in Augustine, a fundamental pessimism about the social life of humanity. According to Ruokanen, this pessimism is defined by a "vitiated *pondus voluntatis et amoris*."[45] The human race bears a misery that arises from the postlapsarian perversion of the harmonious divinely established social order. Indeed, Ruokanen sees an anthropological realism in this portion of Augustine's thought, as the Bishop of Hippo sees all humanity at the mercy of blind, collective, selfish love. Augustine's realism caused him ultimately to

41. Ibid., 93.
42. Ibid., 94.
43. Ibid., 95.
44. Ibid., 106-107.
45. Ibid., 108.

view human social life in terms of "collective self-interested love," not in terms of intact natural justice or of any divine ordination of social structure.[46] As Robert Dodaro has pointed out in reviewing Ruokanen's work, there is also a positive effort called for by Augustine in human social life, namely the need for political leaders to "break with the classical political traditions aligned with *viri optimi* by imitating the apostles, evangelists, and martyrs."[47] Therefore, while Ruokanen, and in a similar way Kaufman, maintain a strong pessimism in Augustine's view of human society, Dodaro notes that the one limited source of optimism that must be affirmed is "[Augustine's] evangelical confidence in the ability of Christians to respond to the grace of conversion."[48]

Ruokanen distinguishes, however, the concept of *saeculum* from this condition of the *civitas terrena*. Building upon the work of Robert Markus, he argues that the *saeculum* is a "transcendentally neutral concept."[49] However, he does not translate such transcendental neutrality into an escape from the misery of human life itself. As a result "it is not neutral but rather a gloomy concept expressing the misery of man."[50] Since the *saeculum* itself has been affected by the Fall, only the eschatological fullness for which man must strive can be positively described as the *futurum* or *novum saeculum*.[51] He concludes his work, therefore, noting:

> Augustine's great work ends with the vision of the eternal felicity of the redeemed society, *civitas dei*, in the new eon. This vision is the only hope of all beings in the world of death and misery.[52]

46. Ibid., 136.
47. Robert Dodaro, review of *Theology of Social Life in Augustine's* De civitate Dei, by Miikka Ruokanen, *Journal of Theological Studies* 45, no.1 (April 1994), 346.
48. Ibid. The presence of this element of optimism is an important point of debate in the work of Dodaro and Kaufman.
49. Ruokanen, *Theology and Social Life*, 111.
50. Ibid.
51. Ibid.

Ruokanen's work is an attempt to relocate the discussion of Augustine's political thought within his theology. He believes only a theological reading allows for an accurate identification of Augustine's main concepts, which Ruokanen identifies as *ordo*, *amor*, and *civitas*. Those three concepts, therefore, can be understood only within Augustine's theology. As a result, his work is characterized as an attempt at contextualizing these terms once again theologically. Ruokanen, like Ratzinger and others before him, identifies a break in Augustine from his classical predecessors. However, for Ruokanen, that break is in Augustine's eudaemonism, which remains not the earthly glory or vanity of classical thinkers, but the eternal fulfillment that is the source of Christian hope. As a result, the Christian life is a pilgrimage, a concept he identifies at the center of Augustine's *City of God*. However, that pilgrimage is plagued by earthly strife and disordered love. What Ruokanen seeks, therefore, is nothing less than a balance between Augustine's discussion of virtue and his fundamental pessimistic realism. Indeed, it is a balance that will be sought and evaluated differently in subsequent authors.

Jean Bethke Elshtain

Defining the Limits of Politics

Jean Bethke Elshtain begins her analysis, like other Augustinian commentators, by diagnosing what she perceives to be a contemporary crisis caused by the disappearance or devaluing of "overlapping associations of social life."[53] The symptoms of such a disease are readily evident in contemporary culture, in which "people

---

52. Ibid., 162.
53. Jean Bethke Elshtain, *Augustine and the Limits of Politics* (Notre Dame, IN: University of Notre Dame Press, 1995), 2.

roam the prairie fixing on objects or policies or persons to excoriate or to celebrate . . . until some other enthusiasm sweeps over them."[54] For Elshtain, our society suffers from the loss of "the sturdiness and patience" that should ground our democracy and culture. Such an absence is based on a misguided individualism, which Elshtain describes as a grounding of the "Selfsame" in itself. Here an appeal must be made to Augustine, who undercuts such "subjectivist expressivism" by connecting the self to its yearning for the God who is "the Same Yesterday, Today, and Tomorrow."[55]

> From an anthropocentric presumption of the Selfsame, no open hearted action nor loving dialogue can come, only the insistencies of a clamorous, triumphalist self, full of demands, shorn of pity, incapable of critical self-examination, disdainful of the only solidarity possible on our torn and tattered globe.[56]

Augustine, therefore, while vilified by numerous thinkers and dismissed by others, still "retains his power to provoke" and is increasingly relevant to our contemporary political and cultural crisis.[57] As James Schall in his review of Elshtain's work elucidates, "Augustine's City of God provides the proper context for distinguishing what we can expect from a limited politics and what we can expect from the transcendant sources of faith and philosophy that often have been confused in modern philosophy."[58] This distinction is central, therefore, in understanding Elshtain's view of Augustine. Her analysis of Augustine begins by recognizing the fundamental flaw of attempting to perfect human society or build a society upon the political order. "Augustine was subversive, shifting

---

54. Ibid., 2.
55. Ibid., 17–18.
56. Ibid., 18.
57. Jean Bethke Elshtain, "Why Augustine? Why Now," *Theology Today* 55, no. 1 (April 1998), 5.
58. James Schall, review of *Augustine and the Limits of Politics*, by Jean Bethke Elshtain, *Theological Studies* 58, no.2 (June 1997), 389.

the center of earthly gravity away from the political order to the 'solid rock' of the *civitas Dei* on pilgrimage."[59] Such a shift was necessary, as Augustine recognized that no earthly institution could legitimately "aspire to the absolute."[60] Augustine acknowledged the sinfulness, or tendency towards *cupiditas*, which darkened all levels of human society: the home (*domus*), the city (*civitas*), and the earth itself (*orbis terrae*).[61] For Elshtain, this acknowledgement of sinfulness within the earthly city has a number of repercussions:

> [T]he quest for insular self-esteem and self-aggrandizement; an urge to dominate over others, to be a self only in relation as a master to a slave, or as a slave who would be master; an urgency toward order that all too readily slides over into the massive dis-order of a coercive *imperium*. [62]

However, another repercussion of human sinfulness is the marring of the priority of peace by the human tendency towards the *libido dominandi*. The problematic nature of earthly dominion, or *potestas*, which excludes any sacralization of the state, is a constant reminder that such peace is only truly manifested in the *civitas Dei*, "which is turned toward God's will."[63] Here, Elshtain draws upon the insights of Robert Markus, whose work *Saeculum* she describes as "the single most astute volume on Augustine's social and political thought."[64] Like Markus, Elshtain sees the *saeculum* in Augustine as the place of human social life, but one in which all human accomplishments are ambiguous towards true human fulfillment. Such fulfillment can only be found in the heavenly city.

---

59. Elshtain, *Augustine and the Limits*, 26.
60. Jean Bethke Elshtain, *Just War Against Terror: The Burden of American Power in a Violent World* (New York: Basic Books, 2003), 32.
61. Elshtain, *Augustine and the Limits*, 27.
62. Ibid., 93.
63. Ibid., 95.
64. Elshtain, "Why Augustine? Why Now?," 6.

Although the earthly city is inescapably marked by sin, including an urge to dominate over others, there are also remedies available. He [Augustine] begins, not with an ontology of violence, but with the presumption of the priority of peace over war. This peace is attained fitfully in the earthly city and achieved in its full richness only in the city of God, but earthly peace is a real good.[65]

Elshtain's work is centered on Augustine's concern for the establishment of earthly peace through the "bonds of affection and necessity" present in human life. As Frances Adeney notes about Elshtain's work, "[u]nlike Augustine, however, she makes little reference to the heavenly city, thereby muting the theological chasm created by Augustine's two-city approach."[66] For Elshtain, this "muting of the theological chasm" is caused by an allegorical dynamic that she observes between the two cities. The Christian must maintain a pilgrim's ethic, attending to the relationships of one's earthly existence, but recognizing that those bonds are neither final nor absolute. "The life of the saint, like the life of the citizen, is a social life . . . There must be a balance in our attention to earthly affairs."[67]

Augustine and *Caritas*

Elshtain's approach is based on a level of individualism, as she believes that it is the individual who is connected to the state by virtue of a series of rights and obligations.[68] However, she grounds those rights and obligations not in themselves, but rather in *caritas*. For Elshtain, the ontological gap between the human person and his

---

65. Ibid., 12.
66. Frances S. Adeney, "Jean Bethke Elshtain: Political Theorist and Postmodern Prophet," *Religious Studies Review* 27, no.3 (July 2001), 247.
67. Elshtain, *Augustine and Limits*, 96.
68. Ibid., 25.

obligations to others, which is an issue that has been grappled with by numerous authors, is answered only in *caritas*. For Augustine, such *caritas* is the sacrificial offering of oneself and hence the "abundant overflowing of the fullness of life."[69] Indeed, Elshtain argues that Augustine's theology of household and theology of city are centered on "interpretive charity," namely the compromise of human wills which flows from love of God and love of neighbor. Her analysis here is based upon Augustine's interpretation of Cicero's definition of the *res publica*. She comments that unlike Cicero, Augustine's definition begins with love, not justice. "That household and city are alike containers for charity and cauldrons for ill-will there can be no doubt . . . we must look to an assemblage of persons bound together by common agreement as to the objects of love."[70] Elshtain's reading of Augustine causes her to argue that friendship is the glue that holds together human ties, binding "husband and wife, brother and sister, friend to friend, citizen to citizen, even in the limited and flawed realm of earthly life."[71] Indeed, human sociability and the desire for peace, she observes, are the very signs of the "heavenly city in this earthly life."[72]

The household in Augustine is also of supreme importance within Elshtain's analysis, as she notes that "the household is a component part that contributes to the completeness of the whole."[73] For Augustine the household is firstly built upon the "ontological equality" of men and women, who occupy different positions.[74] The father of the household, however, must himself tame *cupiditas* and the tendency towards the *libido dominandi* by not exercising arbitrary

---

69. Ibid., 36.
70. Ibid., 39.
71. Ibid.
72. Elshtain, "Why Augustine," 11.
73. Elshtain, *Augustine and the Limits*, 96.
74. Ibid., 39. This ontological equity played out in different roles, Elshtain notes, is present in both convention and nature.

authority and by showing concern for the welfare of all in his household. Augustine sees this concern as contributing not just towards domestic peace, but towards the peace of the *civitas*. Indeed, he posits that a righteous domestic order, founded in compassion and justice (which is tempered by mercy), is "a *civitas* in miniature ruled by love, compassion, and authority in the person of Christian parents."[75] The family in Elshtain's reading of Augustine is an essential association of people and its erosion poses great risk to our society and culture. Second to the family is another mediating association of friends, the Church, whose Augustinian conception Elshtain sees as helping to redefine the pre-Christian order. Fundamentally, the recovery of a Christian *caritas* on all levels of human association, a *caritas* that informs the ends of human action, is the basis of Elshtain's proposal of an "ethic for contemporary society."[76]

Elshtain's analysis of Augustine remains rooted in the fundamental Augustinian distinction of an imperfect earthly city with a tenuous political order and a solid, complete, and perfect heavenly city that remains the fundamental goal of the Christian life. Here, insistence upon political limits is drawn from what she perceives as an Augustinian realism towards political life. However, while some authors move toward abandoning this Augustinian framework, she sees it as essential in understanding the individual's struggle between holiness and attention to earthly affairs. Like other authors we have discussed Elshtain places charity at the center of her ethical interpretation of Augustine, but unlike others explains in detail how that virtue is manifest in human friendship and relationships. Elshtain, therefore, insists upon a broader realm of Augustinian interpretation, namely one that includes all levels of human sociability, especially the

75. Elshtain, *Augustine and Limits*, 40.
76. Adeney, "Jean Bethke Elshtain," 247.

family and local community. Such "limits" upon the role of politics allow for a more well-rounded and comprehensive interpretation of Augustine's political and social thought.

Oliver O'Donovan

O'Donovan's "TheoPolitical Framework"

Although there is an obvious divergence in opinion over Augustine's vision of social and political life and the relationship of the two cities, much of the discussion takes for granted a certain secular framework largely put forward by Robert Markus and his interpretation of Marrou's call for a *tertium quid*. However, Oliver O'Donovan's work, like that of John Milbank, although respectful of Markus's monumental role in Augustinian interpretation, dissents from that accepted framework. Instead, O'Donovan proposes a theopolitical framework which rejects a secularist structure of society and Church and sees in Christ's resurrection and ascension the source of true "ethical illumination."[77] O'Donovan's interpretation of Augustine, especially his *City of God*, leads him, therefore, to clearly and unabashedly reject the notion of a *tertium quid*.

Like Milbank, O'Donovan disagrees with Markus and others over the nature of the "shared ends" and "goods" of the earthly city in relation to the heavenly city. Through his examination of *City of God* XIX, he concludes that, in fact, the discussion of common ends, so often cited in Augustine's notion of a *res publica*, actually connects the shared ends of the earthly household and the earthly city, rather than both the heavenly and earthly cities. That common shared end is unequivocally "eternal death . . . there is no utility,

---

77. Oliver O'Donovan, *Resurrection and Moral Order: An Outline for Evangelical Ethics*, 2nd ed. (Grand Rapids, MI: Eerdmans, 1994), 13.

no final good which gives real value to the pursuit of intermediate goods."[78] O'Donovan categorically denies the possibility that the earthly city can be a "neutral meeting space" or a "naked public square," since Augustine believed that the earthly city and its earthly peace share one loyalty and one ultimate commitment: "the love of self to the exclusion of love of God."[79] The seeking of goods other than and even before God, for O'Donovan and Milbank, renders the earthly city and the liberalism that justifies it as idolatrous and hence irreconcilable with Augustine's conception of the heavenly city. As David McIlroy has noted, "What renders closed liberalism idolatrous is not that the ends it pursues are not genuine goods. What renders closed liberalism idolatrous is that these genuine goods are sought without reference to God."[80]

This conclusion bears two important consequences in O'Donovan's analysis of *City of God*. First, O'Donovan sees no possibility of dual citizenship in Augustine's work. While members of the heavenly city might encourage the "consensus of human wills," this is done purely for the heavenly city's "use of the earthly peace in general." "The wills in question are those of the members of the earthly city among themselves, and the heavenly city supports their consensus . . . by not trying to change their various laws and customs."[81] The consensus, therefore, built between wills remains essential only for the earthly city and its projects. Since that city is corrupted in pride, it lacks any relevance to the ends of the heavenly city. While providing comfort, security, and some level of happiness, these effects are all as transient as the earthly goods that provide them.

---

78. Oliver O'Donovan, *Bonds of Imperfection: Christian Politics, Past and Present* (Grand Rapids, MI: Wm. B. Eerdman's Publishing, 2004), 58.

79. O'Donovan, *Bonds*, 58. Citing here *City of God* XIV.28.

80. A comprehensive and synthetic reading of Oliver O'Donovan is accomplished in the work and analysis of David McIlroy. See David McIlroy, "Idols and Grace: Re-Envisioning Political Liberalism as Political Limitism." *Political Theology* 11, no.2 (2010), 210.

81. O'Donovan, *Bonds*, 59.

The second consequence of denying a secularist framework in Augustine is the direct denial of a "true *tertium quid*" and the possibility of a neutral space where secular and profane can meet as "equal partners." Such a meeting, such a space, is inconsistent with Augustine's work; as O'Donovan notes, it "goes beyond Augustine, for whom, it would seem, true Christians were never true Romans (in the sense of being part of the Roman imperial project) nor false Christians true members of the church (in the sense of being part of a pilgrim society)."[82] The notion of a neutral *saeculum* compromises both cities. It is inconsistent with Augustinian Christology and the concept of original sin, which has placed humanity in a particular condition of egoistic self-seeking. In fact, as McIlroy, Dodaro, and others have argued, the reduction by Markus and others of Augustine's concept of an earthly *civitas* to the term and reality of "state" confuses Augustine's meaning. "Only the 'earthly peace,' that temporal peace of the meantime which is shared by good and wicked alike' is common to both communities, not an institution but simply a condition of order . . . the City of God 'makes use of' the peace of Babylon, and the quoting Jeremiah, 'In her peace is your peace.'"[83]

Political Authority and the Paschal Mystery

O'Donovan, both in his ethical analysis of the modern state and his exegesis of Augustine, regards the neutrality of the secular liberal state to be a problematic attempt by political authorities to avoid the limitations that result from the resurrection and ascension of Christ. While O'Donovan sees all political authority as resting on power, tradition, and judgment, both power and tradition are rendered by Christ's paschal mystery as insufficient alone to justify authority.[84]

82. Ibid. Citing here Markus, *Saeculum*, 60ff.
83. Ibid., 59.

As he writes, "They have to be justified at every point by their contribution to the judicial function. The responsible state is therefore minimally coercive and minimally representative."[85] He states elsewhere in clearer terms: "The reign of Christ in heaven has left *judgment as the single remaining political need* . . . The secular princes of this earth, shorn of pretensions to our loyalty and worship, are left with the sole function of judging between innocent and guilty."[86] However, what has occurred in the modern state is the divorce of justice from government and hence the introduction of an "amoralism" into governance. Therefore, secular neutrality accomplishes nothing more than the ability of secular rulers to ignore moral categories and privatize the Gospel. As David McIlroy explains:

> The neutrality of late-modern liberalism is unmasked by O'Donovan and revealed to be a godless or idolatrous oppression of the Church, a subtle and disguised form of humanity's rebellion against God. Neutral liberalism's rebellion takes the particular form of seeking to reduce the Gospel to a private matter, denying its right or power to effect public transformation.[87]

Indeed, far beyond the secularist vision of the relationship of the Church to political and social life, O'Donovan argues that "there may be a conscious facilitation [of the church by the state] based on the recognition of the church and acknowledgment of its mission."[88] O'Donovan's assertion is drawn from the Augustinian principle that the highest good is ultimately the achievement of one's salvation in Christ. As a result, a government, which cannot save the souls of its subjects, should lend assistance to the Church, which bears that very

84. Oliver O'Donovan, *The Ways of Judgement* (Grand Rapids, MI: Eerdmans, 2005), 227.

85. Oliver O'Donovan, *The Desire of the Nations: Rediscovering the Roots of Political Theology* (Oxford: Oxford University Press, 1996), 233.

86. O'Donovan, *Bonds of Imperfection*, 209.

87. David H. McIlroy, "The Right Reason for Caesar to Confess Christ as Lord: Oliver O'Donovan and Arguments for the Christian State," *Studies in Christian Ethics* 23, no. 3 (Aug. 2010): 301.

88. O'Donovan, *The Desire of the Nations*, 217.

mission.[89] For O'Donovan, the opposite has occurred, as the state has marginalized the Church and its activity within society, leading to a dangerous civil religion which "wears the form of the Antichrist, drawing the faith and obedience due to the Lord's Anointed away to the political orders which should have only provisional authority under him."[90] Like Milbank and much of Radical Orthodoxy, O'Donovan regrets the exclusion of the Gospel from elements of public and social life under the guise of the "secular realm." He notes, "To deny political authority obedience to Christ is implicitly to deny that obedience to society, too."[91]

However, the absence of any evangelical principle in social and political life ought to be expected, as the self-love and pride of the earthly city remain unchanged from Augustine's time. "The city of this world loves itself so much that it despises God by comparison, the eternal city loves God so much that it despises itself by comparison."[92] McIlroy explains, "As O'Donovan understands Augustine, the Bishop of Hippo does not deny the existence or reality of worldly goods, but he does deny that these are worth anything *in comparison* with the eternal good of enjoying God. Worldly goods must not be loved excessively."[93] Citizens of the earthly city are incapable of such temperance and are denied the extended exercise of virtue which flows from true *pietas*, namely, the love and worship of Christ. Hence, for O'Donovan, who accepts Augustine's conception of a society bound by common objects of love, "to expect 'law' of a political entity was to expect too much . . . the most that one could reasonably expect of sinful and prideful communities was some

89. O'Donovan, "Behold, the Lamb!" *Studies in Christian Ethics* 11, no.2 (1998), 105.
90. O'Donovan, *The Desire of the Nations*, 22.
91. Ibid., 246.
92. Oliver O'Donovan, *The Problem of Self-Love in St. Augustine* (New York: Yale University Press, 1980), 64.
93. McIlroy, "The Right Reason," 13.

consensus on goals worth pursuing."[94] Indeed, the reality of the earthly city is such that O'Donovan sees "modest claims" in Augustine's expectations, even those for Christian rulers. "The Christian emperor superimposes on the government of his dominions a kind of *iustitia* that it can function quite well without, and which consists principally in his readiness to ask and to offer forgiveness."[95]

Where others view at least an exception from the rest of the earthly city in the Christian household, O'Donovan sees the Christian emperor and the Christian householder as similar. Both, in his view, are exceptional only as much as they are "detached" from earthly privilege and live in service to others with "longing for the heavenly rest where the burden of command will be taken from his shoulders."[96] For O'Donovan, Augustine bears no illusion of "transformation" within any earthly institutions. Rather, O'Donovan posits, the Christian in service to empire or household is only a sign of God's will to restore creation and not the substance of that restoration itself. O'Donovan's reading of Augustine, therefore, must be seen as somber and pessimistic about the fate of the earthly city in a manner distinct from Markus, Gregory, and others. However, to understand why, O'Donovan bluntly explains:

> If it does not trouble us that we are ignorant of what our children are thinking, that our spouse may be sleeping with our best friend, that many inmates of our prisons may be innocent of the crimes for which they are being punished, that foreign relations are built upon a capacity to repel sudden and unforeseen attack; or if we think that there are alternative patterns of political life available which are not vulnerable to treachery, stupidity, or simply conflicts of view, then we will find Augustine's somber rhetoric merely perplexing. But in that case, Augustine will say to us, we are hardly fit to be citizens of

94. Oliver O'Donovan, *Common Objects of Love: Moral Reflection and the Shaping of Community* (Grand Rapids: Eerdmans, 2002), 21.

95. O'Donovan, *Bonds*, 63.

96. Ibid., 68.

the heavenly city, in which each will be transparent to all: *patebunt cogitationes nostrae invicem nobis* (22.29.6).[97]

In considering O'Donovan's conclusions, the question raised by Jean Bethke Elshtain remains, namely what O'Donovan's interpretation of Augustine looks like in human society? It is unclear how the "transformation" of earthly institutions can be understood in light of the pessimism O'Donovan interprets in Augustine. As Elshtain observed, "O'Donovan argues that the only reasonable hope is the coming of the kingdom, but this is not simplistic eschatological yearning, it is a more complex enterprise by far. I do not yet fully understand O'Donovan's thought on this and other points, but I plan to reread him until I have grasped it . . ."[98] Indeed, O'Donovan's interpretation of Augustine's political and social thought is one shaped by Augustine's theology and most especially his concern for humanity's fulfillment in the Kingdom of God.

Robert Dodaro

Recovering an Augustinian Theology of Virtue

Robert Dodaro approaches Augustine's social and political thought in a comprehensive manner by threading together areas of Augustine's theology oftentimes isolated from political questions, especially Augustine's Christology, ecclesiology, and scriptural exegesis. He lays out his method at the beginning of his work. "For me, the question 'How did Augustine conceive the just society?' involves aspects of his thinking about Christ, human knowledge, the church, and scriptural hermeneutics, as well as political thought and ethics."[99]

97. Ibid., 72.
98. Jean Bethke Elshtain, review of *The Desire of the Nations: Rediscovering the Roots of Political Theology*, by Oliver O'Donovan, *Theological Studies* 58, no. 4 (December 1997), 751.

For Dodaro, the concept of the "ideal statesman" in Augustine bridges the concepts of *ecclesia* and *res publica*. One of the innovations of Dodaro's work which facilitates this unique approach is his analysis not simply of Augustine's *City of God*, but also of the *epistulae* written to various public officials. The analysis of such letters is essential because their contents contain "a history of civic virtue and a philosophical discussion of its true nature that form the foundation of Augustine's arguments to public officials such as Nectarius, Volusianus, Marcellinus, and Macedonius."[100] Any discussion, therefore, of Augustine's political vision must account for these letters, as they demonstrate for Dodaro "that Christians in public life can develop the capacity for moral reasoning, aided by grace, in which their practice of civic virtues is transformed by their practice of Christian faith, hope, and love."[101]

Dodaro's movement from the discussion of Augustine's anthropology, in light of his Christology and ecclesiology, to Augustine's vision of the ideal Christian statesman pivots on the theme of virtue. This is due to the object of Augustine's examination, namely the human soul (in this case the soul of the Christian statesman). Augustine asserts that true virtue is always mediated by Christ. According to Dodaro, the mediation of virtue separates Augustine from his classical interlocutors and defines the discussion of the two cities. "Augustine thus opposes Cicero's key assumption . . . that human beings are able to act justly on the strength of their own reason and will."[102] While Robert Markus and others believe that the *res publica* is built upon a "neutral" formula of consensus

99. Robert Dodaro, *Christ and the Just Society in the Thought of Augustine* (Cambridge: Cambridge University Press, 2004), I.

100. Ibid., 9.

101. Robert Dodaro, "Ecclesia and Res Publica," 245. For Dodaro, *ecclesia* here refers to "church" as a society in both its historical and eschatological sense.

102. Dodaro, *Christ and the Just Society,* 26.

on "common objects of love," Dodaro notes that such neutrality is inconsistent with Augustine's appeals for the Christian in the political sphere to exercise Christian virtue.[103] He notes that Augustine views the "just society" not simply as being hindered by man's "moral debilitations," but also as being hindered by moral failings which obstruct the knowledge and love of God necessary for the practice of virtue.[104] For Markus this is precisely the reason why Augustine attempts to reformulate Cicero's definition of *res publica*, namely to produce a formula that accounted for imperfection and the limited achievements attainable by fallen man. Markus writes, "A formula which did not require such perfection was needed to allow discussion of earthly polities; and this is what Augustine set out to provide in his alternative vision."[105] However, Dodaro's work sees the cause of Augustine's "alternative" formulation as a result not just of pessimism, but rather the role and work of Christ in the life of the Christian.

What is required, therefore, of the statesman in Augustine's view is true *pietas*, which Augustine defines as the statesman's public acknowledgement of the limits of his virtue through prayer and penance to God. It is in this way that piety "purifies the intention behind other virtues, such as justice, with the result that these, too, are rendered true."[106] It is for this reason that Dodaro, like others, sees Augustine's emphasis on martyrdom as important.

> If Christians truly desire to create a more just society, they should first renounce the desire to become like their enemies by renouncing the use of violence. Christ and the martyrs testify that the only efficacious way to reform political society is to oppose injustice through nonviolence.[107]

---

103. Dodaro, "Ecclesia and Res Publica," 253.
104. Dodaro, *Christ and the Just Society*, 29. It is, therefore, no coincidence that "moral self-deception" and "self reliance" are for Augustine the twin effects of original sin.
105. Robert Markus, review of *Christ and the Just Society in the Thought of Augustine*, by Robert Dodaro, *Journal of Ecclesiastical History* 57, no. 1 (January 2006), 106.
106. Dodaro, "Ecclesia and Res Publica," 57.

In man's fear of death, his *timor mortis*, Augustine notes that human ignorance and weakness are compounded. However, in this context, the two cities can be directly connected to two distinct sets of goods, the *bona temporalia* and the *bona aeterna*. In Augustine, these goods are connected to the two loves of man, *amor sui* and *amor Dei*. To demonstrate the love of self and the seeking of temporal goods, Augustine points out the false piety practiced by pagan Romans, a piety that prevented the implementation of true justice.

> Because he believes that happiness is predicated upon the knowledge and love of God as the supreme good, he concludes that fear of death epitomizes the fundamental threat to the formation of a just society. Justice is not found wherever fear of death impedes action aimed at the attainment of lasting happiness. Virtue is therefore necessary to overcome fear of death, all the more so because it leads human beings to choose permanent over temporal goods.[108]

The Role of Christ in Augustine's Vision

Dodaro's argument necessarily turns to Augustine's Christology, since for Augustine it is the body of Christ, the whole and just Christ (*Christus totus iustus*), in which the only truly just society is formed. Two Christological doctrines are key to this vision: the unity of Christ's two natures and Christ's identity as head and body of the Church. Christ, the only source and guarantee of virtue, is the only true high priest, the only mediator between God and man. He alone obtains the forgiveness of sins because he alone is true God and true man.[109] The unity of Christ's humanity and divinity assures for Augustine Christ's distinction from the rest of humanity, including

---

107. Robert Dodaro, "Augustine's Secular City," in *Augustine and his Critics.* ed. Robert Dodaro and George Lawless (London: Routledge, Chapman & Hall, 1999), 101.

108. Dodaro, *Christ and the Just Society*, 35–36.

109. Ibid., 105. As Dodaro expands upon this point, it is a central element of Augustine's debate with the Donatists.

even bishops renowned for holiness. For Augustine, the fundamental meaning of Christ's identity in this context remains that Christ's grace alone is that which allows man to act virtuously and obtain the forgiveness of his sins.

The second Christological mystery that is important for understanding Augustine's social thought is the identity of Christ as head and body of the Church: "Faith in a mystery that is impenetrable to reason, accompanied by a humility that renounces the self as the source and repository of virtue, allows members of Christ's body to perceive the hidden, deleterious influence of moral ignorance and weakness on the soul."[110] Dodaro sees this mystery as pointing to an exchange, a *commutatio*. Christ voices our own fear of death, pain, and despair and gives us hope in the face of our experience of those things through grace. This mystery leads to a summary of Augustine's view of justification, in which Christ, the only truly just one, justifies those united to Himself. This union, according to Dodaro, allows for the "only just society in history."[111]

Augustine's view of this mystery also points to the need for the Christian statesman to abandon self-reliance and self-reliant virtue. The human experience of virtue without the mediation of Christ leads to justice that is partial and opaque. Dodaro sees a problematic strand in John Milbank, who argues for a level of justice actualized in the Church on earth, which Augustine would not have seen as possible until its final perfection in the Last Judgment. However, as Dodaro notes, "In Augustine's view, what little insight into true justice the Christian statesman is able to acquire through Christ's grace while exercising his office, he does so largely after sinning, as a result of the grace of contrition and pardon."[112]

110. Ibid., 113.
111. Ibid., 108.
112. Dodaro, "Ecclesia and Res Publica," 267.

To demonstrate this reality, Augustine points to the way that divine revelation, contained in the Scriptures, is encountered, namely through allegories and parables. As a result, the reality that man on his own cannot fully understand revelation is similar to his inability to exercise true virtue without Christ's mediation. Just as it is only in Christ that we have access to revelation's fulfillment, so too only in Christ do we have the complete example of justice distinguished from our natural capacity. "Augustine thus argues the difference between the complete understanding and example of justice found exclusively in Christ and the partial justice of which human beings are capable."[113] For Augustine, Dodaro argues, the statesman must regard himself as a "pardoned sinner" who receives the forgiveness and grace of God and practices true piety formed by faith in Christ. The statesman who does this "transforms civic virtues to arrive at morally sound judgments because he rules the earthly city with his gaze solidly fixed upon the eternal goods of the heavenly city."[114]

Finally, analyzing Augustine's letter to Macedonius, Dodaro argues that, for the bishop of Hippo, the goals of public policies must be viewed always in light of man's ultimate fulfillment. The letters of Augustine to Macedonius and others consistently speak of the need for the ethical horizons of Christians to "be broadened by the love of God," beyond a concern for assuring temporal goods without reference to man's eternal goods.[115] To demonstrate this need in the lives of statesmen, Augustine points to the double meaning of peace. For Augustine, peace is both seen in a restrictive sense as freedom from suffering; it is also that which is attained through the virtues of faith, hope, and love. The Christian statesman, therefore, must strive

113. Ibid., 177.
114. Ibid., 242.
115. Ibid., 246.

for peace and bridge temporal aims and eternal goods by working towards bridging the gap of the two cities.

> He insists that the Christian statesman must govern prudently and justly while recognizing what the virtue of hope teaches: that he not conceive of his primary aim to foster happiness in this earthly life as an end in itself. Were he to do so, he would risk elevating the pursuit of temporal benefits such as health, wealth, and liberty above the pursuit of eternal goods, such as happiness and life in God, which transcend death. Hope therefore redirects the aim of civic virtues away from an exclusive concern with acquiring prosperity and security in the earthly city to the pursuit of the happiness that belongs to the heavenly city.[116]

Charles Mathewes

Mathewes's Particularistic Approach

The work of Charles Mathewes, most especially *A Theology of Public Life*, is dedicated to refocusing the discussion of Christian involvement in politics from the modern state to the necessary engagement of the Christian citizen. Mathewes, largely informed by Augustinian principles and in dialogue with non-Christian political theorists, calls his approach "unapologetically particularistic," meaning:

> It argues that Christians can and should be involved in public life both richly as citizens—working for the common good while remaining open, conversationally and otherwise, to those who do not share their views—and thoroughly as *Christians*—in ways ascetically appropriate to, and invigorating of, their spiritual formation, not least by opening their own convictions to genuine transformation by that engagement.[117]

---

116. Dodaro, *Christ and the Just Society*, 209. See also "Ecclesia and Res Publica," 271.
117. Charles Mathewes, *A Theology of Public Life* (Cambridge: Cambridge University Press, 2007), 2.

Mathewes' central effort in this recovery of Christian "engagement" in the political order is to demonstrate that while the created world is imperfect and violent, the Christian must not simply seek an escape, but must enter and engage it. "Neither immanentists nor escapists can capture the true longings of humans, which inevitably transcend the mere immanent satisfactions or anesthetics they advertise. Both are expressions of impatience."[118] Mathewes seeks to abandon the fear and cynicism that some have called Augustine's legacy and instead argues that the bishop of Hippo calls for the Christian to engage the world with eyes fixed on heaven. "His first and primary polis is the church, the republic of grace, and the fundamental political task for this polis lies in the evangelical extension and ascetical preparation of its citizens to be fit to bear the joy that is humanity's eschatological destiny."[119] For Mathewes, however, such an eschatological perspective must not be confused with a Manichean apocalyptic dualism, as his interpretation of Augustine's vision is one that sees the world and its politics as necessarily theological.

> Hence worldly concerns, far from needing to be made theological, always already *are* theological: care for the world already is a mode of comportment which has as one of its purposes the satisfaction of theological longings, however normally misconstrued these longings (and their 'satisfactions') may be.[120]

Mathewes, unlike many other commentators, does not neglect the metaphysical underpinnings of this Augustinian vision. He recognizes the complexity of Augustine's epistemology and its connection to the metaphysical foundation of Augustine's vision. "Augustine anchors his external realism, that is, in the inwardness

---

118. Charles Mathewes, "A Worldly Augustinian: Augustine's Sacramental Vision of Creation," *Augustinian Studies* 41, no. 1 (2010), 345.
119. Charles Mathewes, "An Augustinian Look at Empire," *Theology Today* 63, no. 30 (2006), 293.
120. Mathewes, *Theology of Public Life*, 85.

of the mind's discernment of God. Objectivity is realized through subjectivity, but only because subjectivity has at its heart an objective reality."[121] Augustine's image of man is fundamentally one who seeks knowledge not isolated from others, but in a "community seeking salvation."[122] Augustine recognizes the existence of truth, a truth that lies in both our exterior and interior realities, precisely because we are always subject to the "Divine other." "Christ's presence within the soul is more a transcendental presupposition of our constitution than a positivistic observation; wherever truth is, there is Christ."[123] Epistemology for Augustine begins with God's action within the soul; as a result, there is an "always already present claim on the self of some value-creating and value-sustaining commitments to the world."[124] Mathewes recognizes the role of love, since memory and mind are only a part of Augustine's epistemological vision. That vision is completed by love, which ultimately directs the will. "Augustine's epistemology turns into ontology, and this ontology finally turns out to be theology."[125]

Human existence, for Augustine, is defined by the experience of "otherness," in that it is broken and estranged, only to be reintegrated and made whole by the reception of grace. "The reception of grace here described has eschatological, ecclesiological, and sacramental dimensions . . . nothing is yet 'accomplished'; all we feel now are the first fruits of an integrity and wholeness that we will properly possess only in the eschaton, and which at present we only proleptically 'borrow' from that coming kingdom."[126] Mathewes argues that Augustine's vision is realized when we acknowledge that man's

121. Ibid., 50.
122. Ibid., 51.
123. Ibid., 54.
124. Charles Mathewes, "Augustinian Anthropology: Interior intimo meo," *The Journal of Religious Ethics*, 27, no. 2 (Summer 1999), 200-201.
125. Mathewes, *Theology of Public Life*, 57.
126. Ibid., 64.

alienation can only be overcome by God's action in Christ, which allows the conviction that God is at the core of the self. The nihilistic despair, therefore, that is experienced often in the contemporary world is caused by a theological and philosophical presumption of self-possession, which alienates the self from others.

The "Liturgy of Citizenship"

Mathewes, after addressing philosophical concerns and theological foundations, turns to what he calls the "liturgy of citizenship," both in a civic and theological sense. Beyond civil obligation, he believes citizenship can be "performed in a way that is continuous with the liturgy of the blessed in heaven that is our eschatological destiny."[127] Mathewes seeks to shift political agency from focusing solely on consent, which has been the traditional liberal political principle, to a politics reflective of our social nature, in which our love is manifest in a collective life: "There is no sense, in contemporary liberal political theory, that politics and public life in general—in the sense of taking responsibility for running the polity—is any sort of intrinsic good."[128]

Mathewes structures his analysis of citizenship based upon the virtues. Virtue itself, he argues, is transformed by Augustine from a sense of achievement to "a language of suffering, of being willing to be shaped (not to shape ourselves) by the medicine of a gracious God."[129] As a result, the theological virtues of faith, hope, and love form the shape of Mathewes' description of Christian political engagement. He argues that faith in public life is essential for the Christian, as faith gives public engagement conditions and places it in its proper context. "Political institutions must not be the object of

---

127. Ibid., 146.
128. Ibid., 157.
129. Mathewes, "An Augustinian Look at Empire," 304.

ultimate faith, and so affirmed, again on grounds of faith, in order to encourage citizens both to be genuinely engaged and . . . to recognize the 'mundaneness' of any particular political disposition."[130] The Church's presence in political discourse is also important because it is the Church's role "to proclaim that politics expresses extrapolitical longings."[131]

Hope, for the Christian citizen, is essential as well, as it alone allows the survival of the "banalities of public life's relentless immanence, its bruising way with our plans and expectations."[132] Mathewes recognizes that we must move beyond cynicism (which he posits as the cultural remedy for despair), especially a cynical disbelief of evil.

> Paradoxically, perhaps the idea of evil captures something fundamental about reality by being fundamentally hopeful—that is, by affirming that realities such as malice, suffering, and injustice do not tell the whole truth about reality, but are in some way partial, perhaps even accidental, to the ultimate nature of reality itself.[133]

Indeed, it is hope that reminds the Christian citizen that the reality of suffering and deceptions of the present will not remain, but rather are "signs of a greater kingdom to come."[134] He affirms, "Hope is more an ontological reality than it is a psychological one—an ontological reality that encourages a certain style of inhabiting time in advental anticipation."[135] Drawing from Augustine, Mathewes introduces the concept of *distensio animi*, the tension or longing of wonder and frustration that we experience in this life. This tension is essential to Christian hope, and characterizes our deepest loves, which reach

---

130. Mathewes, *Theology of Public Life*, 172.
131. Charles Mathewes, *The Republic of Grace: Augustinian Thoughts for Dark Times* (Grand Rapids, MI: Eerdmans, 2010), 206.
132. Mathewes, *Theology of Public Life*, 215.
133. Ibid., 230.
134. Ibid., 241.
135. Ibid.

out to our "eschatological consummation."[136] Mathewes sees the manifestation of this hope concretely in the Eucharist, where the mundane meets the transfigured and where we proclaim that while broken we will be made whole.[137]

Finally, in love we find the "fundamental theological, ontological, and psychological truth about reality" in Augustinian theology.[138] Mathewes seeks to part from liberalism's skepticism that love is accidental and episodic and notes that Augustine's view on love is linked to joy and delight. Love, for Augustine, "is a crucial element in politics, especially around the inevitable exercise of political authority."[139] For Mathewes, love is not simply respect in the political order; it is also transformative, changing both lover and beloved. "It is love, and not the power we exercise in light of love, that makes us intimate with one another. Love is ontologically a real force, not just a word used to mask or admiring manipulation of one another."[140] Like other Augustinian commentators, Mathewes sees love as an ontological category, as it affirms the other, wills the other's being, and respects the other's alterity. "Love understands public life's ambition, because it recognizes the dimension of longing for what it is. It asks less of politics immanently, but expects more of it eschatologically."[141] Mathewes sees love, even when it causes suffering or pain, as "ascetical training" towards our eschatological fulfillment.

136. Mathewes, "An Augustinian Look at Empire," 303. See also Mathewes, *The Republic of Grace*, 229.
137. Mathewes, *Republic*, 233.
138. Mathewes, *Theology of Public Life*, 261.
139. Mathewes, *Republic*, 149.
140. Mathewes, *Theology of Public Life*, 160.
141. Ibid., 286.

Graham Ward

Ward's Analogical-Ecclesiological Project

While the Radical Orthodoxy movement has often been synonymous with the work of John Milbank, it is in fact a composite of different authors from a variety of theological perspectives.[142] Two of Graham Ward's works, *Cities of God* and *The Politics of Discipleship: Becoming Postmaterial Citizens*, demonstrate this diversity, as Ward bears the defining marks of Radical Orthodoxy in his theological critique of contemporary philosophy and uniquely manifests an ecclesiological engagement with the secular city.[143] Ward's starting point, therefore, is in the examination of the secular city's breakdown into what he calls "communities of fear."

> In the collapse of the modern city what takes over is imagined communities which you belong to by buying into what's on offer to you. They are communities of fear; exclusive because the members fear being excluded themselves . . . such communities undermine the very conception of the common good, of public policy, social rationality, and human rights . . . those necessary concepts which make effective political involvement and commitment significant.[144]

Ward sees the main symptom of this breakdown, which was caused by modern individualism, in the construction of a "culture of seduction" or, as he defines it, "a culture of a euphoric grasping of the present in order to forget the present."[145] Responding to this

---

142. This will be seen again in our discussion of Michael Hanby's work.

143. Mary Doak, "The Politics of Radical Orthodoxy: A Catholic Critique," *Theological Studies* 68 (2007): 386. Doak, in fact, calls Ward's approach one of "Critical Engagement," since, unlike the work of William Cavanaugh and Daniel Bell, she argues that Ward recognizes a need for engagement with the "social bodies" of the earthly city, including the state.

144. Graham Ward, *Cities of God* (London: Routledge, 2000), 68. Ward's critique builds on the analysis of postmodernism's effects in the work of Jean Baudrillard, Charles Taylor, Charles Jencks.

145. Ibid.

culture is, for Ward, the mission of theology today, both in the external condemnation of society's self-destructive consumption and in the external analysis of theology's contemporary spokesmen.[146] "As Christians, we bring to God all the concerns we have with the contemporary world: the crisis of democracy, the reduction of life to economics and consumption, and the various roles that religion is playing and being forced to play in the public sphere."[147] In this effort, Ward sees little use for a "liberal theology" that dissolves the Christian mysteries of incarnation and resurrection into "myths and metaphors." Ward, in fact, calls upon Christian theology to recover an analogical sense.[148] This renewed theological effort implies:

> [an] adequate Christian response which listens to the many voices, the many claims for attention in the postmodern city. It risks encounter, knowing that its own voice is never pure, never innocent. It also, speaks: announcing to the postmodern city its own vision of universal justice, peace and beauty, and it criticises the structural injustices, violences and ugliness which resist and hinder the reception of that vision . . . [it is] a constructive theological project which maps our physical bodies on to our social and civic bodies, on to our eucharistic and ecclesial bodies, on to the Body of Christ.[149]

Ward sees the way to overcome the effects of modern individualism in the recovery of a true sense of human connectedness, which he grounds firmly in Christian anthropology and ecclesiology. For Ward, it is necessary that theology recover the doctrine of analogy because, as he observes, it is a "doctrine of participation and causality" that flows directly from intra-trinitarian communion.[150] The human necessity of "mutual participation" in our various relationships is a

---

146. This is a strong point of similarity with John Milbank, who rejects and seeks to overcome what he calls "a theology 'positioned' by secular reason." See Milbank, *Theology and Social Theory*, 1.

147. Graham Ward, *The Politics of Discipleship: Becoming Postmaterial Citizens* (Grand Rapids, MI: Baker Academic, 2009), 281.

148. Ward, *Cities*, 70.

149. Ibid.

defining part of our existence and, as a result, it can be directly connected to the Eucharistic faith Christians are called to live. "Christians living out their faith *will* contribute to the social energies and the symbolic fields outside the specificities of their ecclesial institutions . . . they will reproduce, produce and disseminate a certain social semiotics that are believed to have analogical significance."[151]

However, Ward's conception of the Christian "contribution" to this project is complicated by his view of *civitas*. For Ward, the "Christian city," which emerges from "responses to God's grace" and "the good practices which such responses call into existence," is in fact immanent to the forms of all cities.[152] Yet, while appearing to collapse the Augustinian distinction of *civitas terrena* and *civitas Dei*, he insists that his argument is grounded in Augustine. Ward's initial analysis travels through familiar territory in the political Augustinian discussion, namely Augustine's distinction between *caritas* and the *libido dominandi*, Augustine's use of Cicero's concept of *res publica*, and Augustine's caution in not identifying the Church with the heavenly city. However, Ward arrives at the conclusion that both cities "share not only the same temporal goods and temporal adversities, but also play a part in God's unfolding providence."[153] Hence, Ward contends, "[t]he logic of analogy is here caught up with the logic of parody . . . when love, justice, society, and peace are predicates of the *civitas terrena* then they are parodies of predicates of the *civitas dei*."[154] The result of this logic of parody for Ward is that

---

150. Ibid., 236. One can see here a parallel with the theology of Joseph Ratzinger, who sees "being in relation" as an essential ontological category. See Joseph Ratzinger, *Introduction to Christianity*, trans. J. R. Foster (San Francisco: Ignatius Press, 2004), 134–5.
151. Ibid.
152. Ibid., 226.
153. Ibid., 229.
154. Ibid., 230.

the "heavenly city itself must make possible the earthly city, such that in the *saeculum* 'city' is used figurally, virtually."[155]

The Mission of the Contemporary Theologian

Having made this claim, Ward then calls upon the theologian in today's world to work to conform modern cities into the city of God. Such a prospect is clearly problematic in the view of numerous interpreters, especially in the interpretation of Ratzinger, O'Donovan, Kaufman, and others. All would caution the loss of eschatological tension present in Augustine's work, and many would cite a neglect of Augustine's pessimistic prospects for the earthly city in comparison to the fulfillment of the heavenly city. For Ward, however, the city has always been a "place of transit between the terrestrial and the celestial." He continues, "Because man was created to live in community, the foundation of a city (and, I would add, its reconstruction) is a theological task."[156] He sees the Church's engagement with the secular culture and civil realm embodied in the modern city as a necessity. Any distancing of Christianity from the city would be an act of "neo-tribalism" condemning the city to its fate and would be contrary to the nature of the Church's mission. "Christianity cannot," he asserts, "renounce the secular world. That condemns society to playing out its nihilistic and self-destructive drive to consume."[157]

Ward sees in Augustine, and more so in Aquinas, an interconnected relationship between city and *ecclesia* that is based in a "common anthropology" that requires a "life in common, a

---

155. Ibid., 230. Here, Ward applies the work of Michael de Certeau, who philosophically distinguishes institution and culture, as well as place and space.
156. Ward, *The Politics of Discipleship*, 209.
157. Ward, *Cities*, 69–70.

good in common."[158] The method Ward proposes to engage the secular, the modern city, is based, therefore, on the human openness to eschatological questions. Using Augustinian terms, the theologian must engage our culture's "restlessness" in expectation of the "final city." Ward puts forward three steps to accomplish this.

> I suggest we can move towards a 'thicker description' of the relationship [between the ecclesial and cultural body] by (1) returning to the specificities of urban living today; (2) offering a theological and critical reading of the root or key metaphor of its culture; and (3) responding to the openings and spaces given, in that culture, for specific theological response.[159]

For Ward, the goal of such intervention, and indeed the goal of his analysis of the earthly city, is to "give secularism a legitimacy that saves it from nihilistic self-consumption, from the atomism of *amor sui*, from the drift into the disorders of the *nihil*."[160] Here, Ward demonstrates his concern with contemporary thought and the nihilism, which often defines it. Also, it is here that Ward sees the role of the Church, which will help to bring about the "redemption" of a society traveling on a postmodern path towards self-destruction, not by subsuming it, but by aiding its return to a proper relationship to the Body of Christ. Building on St. Paul's concept of the body, Ward sees such an "incorporation" into the Body of Christ as possible only when an analogical relation is created (in Baptism) and maintained consistently by an eschatological reminder (in the Eucharist).[161]

158. Ward, *The Politics of Discipleship*, 210. Ward here embraces and describes his Thomistic influences, some of which were only alluded to in *Cities*.
159. Ward, *Cities*, 237.
160. Ibid., 236.
161. Ward, *The Politics of Discipleship*, 249.

Michael Hanby

Augustinianism vs. Stoicism

Michael Hanby's *Augustine and Modernity*, while part of the Radical Orthodoxy publishing series, takes a slightly different approach in responding to contemporary critiques of Augustine. Hanby seeks to confront the Cartesian "modern self," which suffers from a metaphysical collapse, by placing Augustine's ideas in their original context, reuniting Augustine's philosophy with his theology.[162] Hanby sees much of what is called "Augustinian" as stoicism's legacy in Western thought. As a result, he seeks to recover a purer and more comprehensive philosophical and theological Augustinian vision. Hanby, therefore, while not specifically addressing Augustine's vision of the state, attempts to fill the ontological void that numerous commentators have found by returning to Augustine's Trinitarian theology and its ontological implications.

Hanby observes that in Augustine's *De Trinitate,* the divine essence is spoken of as love; hence, for Augustine, "essence requires relation."[163] In fact, Hanby notes that Augustine's pneumatology is based in the very concept of *donum*, as in the Spirit, the Divine gifts himself. This gift is present both in the sacrifice on the cross and, for the Christian in the Eucharistic sacrifice, which for Hanby is not a secondary concern. Indeed, the one sacrifice of Christ constitutes His body and is at the basis of Augustine's vision of the one person of Christ as both head and ecclesial body.[164] It is this sacrifice, which also contains the "pentitential machinery," that allows the Christian to grow in humility in front of God's self gift in Christ through the Holy Spirit.[165]

---

162. Michael Hanby, *Augustine and Modernity* (London: Routledge, 2003), 1.
163. Ibid., 14.
164. Ibid., 18.

Like Dodaro, Hanby believes Christology is essential to any discussion of Augustinian thought. The Bishop of Hippo sees in Christ the incorporation of an estranged creation into His own body to restore divine beauty and confront human apprehension. For Augustine, Christ is both the beauty and form of creation; ontologically, therefore, beauty's role in the Trinity is manifested. Soteriologically, that beauty draws humankind into Trinitarian love.[166] This Christological vision gives significance to *cognito historica*, as the apostles and martyrs testify to and pass on in history nothing other than the Father speaking to the Son and the Son's "replying" in the Spirit. Hanby argues:

> Hence the *cognito historica*, preserved and transmitted in the witness of the apostles and martyrs and yet instantiated ever new in the singularity of contingent circumstance, is unfolded within and mediated by the form of this response, a form transcending to those concepts. This historical knowledge is now intrinsic to both the form and content of contemplation.[167]

The Body of Christ is, therefore, at once the temporal manifestation of the love between Father and Son and the form of a restored creation in the image and movement of that love. For Augustine, there is no conflict between hope for the beatific vision and the prescription of ecclesial life in time, as both have been united in the Incarnation.[168] Christ's mediation constitutes the Church as the one body that manifests Trinitarian love, as Christ is both *exemplum* and *sacramentum*. Hanby argues that this forms Augustine's vision of time itself, which is the union of the ecclesial body with its head between two deaths and two resurrections.[169] In the discussion of

165. Ibid.
166. Ibid., 29.
167. Ibid., 37.
168. Ibid., 39.

Christ as *exemplum*, Augustine's Christology and ecclesiology meet his anthropology. Love, Augustine would argue, must have a desirable object. For man, the divine beauty of the Trinity acts as that object and elicits our desire. The *exemplum* manifested to man in Christ and the object of our desire, our *dilectio*, presupposes our knowledge of it. Therefore, "love and knowledge mutually entail one another" in Augustine.[170] Thus, love has an end, a *telos*, and the distance that "the seer and the seen" must travel is collapsed for man into the "distance between the Head and Body of Christ."[171]

Hanby argues that this Augustinian vision results in the "doxologizing" of human action, as we are all members incorporated into the bodies of either of the two Adams, citizens of either of the two cities. That incorporation is characterized by the respective objects of our worship (God or ourselves) and subject to one of two mediators.[172]

> Christ as exemplar provokes in us and draws us on by the love which he himself gives sacramentally, and by which he draws us into the delight between the Father and the Son. The doxalogization of action and the inescapability of gift and mediation, though it displays how Christ incorporates us into the divine love.[173]

Hanby notes that no one is outside of this love. He calls the Trinity the "doxo-ontological" context of Augustine's entire thought.[174] Citing Augustine's *De Trinitate*, Hanby notes the anthropological implication of this principle. "This trinity of the mind is not the image of God because it remembers, understands, and loves itself,

---

169. Ibid., 41. Hanby's analysis here is heavily reliant on Robert Dodaro and his discussion of *sacramentum* in Augustine. See also Dodaro, *Christ and the Just Society*, 147-152.
170. Ibid., 66.
171. Ibid.
172. Ibid., 67.
173. Ibid., 69.
174. Ibid., 66.

but because it can remember, understand, and love Him by whom it was made."[175] For Augustine, the *amor Dei* is not just characteristic of the citizens of the *civitas Dei*, but also the true end of human love. The source of the anterior movement of love that moves man to know the object of his desire is also, therefore, man's end, the Triune God. Love, therefore, was for Augustine inextricably connected to the worship of God, and hence his entire discussion of *caritas* remains in its essence a theological one, even when discussing caritas within the family or community.

Augustine and His Interlocutors

After discussing Augustine's Trinitarian theology, Hanby turns his attention to two interlocutors and battling ideologies that Augustine fought throughout his life, namely Pelagianism and classical Stoicism. Hanby believes that Pelagianism's legacy is still present in Western Christian thought, as Pelagian "pietism" can be deconstructed to a form of *superbia*, or pride. There is a modern correspondence to the Pelagian removal of the self from time and the removal of man from Christ's mediation. This is because the Father's beauty, Augustine believes, was manifested in and mediated by Christ. Indeed, the Pelagians removed nature from that divine beauty making it an autonomous neutral reality.

> They [Pelagians] *institute* that nature as an autonomous and indifferent fact. On the one hand, this makes nature immanently self-contained and subsistent apart from erotic determination within the economy of gift . . . nature becomes immediately locked into an antagonistic mechanical relation with tensional forces deemed intrinsic to any determination.[176]

---

175. Ibid., 68. Hanby here cites Augustine's *De Trinitate* XIV.12.15.
176. Ibid., 115.

The Pelagians, in a trend readily visible in contemporary thought, reduced grace to the indeterminacy of *possibilitas* or the *cogito legis*; as a result, their flawed moral psychology led to a philosophy without a mediator.[177] Hanby notes that Stoicism's impact, building upon Pelagian trends, resulted in a tension and antagonism between passive rational agency and the medium of man's action. The net result was the loss of transcendence and the absence of mediation. "Since finitude and infinity cannot be concurrent, it is to lock them into juxtaposition to an infinity divisible by finitude itself, an infinity which, to an Augustinian point of view, turns out to be finite after all."[178]

This tension and loss of transcendence in the hands of Descartes resulted in the reduction of "God" to an immanent moral causal force, which would separate nature from its end, *esse* from the good, act from motive, and beauty from truth.[179] As Hanby argues, Stoicism's effects, its lack of *dilectio,* and association of free will as choice were delayed by the preservation of monastic charity and the ecclesial focus on *caritas*. However, once that context was removed in the Cartesian system, the stoic legacy was utilized to "de-Trinitize" God and eclipse Christ as mediator and *telos*.

> The loss of *Trinitas* from *Deus*, of *dilectio* from *arbitrio*, is inevitably, from this perspective, the loss of the mediation of the God-man, a rupture of the union binding *scientia* to *sapientia* and time to eternity. As the stoics and Pelagians, the *civitas terrena* and even Augustine's own youth demonstrate, this loss is always accompanied by the substitution of another figure: the Man-God who generated a different of incoherency, one not liable to qualify as philosophical within the narrow limits of that term in a post-Cartesian age.[180]

177. Ibid., 104-105.
178. Ibid., 116.
179. Ibid., 173.
180. Ibid., 177.

For Hanby, the only response possible to this post-Cartesian context is the renewal of the role of the Church. As the prayer of the Church reminds us, it is only God's body that can save man from nihilistic post-Cartesian immanence. A response to God's anterior call to us is, for Hanby, the "only genuinely political, genuinely ontological, indeed only fully human act. And a graceful act indeed."[181]

Eric Gregory

Augustine and "Civic Liberalism"

Eric Gregory's work marks a new generation's examination of Augustinian liberalism. It is both conscious of its twentieth-century legacy, and eager to apply Augustine's principles in the twenty-first century. Gregory outlines the context of his work by identifying three streams of Augustinian liberalism: Augustinian Realism, Augustinian Proceduralism, and Augustinian Civic Liberalism.[182] Gregory argues that the realist school saw politics as a defensive restraining of evil, but notes that it can easily yield to a moral consequentialism. Proceduralists are more positive in their ideals, but they minimize the concept of justice and privatize virtue.[183] However, Gregory argues that civic liberalism "generally corresponds to moderate forms of liberal perfectionism that offer ethical accounts of human flourishing believed to be intrinsically valuable."[184] This is the school which Gregory seeks to advance in the new millennium, as it both promotes a limited authority of the state and goods such as authority and self respect. He clarifies the

181. Ibid., 179.
182. Eric Gregory, *Politics and the Order of Love: An Augustinian Ethic of Democratic Citizenship* (Chicago: University of Chicago Press, 2008), 9.
183. Ibid., 2
184. Ibid., 9.

meaning of this brand of Augustinian liberalism: "The liberalism I wish to defend is that of political practice grounded in moral appeal to the equal dignity of persons and shared goods protected by a constitutional government in which liberty and equality are respected."[185]

Gregory's project is one that admittedly seeks to avoid what he sees as the "pitfalls" of other Augustinian schools, namely, a reliance upon forms of perfectionism and a willingness to abandon the theological context of their arguments for wider acceptability. Gregory's starting point, therefore, like others before him, is Augustine's moral psychology of love. This psychology of love is the cause of Gregory's rejection of both the pessimism of realist schools and the utopian perfectionism of Rawlsian proceduralists: "Augustinian suspicions about the prideful elements of both politics and virtue, like Adam's fall, do not go all the way down."[186] Indeed, love is the dominant virtue of his civic liberalism, a love that "highlights the vulnerability and dependency of human beings, understood as interrelated bundles of love rather than essentially conflicting wills."[187] Robert Markus, in reviewing Gregory's work, highlighted this element of his civic liberalism: "Its characteristic virtue is love. His primary object is, indeed, to avoid the schizophrenia that has separated sin and love in the dominant modes of Augustinian political thought, and to emphasize a dialectical relation between them."[188]

For Gregory, love is central in Augustine's ethics and it unifies all other human virtues. Indeed, the *ordo amoris* both inwardly moves the person and compels them to action. "Augustine's love is not merely an affect of the agent but an intersubjective movement of

---

185. Ibid., 10.

186. Ibid., 32.

187. Eric Gregory, "Augustinians and New Liberalism," *Augustinian Studies* 41, no. 1 (2010): 320.

188. Robert Markus, review of *Politics and the Order of Love: An Augustinian Ethic of Democratic Citizenship*, by Eric Gregory, *Scottish Journal of Theology* 64, no.2 (2011), 249.

self and others. Love is operative throughout the whole encounter between the self and a reality governed by the movement of love as divine compassion."[189] Gregory further explores the metaphysical implications which underlie Augustine's work and concept of love:

> True love of self is now itself taken into the intersubjective triune love of God. It is this participatory love that frees the self from its own needy self-enclosure. Augustine's self (and his needs) finds its rest in God (who, strictly speaking, has no need *in se* but shares love in community as the expression of Godself). The self that is ordered toward God is released to love rather than grasp or possess the neighbor . . . The true good of this self participates in God's good—a good that has a decidedly social aspect in Augustine's Trinitarian theology.[190]

Turning to Augustine, Gregory sees in the bishop's response to Rome's fall the call for Christian pilgrimage on earth. Augustine is innovative here by "leaving this world's political struggles opaque to the kingdom of charity."[191] For Gregory, Augustine successfully extricates the historical political community from the economy of salvation and, following Markus' analysis, opens to a Christian concept of the secular. The *saeculum* for Gregory has an eschatological dimension, all the while remaining the "mixed time when no single religious vision can presume to command comprehensive, confessional, and visible authority."[192] Gregory here unabashedly builds upon Robert Markus's analysis of Augustine, both with regard to Augustine's critique of the ideology of empire and the necessity for "ambivalence" in the view of the Christian citizen. Indeed, in light of the "secular" condition, Gregory posits that "love can be sensitive to the conditions of pluralism and the great political values of justice, equality and respect."[193]

---

189. Gregory, *Politics*, 318.
190. Ibid., 329.
191. Ibid., 78.
192. Ibid., 79.

Ambivalence, therefore, towards matters of state and worldly affairs "delivers Augustine from both apocalyptic hostility to Rome as an apostate demonic order and social identification of Rome as a sacramental vehicle of grace."[194] However, Gregory criticizes and seeks to avoid Markus' movement from a healthy ambivalence to neutrality. He explains this distinction:

> Nothing is neutral for Augustine. The world is saturated with God. For Augustine, it is the (thoroughly-fictional) world that is imagined to exist without God that is unrealistic. There is no religious *adiaphora*. All politics is about fellowship and worship. Politics is either towards or away from God, and our souls are always being shaped in accord with one of the two cities in agonistic struggle.[195]

Gregory clearly sees the Christian political commitment, therefore, as one based upon eschatology and hope in present society, and hence neutrality is not a possibility. Unlike other authors who prefer to downplay the dynamism between the two cities, Gregory readily admits their tension and rejects any idea of an autonomous *terium quid*.[196] Here, Gregory breaks with the interpretation of Robert Markus in order to recover the sense of tension and ultimate concerns of Augustine when discussing the Christian's earthly citizenship. The source of this eschatological dimension and this break from Markus is Gregory's focus on Augustine's Christology, which has been utilized by other commentators, especially Dodaro and Hanby.

Augustinian liberals typically prefer the eschatological deferral to the apocalyptic vision of the resurrected Christ, especially when it promotes apocalyptic secular politics. For Augustine, however, the

---

193. Ibid., 300.
194. Ibid., 91.
195. Gregory, "Augustinians and New Liberalism," 322.
196. Ibid. Here Gregory touches upon Marrou's phrase and, in so doing, also criticizes Markus's concept of a 'value-free' *saeculum*.

drama of Incarnation displays Christ's authority, enacted and realized in the bonds of human community.[197]

One of the most troubling issues, however, that Gregory, who is seeking to promote an Augustinian civic liberalism, and other commentators grapple with is Augustine's use of coercion in the case of the Donatists. Inevitably, the policy of Augustine towards the Donatists poses "problems for the Augustinian lover," as it appears to directly contradict his theology of the *saeculum*.[198] However, while protesting coercion's use, Gregory recognizes the nuanced connection Augustine makes between his actions and love. While Augustine's intentions remained grounded in the benevolent seeking of the good of the other, "[f]ear and compulsion are paradigmatic experiences of sin's consequence for a thinker who values volitional integrity in the way Augustine does."[199] As Gregory concludes, "[t]his benevolent love implies a commitment to the good of the beloved that tries to promote rather than diminish their agency. It should not always be redescribed as a manipulative express of self-love, though it can be that as well."[200]

Conclusion

The authors we have just discussed represent a subsequent generation's attempts at grappling with almost century-old questions. However, in this discussion, the sources at question have expanded, as Dodaro and his examination of Augustine's *epistulae* have added a new dimension to this discussion. Also, Charles Mathewes attempts a more conscientious effort at recovering Augustine's vision by making

197. Ibid., 323.
198. Gregory, *Politics*, 299.
199. Ibid., 307.
200. Ibid., 309.

hermeneutical distinctions that have previously been absent from the discussion. It is hopefully evident that most of the authors we have discussed both in the previous and current chapters have attempted to understand Augustine's concept of two cities and apply "Augustinian" principles to aid in the construction of a contemporary vision of political and social life. In this endeavor, similar issues and questions have emerged, such as the questions of consensus, social ontology, and the role of the Church. Therefore, we are left with examining the hermeneutical foundations that undergird this discussion and those recurring questions that have emerged throughout our synthesis and exploration of contemporary Augustinian interpretation.

5

Interpreting Augustine's Political and Social Thought

Hermeneutical Issues and Contemporary Applications

Contextualizing Contemporary Augustinian Hermeneutics

In October of 1988, a roundtable discussion was held on the issue of contemporary Augustinian interpretation. In my opinion, this meeting was second in importance for our discussion only to the groundbreaking 1954 Augustinian Congress held in Paris. At this meeting, a number of contemporary authors involved in this discussion met at The Union Club in New York City, namely Robert Markus, Ernest Fortin, Elizabeth Clark, Jean Bethke Elshtain, James Schall, Eugene TeSelle, Graham Walker, and Richard John Neuhaus. They debated over the course of two days on various elements of Augustine's thought, including love, friendship, his Neoplatonic influences, the virtues, and values. However, arguably the most controversial and divisive debate in this discussion emerged over the question of how to read Augustine and how to appropriate his thought today.

Indeed, while debating Augustine's understanding of virtue and human nature, Rabbi David Novak interjected to point out the need to consider the hermeneutical question underpinning their discussion. Novak argued from his experience of studying the Jewish philosopher and sage, Maimonides:

> There's a fundamental problem that has to be brought out in the open. The problem that you have with Augustine is the problem that I have with Maimonides. Are we talking about what Maimonides meant or about the truth of what Maimonides said? Now if we're talking about what he meant, then we should incorporate all the linguistic, historical skills that we have at our disposal, and say what he meant in the proper context. If we're asking whether what he's saying is true, then we are asking what Maimonides said is true about Judaism as we experience it here and now . . . That's the hermeneutical problem that you have. Are you looking for the meaning only? Or are you looking for the truth?[1]

Novak's interjection is an important and relevant one for our discussion as well. It must be noted that while Novak sought their separation, the two hermeneutical trends which he identifies, namely the interpretation of meaning and application of truth in Augustine, have been inextricably joined. How one interprets Augustine's writings will obviously influence and determine the subsequent application of his thought. Elshtain illumines this relationship further, "Fortunately, there is a vast body of work—so vast no single person could ever hope to wade through it, much less Augustine's own vast corpus—that tries to understand Augustine in the context of his own time and to situate him in and for our time in a way that helps us to think 'with Augustine' yet again."[2] This hermeneutical

---

1. John R. Muether, "The Story of an Encounter," in *Augustine Today*, ed. Richard John Neuhaus (Grand Rapids, MI: Wm. B. Eerdman's Publishing Company, 1993), 141.
2. Jean Bethke Elshtain, "Why Augustine? Why Now?" *Theology Today* 55, no. 1 (April 1998), 6.

task of thinking "with Augustine," is one that has been taken up by many authors. For example, we have examined how the entire trend of "political Augustinianism" originates in the interpretation and consideration of Augustine's concept of *civitas dei*. In the discussion of this concept, Augustine is subsequently accused by various authors of subverting the political order and ceding temporal authority as a whole to the sacred *imperium*.

From a theological perspective, the interpretation of Augustine's corpus necessarily precedes and lays the foundation for the subsequent application of principles drawn from his work in order to answer modern questions. While many historians will find such efforts as an unnecessary and even foolhardy departure from Augustine, the fact remains that such efforts are part of a larger theological method. The interpretation of the Church's tradition and the application of principles that are discovered within it are both important theological tasks relevant to our examination of Augustine of Hippo. While it is evident that such interpretations rely upon historical context, linguistic analysis, and other critical tools at our disposal, theology still seeks to go deeper. It seeks to study not only a particular text or author, but also to discover principles of importance to the life of the Church in its current social and historical context. As we have seen throughout this discussion, the past century with its turbulence and bloodshed has led many to turn again to the Bishop of Hippo. In this chapter, therefore, what remains is admittedly a theological analysis of the debate that we have surveyed and the Augustinian principles that have been invoked repeatedly over its history. As Charles Mathewes explains, "Application is intrinsic to interpretation; we do not understand Augustine properly unless we try, at least implicitly, to apply his thought to today—thereby bringing new illumination into facets of his thought."[3]

Having laid out over the past four chapters the various commentaries and schools of interpretation in Augustine's political and social thought, it is necessary now to examine some of the major hermeneutical issues that lie underneath our discussion. In doing so, we necessarily will have to evaluate the validity of some of the arguments we have discussed. Aiding this task is the fact that the sources from Augustine's vast corpus that have been invoked are similar, namely Augustine's *De Civitate Dei*, *De Doctrina Christiana*, *Confessiones*, and his letters to Macedonius and Marcellinus. However, the way in which these sources have been interpreted and utilized varies widely. Also, it is evident that the goals of various commentators and scholars differ. Some seek to retrieve Augustine's vision and apply it to our own age, which is the task Elshtain calls "thinking with Augustine." However, others dissent from and seek to "overcome" Augustine's influence in Western political thought and theology in general. This latter school sees in Augustine the source of numerous problematic trends: a paternalistic social ideal, a fixation on sexuality, an exaltation of guilt and self-loathing, a weakened human anthropology, the condemnation of the world and temporal authority, and other social and political "problems." Elshtain criticized this latter effort as:

> Those who credit, or discredit, Augustine as the father of nearly *all* our discontents, the progenitor of nothing less than Western *ressentiment*, a term made famous by Nietzsche that signifies the envy of the strong by the weak yet includes their subsequent revenge as they turn the tables and institute regimes of moralistic repression that wallow in sickly tales of the superiority of victims.[4]

The hermeneutic of this latter group is not one of retrieval, but rather refutation. These authors see in Augustine's corpus not a well from

3. Mathewes, "An Augustinian Look at Empire," 292.
4. Elshtain, "Why Augustine?" 5.

which to draw, but a poisoned tree which needs to be cut down before others reap its fruit. They maintain a rather stern image of the Bishop of Hippo and a harsh condemnation of his continued influence and relevance. However, the hermeneutical question must be posed as to whether this latter image of Augustine is in fact the Bishop of Hippo, or simply a straw man who has borne undue and unwarranted criticism. Similar to the debate over Augustine's connections to the medieval ideal of unified power, much of what is attributed to the Bishop of Hippo must be attributed to his later interpreters. The hermeneutical problem, therefore, in this latter school remains the question of how much of the "Augustinian tradition" can be actually attributed to Augustine himself. Put in another way, what constitutes an "authoritative" interpretation of Augustine's political and social thought? There also remains the related question as to whether an authoritative interpretation is even possible in the first place. These questions will be examined further in this chapter, and have already been alluded to throughout our discussion. For example, the interjections of Henri de Lubac in the discussion of *l'augustinisme politique* exposed early on many of these hermeneutical issues and concerns.

Before beginning this task, therefore, Eugene TeSelle has put forward a helpful summary of the various interpretations at play in our discussion and the different hermeneutical perspectives that necessarily support each of them:

> What is it that we expect of Augustine in the political realm? The patterns of response suggest several answers. Some expect a confirmation of 'political realism' (Niebuhr; Deane), or an anticipation of modern secular politics (Markus), or a putting down of all liberal-to-radical, secular humanistic attempts to change the world, a condemnation of what Charles Cochrane called years ago 'creative politics,' or what is even worse a historical 'gnosticism' that seeks human perfection in the earthly future (Schall). Some look for a whipping boy, a detestable

example of all that Christian ethics ought not to be, guilt ridden over sexuality, fawning toward those in power, eager to praise the martyrs but persecute pagans, heretics, and schismatics let me confess to sharing in his tendency). Some wish to diagnose or dissect a fundamentally wrong-headed theology, one that is excessively dualistic in its conceptions of body and soul, earth and heaven, this age and the next, such that the political 'is not to be seen as productive of or even symbolic of the transcendent destiny of man [sic] in the kingdom [sic] of heaven'.[5]

The Hermeneutics of Retrieval

Recovering an Augustinian Outlook

The prospect of retrieving Augustine's political and social thought begs a very basic question, namely is there even a political and social vision to retrieve? Does Augustine care about the issues that we perceive as "essential" to his *City of God*. Indeed, various authors have proposed a retrieval of Augustine's fundamental ambiguity towards the political order, and his pessimism towards any prospect of a Christian improvement of the earthly city. Peter Iver Kaufman has argued that Augustine must be seen as fundamentally pessimistic at the prospect of any "extensive, redemptive changes" to social and political life.[6] Indeed, Kaufman demonstrates this hermeneutical pessimism as he explains the fundamental purpose of *City of God*:

> But the *City* is not simply Christian apology. It is an extended sermon exposing preoccupations that kept Cain's heirs from becoming pilgrims. The crisis of contemporary political culture provided Augustine a splendid contrast when he juxtaposed perishable political cultures with the eternal kingdom that awaited citizens who placed their mourning in the context of their faith, as pilgrims should.[7]

5. Eugene TeSelle, "Toward an Augustinian Politics," Journal of Religious Ethics 16, no. 1 (Spring 1988), 87.
6. Kaufman, *Incorrectly Political*, 228.

For Kaufman, Christians engaged in political office, or generally carrying out their civic obligations, remained in "dangerous waters." He recognizes that Augustine called for obedience to the law and allowed for the use of earthly peace, but insisted no obligation, political or otherwise, was to hinder the practice of the Christian faith. "The faithful, that is, ought to obey and defer, yet without compromising their faith. Augustine was edgy when he contemplated what is known today as institutional charisma, the reach and seductiveness of political authority."[8] This "edginess" on the part of Augustine leads to his frequent use of the term *peregrinus*, and also makes it difficult to determine the subtle boundary between despising (*contemnere*) and disdaining the world.[9] Kaufman sees no prospect in Augustine for Christianity's ability to somehow influence or better the political structures of human community. In fact, he rejects the use of Augustine in justifying any such effort. Citing the frequent use of Augustine's reference to *remota justitia*, Kaufman notes that Augustine calls "Christians to be helpful politically but also advised them not to be hopeful about politics." He continues, "Readers must choose whether the optimism or pessimism of interpreters corresponds with Augustine's views, passage by prickly passage . . ."[10]

Kaufman's pessimism is generally accepted by Charles Mathewes, who argues that Augustine's concern is not the political and social well being of the earthly city, but the cultivation and promotion of the Church. Mathewes argues, "His first and primary polis is the church, the republic of grace, and the fundamental political task for this polis lies in the evangelical extension and ascetical preparation of

7. Peter Iver Kaufman, *Redeeming Politics* (Princeton, NJ: Princeton University Press, 1990), 134.
8. Kaufman, *Incorrectly Political*, 104.
9. Ibid., 106.
10. Ibid., 230.

its citizens to be fit to bear the joy that is humanity's eschatological destiny."[11] Mathewes sees any application of Augustine for the general good of the entire population as a reduction of the Bishop of Hippo to mere platitudes and a loss of the fundamentally "heaven-minded" nature of his thought. Augustine's work cannot be translated into a political vision, therefore, because ultimately human activity is ordered towards heaven. Mathewes echoes Kaufman's pessimism, "Our politics until heaven are but a sad and thin shadow of this divine charged 'politics' of recognition."[12] Such a reading of Augustine allows little prospect for a social and political vision, and indeed such an absence of that vision is exactly what Kaufman and Mathewes believe needs to be retrieved.

Ernest Fortin can also be seen in agreement with such Augustinian ambiguity towards political affairs, as ultimately the earthly city remained for Augustine an imperfect reality remaining fundamentally a "compact of wickedness."[13] Fortin argues in a similar vein as Kaufman and Mathewes, "There is, strictly speaking, for Augustine no such thing as a Christian polity. Christianity was never intended as a substitute for the political life. It transcends all regimes and is of necessity limited in its practical application by the modalities of its existence in this world."[14] Fortin believed that Christianity at best places limitations on human wickedness and often violent conditions, as is evidenced by Augustine's view of war. However, the political order is granted little prospect of achieving any lasting success at either improving man's condition or moving the citizenry towards a more virtuous existence. Any vision of Augustine as a patron for Enlightenment thought is quickly extinguished by Fortin's

11. Mathewes, "An Augustinian Look at Empire," 293.
12. Ibid., 305.
13. Fortin, *Classical Christianity* vol. 2, 47.
14. Ibid.

pessimism, and the connection between Augustine and modernity is to be quickly and decisively broken.

It must be said that a level of pessimism is the starting point of John Milbank's system as well, as he argues that politics (and the privacy and property rights it protects) remain products of the Fall and sources of human discord. While Milbank's progression from this pessimism takes a different course than Mathewes and Kaufman, there is an initial point of agreement. As Milbank argues:

> Pagan political *dominium*, or in other words absolute political sovereignty and private property rights, are, for Augustine, consequences of the fall. Although *dominium* inhibits the effects of the fall, it also constantly reestablishes and reinforces human sinfulness and conceals our fallen character from our view . . . it is quite precisely the *political* order (the order of the *polis*) that we are to be saved *from*.[15]

Kaufman himself has recognized how others argue that human politics and society in Augustine are considered goods, or at the very least are neutral blank slates of human expression. Chief among these interlocutors and credited with transforming the discussion as a whole is Robert Markus, who as we have discussed argues that for Augustine "political institutions, social practices, customs" are autonomous and neutral.[16] The political order in Markus's work is not condemned nor is it exalted; rather, it is a shared sphere in which Augustine wanted to convey that both Christian and pagan "had a stake."[17]

While Markus will emerge again in our hermeneutical discussion, his voice is not the only interlocutor against a pessimistic reading of Augustine. John von Heyking has characterized the debate between the different interpretations of Augustine's political thought as

---

15. Milbank, "An Essay Against the Secular Order," 209.
16. Markus, *Christianity and the Secular*, 40.
17. Ibid., 39.

"schizophrenia between political minimalism and sacralism."[18] Here one can see an implicit criticism of the more pessimistic reading of Augustine. Von Heyking in a manner similar to Markus argues that politics is a negotiation of the "conflicting longings and desires" of man, and sees the political realm as a "shelter or sanctuary from the disruptive anxieties and fears about the possibility of the senselessness of mortal life."[19] Milbank would reject this position directly and express his own by arguing that the only "shelter" or "sanctuary" in Augustine's thought remains the *ecclesia*. However, von Heyking goes on to argue that Augustine saw politics as a natural human expression and the cooperative construction of a "community as an expression of their loves."[20]

Von Heyking posits that while admittedly a limited and flawed effort, Augustine assigned politics an exalted role on the level of earthly goods, as amongst human endeavors it is the "highest practical achievement." "Augustine's criticism of prideful passions leaves room to affirm that politics can secure a happiness that is not eternal even when he does not always argue this explicitly."[21] Rosemary Radford Reuther stands in agreement with this perspective and goes further by arguing that man's political reality is part of the Creator's design, and hence is a good to be engaged fully by the Christian. She argues in line with Markus and von Heyking: "The empire, with its functions of political and economic well being, pursues ends which are good and legitimate in themselves and stand within the ultimate purposes of God, even though these material ends become evil when they are absolutized as the ultimate ends of man."[22] Jean Bethke Elshtain, in

18. John von Heyking, *Augustine and Politics as Longing in the World* (Columbia, MO: Univ. of Missouri Press, 2001), 13.
19. Ibid., 51.
20. Ibid.
21. Ibid., 52.
22. Rosemary Radford Reuther, "Augustine and Christian Political Theology," *Interpretation* 29, no. 3 (1975), 260.

a manner more nuanced than the others, argues that Augustine is "redefining" the public itself, and sees the fundamental opposition not between "public and private, church and world, but between political virtue and political vice."[23] For Elshtain, the centrality of *caritas* to the Christian life compels the offering of oneself without fear and brings "an abundant overflowing of the fullness of life."[24]

In evaluating the hermeneutical differences between these readings, I believe that Augustine does bear a clear pessimism towards the political order. Corruption, vanity, oppression, and self-serving motives were not simply proper to the political apparatus of his day, but were for Augustine part of man's fallen nature. Augustine's pessimism towards political structures is consistent with his anthropology, as the sinfulness of the human condition is necessarily reflected in the human community, and is only remedied by the supernatural order of grace. There is little evidence to suggest that Augustine held any sweeping prospects of a change with the introduction of Christians into the political structures of Roman society, and I believe Kaufman's analysis is logical and correct. As Kaufman states, "Regimesreformed or transformed or exchanged for something totally new—to the extent they were political, were fragments of the terrestrial city and not creations capable of trifling perfections in some neutral zone."[25]

While other authors have sought alternatives to this pessimism, often they have done so at the expense of the Augustinian identity of their arguments. Augustine, unlike the contemporary social and political scientist, is not ultimately concerned with human social and political affairs in themselves. They are a means to an end, as the peace and harmony created on earth allows for the Christian

23. Elshtain, *Augustine and the Limits of Politics*, 35.
24. Ibid., 36.
25. Kaufman, *Incorrectly Political*, 126.

to live the Gospel and undertake his earthly pilgrimage without the external pressures of conflict or persecution. However, when such persecution occurs the Christian is called to remain steadfast nonetheless, as Augustine demonstrates in his treatment of the Christian martyr. Unable to find consistency with Augustine on such points, Markus and others have evoked a vision of social consensus, which owes much to John Rawls. In this vision, the emergence of flaws in human political community is seen as the result of human institutions themselves. Edmund Santurri advocates this type of argument:

> Over and against relatively pessimistic accounts of human possibility, Rawls insists that 'human nature is good' in the sense that 'citizens who grow up under reasonable and just institutions . . . will affirm those institutions and act to make sure their social world endures.' Rawls goes so far as to propose that the 'great evils of human history' (for example aggressive war, religious persecution, famine) are themselves a consequence of unjust social and political structures and that with the elimination of such structures 'these great evils will eventually disappear.'[26]

Such a romantic view is, in my opinion, contrary to the anthropology of Augustine, and fails to assign sin the gravity it necessitates. Human political community is flawed not just on an institutional level, but because human beings are sinful. Political vice is present not because of political and social institutions in themselves, but because such vice is the result of our pride and our sinfulness. Therefore, Augustine finds the solution for social ills and human weakness not in human structures, but in the intervention of God through grace. Building upon the work of Fortin and Dodaro, I believe it is here that a proper vision of Augustine's relevance to political questions emerges. In the midst of human sinfulness in all realms of life, Augustine seeks the

---

26. Edmund Santurri, "Global Justice after the Fall: Christian Realism and the 'Law of Peoples," *Journal of Religious Ethics* 33, no. 4D (2005), 289.

promotion and practice of virtue brought about through the effect of grace. However, while Augustine's vision is certainly marked by a strong pessimism, it is not and cannot be completely pessimistic precisely because of the prospect of grace's work within the human soul.

Augustine cannot be called purely a pessimist on the political and social realm because of the continual prospect of conversion and the social benefit brought about by the practice of Christian virtue. Such limitations, as Fortin has argued, are positive effects of Christianity, but do not amount to an optimistic shift in the entire human political and social structure. Augustine's pessimism towards the earthly city is mitigated only by his understanding of Christian virtue and the limited but positive effects that it offers to citizens of an often difficult social and political context. The main proponent of this hermeneutical solution remains Robert Dodaro. Recognizing the validity of Kaufman's pessimism toward any Christian betterment of political and social life and acknowledging Augustine's refusal of any "specific Christian political program," Dodaro maintains that Augustine believed, "Christians in public life can develop the capacity for moral reasoning, aided by grace, in which their practice of civic virtues is transformed by their practice of Christian faith, hope, and love."[27]

Dodaro's position avoids Markus's sweeping neutrality of the public square, and also the sacralization of political authority in Milbank's ecclesiology. All the while, it allows for a limited Christian contribution to political and social life through the personal exercise and promotion of virtue. A Christian's call to virtuous living and responsible citizenship is a necessary element of Augustine's vision of the earthly "pilgrimage." And indeed, the aim of government for Augustine remains "to assist people in living virtuously in this life,

27. Dodaro, "Ecclesia and Res Pubblica," 245.

so that they may achieve happiness in the life to come."[28] Dodaro's perspective here, in my opinion, is faithful to Augustine's concern for the welfare of Christians engaged in public service, and maintains the overarching sense of *distensio* that is part of his vision of the Christian's earthly life.

Dodaro convincingly roots this virtue-centered perspective in Augustine's *Epistula* 155 written to the imperial vicar for Africa, Macedonius. Macedonius is complimented by Augustine based upon his exercise of virtue. In granting clemency in a capital case, Macedonius is told by Augustine that he exhibited charity. Also, in holding fast to Christian doctrine despite the potential outside pressures, he exhibited faith. Finally, by rejecting the vain glory of other Roman statesmen in the exercise of his office, Augustine reminds him that he exhibited Christian hope. Dodaro summarizes:

> For Augustine, faith, hope, and charity are alone capable of drawing the Christian statesman beyond the limited, temporal perspectives of the earthly city into a deeper love of God, and therefore into the eternal reality of the heavenly city. Augustine believes that the theological virtues accomplish the because they alter the way the statesman understands and practices the political virtues in the performance of his public duties. When Augustine congratulates Macedonius for governing in the earthly city 'with his mind fixed on the heavenly city,' he is acknowledging the effects of these three virtues on the imperial vicar . . . the theological virtues alter the Christian statesman's practice of the political virtues.[29]

Dodaro's argument is in line with that of Ernest Fortin, who excludes any notion of a "Christian polity" in Augustine. However, unlike Milbank, Fortin also argues that Christianity is not an Augustinian substitute for political life. "It transcends all regimes and is of necessity

---

28. Robert Dodaro, "Augustine on the Statesman and the Two Cities," in *A Companion to Augustine*, First Edition, ed. Mark Vesey (Oxford: Blackwell Publishing, 2012), 390.
29. Dodaro, "Augustine on the Statesman and the Two Cities," 389.

limited in its practical application by the modalities of its existence in this world."[30] Fortin argues that Augustine envisions the Christian citizen "not that they allow their souls to be molded and determined by taste and opinions of the regime under which they happen to live."[31] Christianity, therefore, is "neither subversive nor conformist" towards political life, and calls upon its members to "bear with equanimity the inescapable evils of life without ceasing to toil unwearyingly for the suppression of those evils which can be successfully overcome by human effort and perseverance."[32] Fortin admits the possibility in Augustine of a Christian ruler, but even here notes that Christian wisdom and political power are distinct forces acting in a single subject.

This latter distinction, however, is problematic, and it appears to rely upon a dualism that separates the individual's identity by virtue of the role of believer and politician. As Dodaro has noted, this reading of the Christian in political life implies a "moral compromise between the two poles of civic responsibility and Christianity." He continues, "By this reading, either the Christian ruler/citizen gives more weight to the tenets of the Christian religion and less to the sometimes harsh obligations of public office, or he fulfills his public duties while paying less heed to the 'other worldly' claims on his soul made by his faith."[33] Dodaro, therefore, sees in Letter 155 a clear demonstration that "the concept of justice, as of the other political virtues, undergoes significant change in the statesman once he considers his public responsibilities in the light of the claims of Christian faith, hope, and

---

30. Fortin, *Classical Christianity*, vol. 2, 47.
31. Ibid.
32. Ibid.
33. Dodaro, "Political and Theological Virtues in Augustine, Letter 155 to Macedonius," *Augustiniana* 54 (2000), 472.

love."[34] There is little room for such a transformation in the analysis of Fortin and the later interpretation of Kaufman.

Kaufman's pessimism could be used to discourage any effort of the Christian in public life, as such an effort would seem futile and the outcome almost certainly negative. However, Augustine does not call for a withdrawal from public life, but rather a distinction between the source of Christian virtue, namely grace, and the place where public testimony is given and virtue is exercised, namely the world. As Robert Dodaro explains, the Eucharist itself reminds Christians that "they should not esteem themselves for their virtuous deeds. Instead they should recognize that the source of their virtue is found not in themselves, but in Christ."[35] The Christian's avoidance of the vanity and egoistic vision of virtue often prevalent in Roman society is in itself a differentiating mark of the Christian in public life. Such true virtue once again rests on the Christian himself and not on larger changes to political and social structures. "[Augustine] urged readers to accept God's grace and God's governance and to stay within the pilgrim city: to love God and neighbor, to endure disappointment patiently and with undiminished faith in divine sovereignty and benevolence, and to yearn for the consolations of faith, which restored the will to obedience."[36]

A clear point of divergence emerges, therefore, in regards to Augustine's view of Macedonius, and the relevance of their correspondence to our discussion. The question remains whether Augustine believed Macedonius was an exceptional Christian leader never to be expected again, or whether he was paradigmatic for the Christian ruler in general. Such a question, therefore, bears a clear hermeneutical significance in the analysis of Letter 155. For

34. Ibid., 473.
35. Dodaro, *Christ and the Just Society*, 104.
36. Kaufman, *Redeeming Politics*, 135–136.

Fortin and Kaufman, this letter remains an isolated incident, as the responsibilities of office and public life, in general, often precluded the Christian from exercising Christian virtue. For this reason they both view a certain wariness predominating Augustine's view of politics and public responsibilities. However, for Dodaro this letter remains a significant element in piecing together Augustine's view of the Christian in public life. In his view, there should be a change present in the Christian's practice of justice and other political virtues. Such a transformation is accomplished with the help of grace and by a living of Christian faith, hope, and love. However, it is important to note that Dodaro does not see such a transformation as applying to every Christian ruler, nor simply because a ruler is Christian. The rarity and uniqueness of the Christian, who allows supernatural grace and Christian virtue to inform his or her rule remains unmitigated. Also, to support his argument Dodaro notes that such a transformation is alluded to in Augustine's *Epistula* 138 to Marcellinus and is consistent with Book V of the *City of God*.[37] Dodaro's position does not deny that the Christian politician will sin, but rather reinforces the uniqueness of some Christian rulers in their humility to accept the inevitability of error and their use of penance to admit sin and ask forgiveness for it.[38]

It is here that Augustine's pessimism is tempered, and his assertions to Macedonius are concretely manifested. In my opinion, however, the positions of Fortin and Kaufman and that of Dodaro do not appear to be mutually exclusive. While it might be paradigmatic, Augustine's letter to Macedonius does not deny the fact that rulers like him will be rare and unexpected. Furthermore, the wariness of Augustine towards the Christian's capacity of exercising such transformative virtue while in office remains justified, as certainly

37. Dodaro, "Political and Theological Virtues," 471.
38. Dodaro, *Christ and the Just Society*, 193.

Augustine knew Christians in such positions who were unlike Macedonius. As a result, it appears that Augustine's correspondence remains significant to our discussion and can be viewed integrally with the realism and wariness expressed by Kaufman, Fortin, and others.

The answer, therefore, to the initial question at the beginning of this section of whether Augustine has a particular political vision must be answered negatively, as the political realm itself is of little concern when compared to the Christian's citizenry in the eternal city. It is this latter citizenship which must remain the goal of every follower of Christ. If anything, the earthly city and its glory continually offer a temptation to Christians, who could become attached to the love of worldly glory, which in turn distracts the Christian from the love of the Creator.[39] As Peter Kaufman notes, "[Christian magistrates] risked developing passions for power which would soon overwhelm them . . . It was incumbent on the Christian official to devise measures to resist evil but to avoid politicizing the good, because of the pull of politics in this vexed existence, in time, was always a pull toward *amor sui*."[40] However, this discussion is in no way completely futile. Augustine did bear concern for political and social issues, inasmuch as they determined the context in which Christians were to exercise virtue, practice their faith, and testify to that faith under persecution. To demonstrate his level of concern and the balance in his thought between man's final goal and temporal reality, it is helpful to view his treatment of the Christian martyr.

I find it interesting that the role of the martyr is given little treatment in Robert Markus's *Saeculum* and in his *Christianity and the Secular*. The martyr in his martyrdom, which is both the supreme act of testimony to faith and also continued obedience to the law,

39. Kaufman, *Incorrectly Political*, 124.
40. Ibid., 132.

clearly exemplifies for Augustine the role of the Christian in society and the method of true "activism." As Joseph Ratzinger has noted, the concept of martyrdom is essential for Augustine in that the Christian martyr is the "counterpoint of the pagan hero . . ." Ratzinger continues, "His victory is suffering, the saying of no to powers that determine public opinion. Augustine sees in the martyr the particular form in which Christian victory is affirmed in this age of the world and in the martyr the sign of the Church: that it lives and conquers in this world in the form of suffering."[41] The Christian martyr, therefore, stood as a living reminder to every Christian of the pilgrim nature of this life and the eternal nature of the victory promised through Christ. The martyr, therefore, embodies both the cause for Augustine's apathy towards politics for its own sake, but abiding concern for how it affected his flock and the Church on earth.

Dodaro, like Ratzinger, has noted that the martyr in Augustine exemplifies true virtue, in that such virtue seeks the acquisition of "permanent goods, such as eternal life; therefore it culminates in the knowledge and love of God."[42] It is the martyr, therefore, not the Roman hero, who overcomes all fear of death and forsakes even earthly glory in conformity to Christ for the achievement of the only true and eternal end, namely life eternal.[43] Dodaro argues that it is in Augustine's sermons on the feasts of the martyrs, especially *Sermon 302* on St. Lawrence, that the Bishop of Hippo puts forward his vision of civic virtue, "namely justice, piety, and the love and forgiveness of enemies."[44] Ultimately, therefore, it is in the context of

41. Ratzinger, *L'unita delle nazioni*, 105-106.
42. Dodaro, *Christ and the Just Society*, 55.
43. Ibid., 56.
44. Dodaro, "Between the Two Cities," in *Augustine and Politics*, 101. See also Robert Dodaro, "Augustine's Use of Parallel Dialogues in his Preaching of Nonviolence," in Ministerium sermonis: Philological, Historical, and Theological Studies on Augsutine's Sermones ad populum, *Instrumenta Patristica et Mediaevalia* 53, ed. Gert Partoens, Anthony Dupont, Mathiajs Lamberigts (Turnhout: Brepols, 2009), 327-344.

martyrdom that Augustine lays out his vision of Christian activism, namely seeking a more just society by acting contrary to the enemies of Christianity. It is, therefore, ultimately, a call for "opposing injustice through nonviolence."[45]

Preserving the Theological Nature of Augustine's Vision

Retrieving Augustine's political and social vision, no matter what school of interpretation is in question, also implies retrieving the wider theological context in which Augustine's vision was formulated. While sounding like an obvious observation, it bears repeating that Augustine was not a political scientist, sociologist, or social commentator, but rather a bishop and theologian. As a result, he commented on certain political and social themes when they touched upon the Church and the souls whom he was charged with shepherding. For this reason, Rowan Williams has argued, "We should look less for a systematic account of 'church' and 'world' (let alone church and state), and more for a scheme for reflecting on the nature of social virtue."[46]

Indeed, Williams, Dodaro, and others freely admit the lack of a systematic discussion of the political and social questions at hand, but they also readily admit the larger theological context from which Augustine's political and social principles are drawn. Robert Dodaro has noted, I believe quite fairly, that numerous studies of Augustine's political thought "invariably pay little attention to his thinking about Christ and scriptural interpretation, and make almost no effort to ask what role these and other areas in his thought contribute to his political ethics."[47] Eric Gregory has argued as well that "political

---

45. Ibid.
46. Williams, "Politics and the Soul," 57.
47. Dodaro, *Christ and the Just Society*, 1.

Augustinianism" has been "neither politically nor theologically Christian. It likes religious language, but it is conceptually atheistic."[48] What is often ignored in this discussion, therefore, is the fact that Augustine's Christology, ecclesiology, anthropology, and scriptural exegesis are not isolated topics, but rather flow together as part of his larger theological vision. It is in this theological framework that Augustine engages political and social themes. Hence, to borrow Gregory's term, the "conceptually atheistic" discussion of Augustine's political and social "doctrine," is in itself highly problematic.

Nevertheless, it can be argued that Arquillère's *L'Augustinisme Politique* began this wider trend of divorcing Augustine's thought on politics and society from their theological context. Augustine, as Deane's work exemplifies, is defined in this context as a "political thinker," whose "political theory" is evaluated and transmitted to subsequent thinkers. Indeed, Augustine has been compared and connected to numerous subsequent thinkers ranging from Giles of Rome, Pope Gregory VII, Machiavelli, Hobbes, Max Weber, and others. However, in these comparisons what is forgotten is Augustine's true concern, which is not the exercise of power or political authority, but indeed the attainment of beatitude in the heavenly city. Another cause of this loss of Augustine's theological context rests in the work of Reinhold Niebuhr and his realist interpretation of Augustine.

For Niebuhr and the realist school, man's true freedom, nature, and deepest concerns were intertwined in his political and temporal reality, and as a result the theological vision of Augustine was consequently deflated. We have previously discussed the Niebuhrian interpretation of original sin, and his firm rejection of any anthropological effects in post-lapsarian humanity. Indeed, as Gerald

---

48. Gregory, *Politics and the Order of Love*, 127.

Schlabach has explained, "For Niebuhr, the transcendent, the eternal—the realm wherein an ethic of pure mutuality through pure self-sacrifice could function—was like Kant's noumenal realm. It was ultimately real, but currently inaccessible to all but a very few; even for them, Jesus' ethic constituted a 'tangent toward eternity' and out of history."[49] As Schlabach points out, the category of transcendence and eternity, which is an essential component in Augustine's work, was placed by Niebuhr beyond history's grasp, and was hence rendered irrelevant to the concerns of human life and society. The problem here is that such a vision loses Augustine's concern with our eternal end, and leads to a merely socio-political reading of the Bishop of Hippo. Eric Gregory aptly explains, "Despite his accent on gratitude and contrition, [Niebuhr] was devoted to giving American civilization just enough religion he thought it needed without giving it too much theology."[50] However, while Niebuhr saw himself as introducing realism that is free of cynicism, the results of his project have in part caused a loss of the integral unity of Augustine's vision. Indeed, Augustine's thought and principles cannot be extricated from their theological context and their fundamentally transcendent goals and still honestly be called Augustinian.

Maintaining the Eschatological Nature of Augustine's Vision

Augustine's *City of God*, as we have seen throughout this discussion, has been embraced by numerous thinkers and utilized quite often in disciplines outside theology. However, in many of these interpretations of Augustine, and even in the Niebuhrian realist reading, what is quickly lost is Augustine's eschatological sense. This

49. Schlabach, "Is Milbank Niebuhrian?," 35.
50. Gregory, *Politics and the Order of Love*, 14.

can be defined as his fundamental concern with humanity's fulfillment and the fulfillment of history itself. Eugene TeSelle, I believe, correctly points out that much of the indecision and tension in Augustine's thought towards political questions "relaxes" exponentially when the Bishop of Hippo turns toward the end times. TeSelle explains, "This eschatological or teleological framework seems to alter Augustine's stance toward political life, not only his train of reasoning but his posture and his muscle tone . . . He seems to relax and gain perspective only when he thinks 'from the end.'"[51] Indeed, the cause of Augustine's ambiguity towards political issues themselves is precisely because of their earthly nature, and hence they pose little ultimate concern for him or his flock. Eric Gregory, in fact, disagrees with Markus in his attempt to place Augustine's concept of the "secular" back within the context of his eschatology. Gregory argues, "This definition does not deny the Christian claim that the state remains under the lordship of Christ, providentially secured in its identity 'in Christ.' But it does claim that the secular is the 'not yet' dimension of an eschatological point of view."[52]

The commentary of Charles Mathewes is of great value here, as his work insists on the connection between Augustine's political ambivalence and his fundamental concern with Christian eschatology, the theology of the ultimate ends of humanity and the cosmos itself. He writes, "Augustine's goal was always the same: to refuse the mythology of the state. Political entities are fundamentally secular realities, this worldly, and are useful in securing us space and occasion to fulfill our doxological longings to give gratitude to God and praise God's glory."[53] Indeed, the innate desires of humanity are responded to in Augustine's vision not in the political and social

---

51. TeSelle, "Toward an Augustinian Politics," 99.
52. Ibid., 79.
53. Mathewes, "An Augustinian Look at Empire," 300.

issues of his day, but in the faith which he, as a Christian and bishop, was called to preach and defend. Therefore, the political sphere, the earthly city, did matter, inasmuch as it was "extension," space in which man is called to prepare for his final and complete fulfillment in the heavenly city. "[Augustine's] first and primary polis is the church, the republic of grace, and the fundamental political task for this polis lies in the evangelical extension and ascetical preparation of its citizens to be fit to bear the joy that is humanity's eschatological destiny."[54] Without this hermeneutical key, in my opinion, it becomes very easy to misread Augustine's *City of God*, and hence distort his fundamental goals.

It is also a recovery of the eschatological nature of Augustine's vision that prevents what can be viewed as two excessive readings of Augustine. The first, which is feared by Robert Markus and others, is the emergence of Christian triumphalism. This is the call for a new Christendom, where secular *imperium* is anointed and divinely ordained. Even Oliver O'Donovan, who is sympathetic with such a concept of Christendom, notes, "It is not, as if often suggested, that Christian political order is a *project* of the church's mission, either as an end in itself or as a means to the further missionary end. The church's one project is to witness to the Kingdom of God."[55]

The other extreme reading that is also avoided by a "healthy" eschatology is the Marxist-inspired interpretation of Augustine in which humanity bears a "temporal task" of actively "transforming" the world. In this reading the world is made the primary *locus* and *telos* of humanity, and the Kingdom of God becomes a political project. The danger of this reading of Augustine is well identified by James Schall. He recalls the key distinction introduced by Jacques Maritain in his confrontation of Marxism, namely that the Kingdom

54. Ibid., 293.
55. O'Donovan, *The Desire of the Nations*, 195.

of God in glory is not a "definite advent of justice and peace, and of human happiness . . . for this progress is not capable of any final term."[56] Eric Gregory, who advocates for a recovery of "civic liberalism," also notes, "Augustine did hold that Christians should not zealously try to rush in the eschaton by fully enacting the good in secular politics. If it is a matter of God's grace, he argued against Donatist perfectionists, Christians should not desire a pure community of the holy 'before the time is right.'"[57]

Schall notes that each person's destiny is the inner life of God, freely presented and mediated in Christ. Hence in reflecting on Augustine's heavenly city and its relation to the Kingdom of God we must remind ourselves, "The Kingdom of God, in the strictest sense, can only be composed of those who have made this choice as their individual and thus common good." The central question, therefore, is not citizenship and activism in this world, but the openness to grace which allows us entrance into the heavenly city, the *civitas dei*. TeSelle, as well, confirms that humanity's ultimate goal is the fundamental lens by which Augustine discusses Christian practice and living. "He offers us something more in his reflections on Christian practice. Contrary to what one might expect, they find their center in his eschatology, that is, his discussion of ends in human life."[58] In attempting to understand how Augustine envisioned the role of the statesman, it should be no surprise that there is a deeply "eschatological" character to the Christian's role in public office and political life. As Dodaro pinpoints, this role is "to harmonize secular virtue with true virtue, understood as a life of happiness in God, and not merely as freedom from need or want."[59]

56. Schall, *The Mind that is Catholic*, 27.
57. Gregory, *Politics and the Order of Love*, 15.
58. TeSelle, "Toward an Augustinian Politics," 98.
59. Dodaro, *Christ and the Just Society*, 210.

Interpreting Augustine's Ecclesiology

Augustine's vision of the Church is of primary importance in understanding the differences, and at times the hermeneutical extremes of Robert Markus and John Milbank. Markus's vision of an Augustinian *saeculum* emerges as a response to "Constantinian Christianity," where "the world was flowing into the Church, being taken over wholesale by the Church, and the Church was expanding its influence into more and more areas of the culture of Roman society and dominating its ever-growing areas of daily life."[60] Therefore, the response to this trend in Markus's work is a secular shared space where bishop and magistrate act freely in their own realms and on their own principles.[61] This shared space in itself is consistent with Augustine's understanding of the earthly city, and Marrou's *tertium quid*. However, in Markus's *saeculum* political institutions, social practices and customs must remain doctrinally neutral. As a result, political discourse and public debate are to be divorced from the discussion of the ultimate realities of human salvation. What becomes dominant instead are so-called "penultimate" concerns.[62] A "secularist" interpretation of Augustine is facilitated by Markus's vision and, as we will discuss below, excesses in this reading allow for the complete privatization and absolute separation of religion from public life and the public square in general.

On the other side of this debate, John Milbank's vision of the Church and his interpretation of Augustine's ecclesiology are also reactionary. Milbank's purpose is to respond to the secularization and individualism, which he believes has unfairly been attributed to Augustine. He lays this out quite clearly:

---

60. Markus, *Christianity and the Secular*, 23.
61. Ibid., 39.
62. Markus, *Christianity and the Secular*, 42.

Augustine, in particular, has been interpreted as foreshadowing protestantism and liberalism. It is contended that he invents an individualistic understanding of both Church and state, because, on the one hand, he interprets the state as merely a compromise between individual wills for the satisfaction of material conveniences, and, on the other, he understands the true Church, the *Civitas Dei*, as the collection of elect true believers known only to God.[63]

In response to these assertions, which Milbank and others believe Markus has helped to promote, Milbank seeks to recover a vision of the Church as *civitas*. He asserts plainly, "The Church on earth is part of *societas perfecta*, a properly self-sufficient society with its own means of establishing and maintaining norms, its own mode of social organisation."[64] For Milbank, the Church is a new social order, which provides refuge to its children from the "ravages" of the state and secures unity and peace.[65] The Church, therefore, is the alternative to the polis, and not its partner. Milbank rejects the Thomist placement of political and social life in the natural order, and the subsequent divisions that emerge between the secular and spiritual realms. Indeed, the Church must for Milbank recover activities it has previously ceded to the "secular" realm.[66] Milbank argues that it is only the Church that can achieve an "ontological priority of peaceful unity." That peace is achieved by its "counter-history" told through the event of human redemption in Christ. This event provides a "counter-ethics" exposing the difference between society within and outside the Church. It is nothing less than a "counter-ontology," which differentiates the Church from other systems and secures true peace.[67]

---

63. Milbank, *Theology and the Social Theory*, 400.
64. Milbank, "An Essay Against Secular Order," 207.
65. Ibid., 210.
66. Milbank, *Theology and Social Science*, 403.
67. This position is presented and critiqued by Michael Hollerich, see Michael Hollerich, "John Milbank, Augustine, and the 'Secular,'" 11.

As Michael Hollerich argues, in my opinion justifiably, Milbank's work is a positive step forward in that it responds to the "disappearance" of the Church in the public square that is present in the vision of Robert Markus and others. Hollerich rejects the tendency in Markus's interpretation "to maximize the gap between the visible, historic Christian Church on the one hand, and the city of God on the other."[68] Such a tendency pushes the Church on earth to irrelevance and disconnects it completely from its heavenly fulfillment. Milbank, therefore, seeks to recapture Augustine's vision of the Church as the "community of salvation insofar as its social practice, replicating its narration of the story of Jesus, embodied the forgiveness of sins and realized the bond of charity among its members."[69]

While Milbank's project is laudable, I believe that his vision of the Church can also be problematic. It appears to me that at times his ecclesiology focuses completely on the Church's heavenly reality, while leaving little room for its institutional and human manifestation.[70] If Markus concentrates on the *ecclesia permixta* at the expense of the Church's mediating role on earth, I believe Milbank at times does the opposite. In identifying the Church as the *civitas dei* on earth without qualification, there are inevitable problems that emerge. It becomes difficult to explain, for instance, the presence of human sinfulness within the members of the Church and the need for continual renewal. The Church for Augustine is not forever destined to remain an *ecclesia permixta*, and hence it awaits its final completion. Such a tension between its foundation by Christ on earth

68. Ibid., 10.
69. Ibid., 12.
70. Dodaro observes this strain in Milbank as well. See Dodaro, "*Ecclesia and Res Publica*," 258–259. This distinction is the essence of *Lumen Gentium* 8 which presents both the "society structured with hierarchal organs and the Mystical Body of Christ," as forming "one complex reality which coalesces from a divine and a human element."

and its heavenly fulfillment is the essence of the famous formula of "already and not yet," whose essence is enshrined in *Lumen Gentium*, 5. "While it slowly grows, the Church strains toward the completed Kingdom and, with all its strength, hopes and desires to be united in glory with its King."[71]

I believe this concern is consistent with Joseph Ratzinger's insistence that there remains a sense of free adhesion to the faith secured by a duality between state and church. By maintaining, therefore, the autonomy of political authority, the integrity of the Church and its testimony of faith is also secured. In this way, Ratzinger's call for such autonomy can also be seen as a counterpoint to Milbank's project. Ratzinger notes, "Only in those places that the duality of state and church, of sacral and political authority, is maintained in some form or another do we find the fundamental prerequisite for freedom . . . Church and state remain separate and that membership in the Church clearly retains its voluntary character."[72]

However, despite these issues it also appears that Milbank's work remains an important corrective in the discussion of Augustine's political and social vision. His insistence that the life of the Church does matter and is central to Augustine's conception of society is a necessary reminder in the face of numerous commentaries that simply relegate the Church's life to a socially helpful "Sunday activity." The Church's life: its liturgy, its preaching, its charity, and its fundamental unity, are not ancillary to Augustine's vision of society, but rather remain central components of it. As Eric Gregory points out, "*Caritas* grows only in the community of faith grounded in the body of

---

71. *LG*, 5.
72. Joseph Ratzinger, *Church, Ecumenism, and Politics*, 157. Ratzinger here is consistent with *Gaudium et Spes* (GS) 76 which states, "The Church and the political community in their own fields are autonomous and independent from each other. Yet both, under different titles, are devoted to the personal and social vocation of the same men."

Christ. It is a collective body that contains each member within itself, suffering with each other, united by a common love of the God of Jesus Christ."[73] For Augustine, this ecclesial life offers to Christians the supernatural grace they need to live virtuously in the world and offers a foretaste of their true homeland, namely the heavenly city.

The Centrality of Christ in Augustine's Theology

In recovering the theological nature of Augustine's social and political vision, the discussion of Christ and the central importance of Augustine's Christology is often absent in many commentaries. Indeed, beginning with the "political Augustinian" shift towards external political and social concerns there has been a loss of the Christological vocabulary and themes utilized by Augustine himself. However, as Robert Dodaro has shown in his work, "Augustine maintains that justice cannot be known except in Christ, and that, as founder (*conditor*) and ruler (*rector*), Christ forms the just society in himself."[74] Augustine's vision of the city of God is dependent on his Christology. As Dodaro reminds us, the city of God is the "body of Christ," or the members of Christ's body united as a whole who together constitute the whole, just Christ (*Christus totus iustus.*)[75]

In reaffirming the Christological context in which Augustine formulates his vision of the *civitas dei*, Dodaro is able to show how it is Christ's mediation by the humility of His incarnation that allows for the creation of the only truly just society. It is only through his Christology that Augustine is able to reject the "autonomous moral reason" of classical philosophy so popular in his time. Rather, he affirms Christ as the only source of lasting virtue, and the only true

73. Gregory, *Politics and the Order of Love*, 237.
74. Dodaro, *Christ and the Just Society*, 72.
75. Ibid., 72.

model of perfect virtue.[76] It is only by the adhesion of the human intellect and will to the example of Christ and openness to His grace that ignorance and weakness (characteristics of post-lapsarian humanity) are overcome. In this way, as well, the practice of true justice is learned. Dodaro argues that the inescapable source of such weakness and the ultimate effect of original sin remains the fear of death. This ultimate fear for Augustine marks the limit of all natural virtue and is the fear that Roman glory-seeking never successfully assuages.

It is, therefore, only in the "wondrous exchange" (*mira commutatio*) of Christ on the cross that Christ makes "his justice our justice." Dodaro explains, "Christ assumes the fear of death that all members of his body experience, while he communicates back to them his own hope as consolation."[77] Here, therefore, is the uniqueness of Christ's justice and the fundamental differentiation of all human virtue from that virtue which is mediated through and learned from Christ. It is for this reason that Dodaro notes, "Augustine proposes Christ as the statesman (*rector rei publicae*) whose unique condition as God and man means that he alone in history is capable of sustaining a just society, because he alone is both completely just and capable of healing other human beings from original sin, thus making them just."[78]

Dodaro, therefore, insists that the very concept of justice for Augustine is necessarily theological. While Markus appeals to a Rawlsian conception of justice in society, Augustine's vision of justice is scripturally based, and any alternative neglects this fundamental Christological meaning.[79] Justice is "to stand in right relationship to God and, therefore, to obey God and his commandments . . . Augustine argues that justice is interchangeable

76. Ibid.
77. Ibid., 196.
78. Ibid., 71.
79. Markus, *Christianity and the Secular*, 67.

with love (*caritas*)."[80] In affirming Augustine's theological conception of justice, Dodaro transforms the discussion of Augustine's political and social vision. Augustine's discussion of justice cannot be simply a political and social debate concerned with civil society and political structures, but must retain a theological character concerned with true justice offered to humanity in Christ. Indeed, "Christ's justice united political and religious concerns."[81] In my opinion, this is also the essence of Rowan William's observation about Book XIX of the *City of God*, "[Augustine's] question in Book XIX is, rather, about the optimal form of corporate human life in light of what is understood to be its last end . . . *De Civitate* is not at all a work of political theory in the usual sense, but sketches for a theological anthropology and a corporate spirituality."[82]

The theological anthropology being sketched by Augustine is based upon and modeled after Christ and the true justice, which he alone can offer humanity. Joseph Ratzinger, as well, connects Augustine's anthropology to his Christology, seeing in the latter an exegetical key of central importance:

> The Christian faith—following the way shown to us by Jesus—banished the ideal of political theocracy . . . it promoted the secular character of the State, in which Christians live together in freedom with those who hold other beliefs, united by the common moral responsibility founded on human nature, on the nature of justice. The Christian faith distinguishes this from the Kingdom of God, which does not and cannot exist in this world as a political reality, but rather comes into being through faith, hope, and charity and must transform the world from within.[83]

---

80. Dodaro, *Christ and the Just Society*, 76.
81. Ibid., 77.
82. Williams, "Politics and the Soul," 58.
83. Ratzinger, "Europe: Today and Tomorrow," 98–99. I will return to this concept of "transforming from within," later on as it provides an important paradigm for the role of Christianity in the contemporary world.

The interplay here of Christ's "exemplary and sacramental functions" is also taken up by Michael Hanby, who in building upon Dodaro's analysis presents the intertwined nature of Augustine's Christology and human anthropology. Hanby argues that Christ's exemplary role reveals to humanity an "inexhaustible" fullness, that causes us to increasingly "let go" and partake in the "Son's response to the Father."[84] As Hanby eloquently points out, "So in making Christ an exemplar, who is the object of our love and intention, Augustine opens an infinite distance between the body and the head, between the exemplar and the less than exemplary. This distance is the distance of *faith*."[85] The *eros* that Augustine introduces in his anthropology becomes for him nothing less than the distance between "lover and beloved, seer and seen," and it can only be filled by the *sacramentum*, where Christ mediates and fills that distance with a gift of His grace.[86] Augustine's Christology, therefore, contains a direct connection between *exemplum* and *sacramentum*, in which humanity is directly implicated. "Our love of and intention of the end as *exemplum* requires for its intellgiibility the mediation and giving of that end as *sacramentum* . . . it is this gift, this *dilectio*, 'that makes us abide in God, and Him in us."[87]

The Call to Virtue and the Role of Grace

As we have already touched upon, the pessimism towards the earthly city that Kaufman and Fortin see as pervading Augustine's thought must be conditioned slightly precisely because of Augustine's concept of grace and the virtue it cultivates. Augustine's concern for this

---

84. Hanby, *Augustine and Modernity*, 63. See also Dodaro, *Christ and the Just Society*, 147-159.
85. Ibid., 64.
86. Ibid., 65.
87. Ibid., 67.

theme is directly related to his struggle with Pelagianism, and as Dodaro notes, "[Augustine] dismisses their concept of moral reasoning as deficient, because they conceive divine wisdom as a rhetorical enticement to obey scriptural mandates whose full significance is assumed to be transparent to an autonomous moral reason."[88] While the Pelagians focused on following Christ's example, Augustine focused on Christ's sacrament and a concept of grace as "participation." By participating in the mystery of Christ, "deeper meanings" of religious truth are reflected upon which move the Christian to a deeper understanding and humility towards God. Grace, therefore, is directly connected to virtue in Augustine, as faith and humility are required in order to "heal the presumption which inhibits a fuller understanding of moral lessons contained in the example [of Christ]."[89]

This conception of grace has a direct impact on Augustine's conception of the just society, which as Dodaro has demonstrated is formed and created only by Christ. It is, therefore, on this point that Augustine breaks with Cicero's conception of the statesman. The true statesman must no longer simply "speak persuasively about justice," but rather to be just must appeal to the one who alone "is capable of purifying his listeners' souls."[90] It is the grace of Christ, which demonstrates to the human soul that its previous understandings of justice are nothing more than a reflection of the soul's own self-righteousness.[91] Indeed, only grace allows the soul to recognize and reject the pride and vainglory rampant in civil society. Through the mediation of Christ alone and membership into his body can one truly begin to overcome the weakness and ignorance that characterizes fallen man. This understanding of Augustine's concept

88. Dodaro, *Christ and the Just Society*, 180.
89. Ibid., 180.
90. Ibid., 75.
91. Ibid.

of grace and how it informs human action is a crucial element often forgotten in the application of Augustine's thought to the political and social questions that face Christians today.

James Schall reminds us of another important element of Augustine's concept of grace, namely that it separates his realism from the Machiavellian realism so often seen as his heir. Augustine's realism is the belief that "the state is indeed a divine institution, but it is not the location of perfection or grace. It is a remedy that must deal with disordered souls as they manifest their desires and degeneracy in public."[92] For Schall, however, this realism is not mere pessimism or a passive admission of the need for intervention among fallen beings. It includes the fact that there are those who "lived good lives under grace, even amidst the many who lived bad lives rejecting the same grace."[93] Here Schall, like Dodaro, is willing to go beyond the Niebuhrian realism that has been so prevalent in Augustinian interpretation for nearly a century. For unlike Niebuhr, who largely sought to circumvent the issue of post-lapsarian humanity and Augustine's understanding of original sin and its effects, Schall readily admits that "Augustine knew that grace was present even in the most disordered life, because he knew his own life. His realism included grace, and grace included a challenge to the classical virtues precisely in their own failures."[94] This theological conception of grace, therefore, separates Augustine's understanding of virtue and his vision in general from both the classical pagan tradition and from the Machiavellian and Hobbesian traditions so often cited as his successors.

92. Schall, *The Mind That is Catholic*, 205.
93. Ibid.
94. Ibid., 206.

The Question of Consensus

In recovering Augustine's Christological vision, it becomes clear that Augustine envisions in Christ the creation of the truly just society, as his "virtue takes hold in human beings when they believe in the mystery of the incarnate God."[95] As Ernest Fortin demonstrates, the Christian embrace of all peoples regardless of social status, class, or any other classification allowed for "an expression of common life that stands above its individual members and binds them together as fellow citizens."[96] However, this theologically-based social ontology, which Augustine relied upon, has been abandoned by Markus and subsequent interpreters, such as Edmund Santurri and Paul Weithman. As we have previously discussed, Markus believes that utilizing Augustine's principles a pluralistic society demands some "version of overlapping consensus . . . a shared area of social ethics which binds people together in a nation-community."[97] The result is a society that is "intrinsically 'secular' in the sense that it is not as such committed to any particular ultimate loyalty . . . a pluralistic, religiously neutral civil community."[98] Such an absence of "ultimate loyalty," however, stands in direct contradiction to the ultimate loyalty and fidelity that Augustine insists the Christian must maintain to the *civitas dei*. For Augustine, the Christian's ultimate fulfillment is not a distraction that is to be ignored in his public life, but indeed an essential component of his identity that is to inform and shape who he is and what he does.

One major difficulty, therefore, that emerges immediately is how such an "overlapping consensus" is grounded in a neutral social sphere. Markus seeks to answer this question by making an appeal to

95. Ibid., 72.
96. Fortin, *Classical Christianity,* vol. 2, 39.
97. Markus, *Christianity and the Secular,* 67.
98. Markus, *Saeculum,* 173.

John Rawls, but what results, regardless of his philosophical appeals, is a post-Enlightenment secular individualism wrapped in Augustinian vocabulary. In Markus's vision, the individual, shielded from any previous loyalties or religious principle, adheres freely to civil society and acts in society by uniting their own ends with those of the *polis*. Augustine, in this view, once again becomes an ancestor of Hobbes, Mills, and other individualist thinkers, for as Oliver O'Donovan has pointed out the *compositio voluntatum*, or consensus of human wills, becomes in this perspective a consensus of individuals within the earthly city.[99] Furthermore, the "ends" of the Christian can never rest solely in the earthly *polis*, but more importantly must remain fixed on his or her fulfillment in the heavenly city.

The fundamental problem is not simply that Markus wants to maintain social obligations without an ontology, as this has been attempted before by others. The problem also, as it relates to this discussion, is the claim that Augustine can somehow be identified with originating or setting the stage for such an effort. Eric Gregory seems to fall into a similar trend when he writes, "Augustinian political ethics have flourished without sustained recourse to the theology that animates his social ontology."[100] While political ethics might be flourishing, if such ethics are not referencing the Christian social ontology that flows from the Trinitarian mystery then such ethics can hardly be called Augustinian. Eugene TeSelle admits that social ontology is at the basis of Augustine's *res publica* and political ethic. He notes, "It is this ethic—ontologically rooted, sanctioned by eternity, and inwardly realized in the virtue of justice—that Augustine defends against the 'realists' of his own day. It is rather ascetic, as such things go, concerned to maintain the integrity of

---

99. O'Donovan, *Bonds of Interpretation*, 58.
100. Gregory, *Politics and the Order of Love*, 245.

the individual and the body politic, and willing to risk temporal discomforts for the sake of civic virtue."[101]

One important reason that such a lack of Christian social ontology is inconsistent with Augustinian thought remains that the Bishop of Hippo's ontology is tied to the search for truth, which has been revealed fully in Revelation. As Joseph Ratzinger argues, the monumental shift in Augustine is that religion is no longer based in "consensus but truth, that is the absolute, that is not instituted by the state, but has been instituted for itself a new community, that embraces all in as much as they live out the truth of God."[102] In Augustine, the good does exist and Truth has taken flesh in the Incarnation. The *summum bonum* for Augustine is unequivocally God. Hence, any attempt to create a neutral public square in the name of pluralism evacuates what Augustine argues is the very source of consensus upon which society is based. As Rowan Williams aptly explains, "Where there is no *jus* toward God, there is no common sense of what is due to human beings, no *juris consensus*. And this theme proves to be the main burden of the *De Civitate*'s vision of political virtue."[103] As a result, the perspectives of Markus, Von Heyking and others, who seek at times to circumvent a Christian ontology in the name of Augustine betray the basic ontological categories and theological foundations upon which the Bishop of Hippo relied, and which Augustine would maintain every society still requires in order to create true consensus.

Ratzinger's vision embraces these Augustinian categories and recognizes the dangers of a society that lacks an objective sense of the good: "'The liberated society' has to be independent of morality. Its freedom and justice must be produced, so to speak, by its

---

101. TeSelle, Toward an Augustinian Politics," 89.
102. Ratzinger, *L'unità delle nazioni*, 81–82.
103. Williams, "Politics of the Soul," 59.

structures . . . The ethos does not support the structures, but rather the structures support the ethos, precisely because the ethos is the fragile thing, which is at the root of the myth of the better world, the real essence of materialism . . ."[104] What Markus's neutrality accomplishes, therefore, is a justification of Christianity's removal from the public square, and with that removal the loss of the very ethical foundations of Western society. His mission for a Rawlsian-inspired neutral public square is part of a larger post-Enlightenment quixotic project, and rests far from the vision of the Bishop of Hippo. As Ratzinger has stated, "Reason needs revelation in order to be able to function as reason. The reference of the state to the Christian foundation is indispensable for its continuance as a state, especially if it is supposed to be pluralistic."[105]

The neutrality of the public square is something never envisioned in Augustine, as Ratzinger reminds us, the earthly city remained in proximity to the "city of the devil" and in Augustine's work there is "no further positive basis for the earthly state."[106] I believe that Peter Kaufman is correct, therefore, in noting that "when Augustine pressed readers to 'mark the contrast' between the terrestrial and celestial cities, he also appears to have precluded any significant, religiously neutral or uncommitted political practice from which anything truly just might come."[107] While Markus in his later work, *Christianity and the Secular*, steps back from the "neutrality" of human action, recognizing Augustine's insistence on ultimate ends, he still insists that there remains a neutral public square in Augustine's vision. "It is not necessary to think of such a sphere as the sum of a multiplicity or a fabric woven of many actions by many people . . ."[108]

104. Ratzinger, *Church, Ecumenism, and Politics*, 196.
105. Ibid., 206.
106. Ibid., 205.
107. Kaufman, *Incorrectly Political*, 123.
108. Markus, *Christianity and the Secular*, 44.

However, his concession of the impossibility of neutral human action does not mitigate the fact that his argument remains a contradiction of Augustine's vision of a Christ-centered just society. Furthermore, it is inconsistent with the fundamental pessimism with which Augustine treats Roman society in general and any prospect for that society's promotion of true and lasting virtue.

In fact, in examining Marrou's introduction of a *tertium quid*, one observes not a neutral public square, but the understanding that citizens of the two cities will coincide and interact in human history. For Augustine, this overlap in the world is the space in which the human person exercises their freedom by acting towards their ultimate end. Indeed, Augustine's focus on the human action is a central element of his thought, as Markus has admitted. As Eugene TeSelle has argued, it is within the human act that we see Augustine's intentions emerge clearly, "There may be a certain contemporary appeal in Augustine's mature focus upon human action, for the word which he seeks is not in heaven (that is, in the *lex aeternae* alone) and not in the depths (that is, in the social world of an errant humanity) but at the juncture of both, in a heart that looks beyond itself and is for that reason all the more capable of acting in its own situation."[109] The *saeculum*, therefore, can be seen as the place of this juncture. However, it is not a neutral space, for it holds the possibility of perdition if one is overcome by the pride, vanity, and weakness so common in the world. The "world" that Markus believes Christians must "dialogue" with is for Augustine the *civitas diaboli*, whose transitory peace is to be utilized, not prized.[110] Indeed, this *tertium quid* is also at times a place of conflict, where the "contrast" of the two cities is made plain and the citizens of the heavenly city will find their

109. TeSelle, "Toward an Augustinian Politics," 105.
110. O'Donovan notes that such earthly peace is shared by good and wicked and is a condition of order, not an institution. See O'Donovan, *Bonds of Interpretation*, 59.

fidelity tested. While Augustine would not deny that the Christians must bear loyalty to the political community in which they live, he also recognized that this loyalty, as Rowan Williams has pointed out, is limited by the Christian's previous and more important loyalty, namely to God.

There are moments in this "overlap" of the two cities where, as Williams writes, "loyalty to God trumped the demands of the *civitas*. The state's power was not the ultimate and sacred sanction."[111] Augustine recognized this reality, and for this reason exalts the role of the martyr, who bears witness in the public square to the "hierarchy" of loyalties that exists and bears the consequences of the conflict between them by his or her death. However, Markus's insistence on a "neutral" public square disqualifies the possibility of any such previous loyalties, and seems to be based in a romanticism that is at its core inconsistent with Augustine's theology and vision. Also, as Rowan Williams demonstrates, this neutrality precludes the positive benefit of Christianity imbuing public life with "depth and moral gravity that cannot be generated simply by the negotiation of practical goods and balanced self interests."[112] Far from Markus's neutrality, Williams makes clear that what Augustine is advocating is neither a rejection of the public sphere by the Christian nor a privatization of the Christian's faith, but rather a *"redefinition* of the public itself." As Williams explains, "The opposition is not between public and private, church and world, but between political virtue and political vice. At the end of the day, it is the secular order that will be shown to be 'atomistic' in its foundations."[113]

---

111. Williams, *Faith in the Public Square*, 29.
112. Ibid., 35.
113. Williams, "Politics and the Soul," 58.

An Augustinian Criteria of Authenticity

The debate over Markus's concept of *saeculum* serves as a reminder that a retrieval of Augustine's thought requires boundaries to define what can truly be called "Augustinian." Amidst the numerous interpretations and applications of his thought, it is readily clear that the title "Augustinian" has been used in at least three ways throughout the various authors we have discussed. The first describes an argument that generally uses Augustine's vocabulary or even his historical biography, but whose actual substance would not be recognizable to the Bishop of Hippo. As a result, I propose this use of Augustine as a "nominal Augustinian" argument. Reinhold Niebuhr is a primary example of this type of Augustinian interpretation. Niebuhr embraces Augustine's categories when they fit his realist vision, but adapts others to fit his position outside of Augustine's meaning.

The second use of the adjective "Augustinian" flows from an "intellectual history" perspective, and views Augustine as a thinker amidst the "pantheon of Western thought." In this school, Augustine's work is plumbed for "relevant" ideas that fit predetermined historical and intellectual narratives. His theology, pastoral life, and the very context of his thought are of little interest, and he is largely reduced to the status of "philosopher," or "political thinker." An example of this usage can be seen in Herbert Deane's work, which admittedly is written from a political science perspective. However, it must be argued that this second use of "Augustinian" is also a temptation to which many commentators can succumb. Such a perspective has been contributed to by the work of Arquilliére and the "political Augustinian" tradition, which has helped isolate Augustine's political thought from his theology and wider vision.

The third major use of the title "Augustinian" falls on those interpretations, which genuinely seek to both authentically interpret and apply what Augustine believed about political and social life through an examination of his *corpus* of literature, and by taking into account the breadth of his theological vision. While these interpretations will vary widely (one need only to consider the difference between Markus and Milbank), they are engaged in the search for Augustine's understanding and its contemporary relevance. Augustine's theology and his pastoral concerns, often enumerated through polemics with hostile neighbors, e.g. the Donatists and the Pelagians among others, are seen as essential in understanding his thought. However, a question inevitably arises within this last category of writers as to the nature of an authoritative reading of Augustine's vision.

Before laying out what I believe are the beginnings of a basic criteria in determining Augustinian authenticity, it is important to note that certain aspects within an interpretation might conform to our criteria while other areas do not. Also, it cannot be forgotten that some interpretations might limit their scope or focus on one aspect of Augustine's thought. As a result, it is difficult to generalize among Augustinian interpretations. However, it is necessary to set at least some boundaries to aid in the determination of "Augustinian" identity.

The first characteristic essential to an authoritative interpretation of Augustine on the issues we have discussed must be consistency with his theological vision, especially his skepticism towards the optimistic prospects of unaided postlapsarian society and his fundamental concern with humanity's ultimate end. It is not a coincidence that we have surveyed Augustine's main theological concerns on this question, as they form the basis for his political and social vision. There can be no such thing as a "non-theological" vision of

Augustine's social and political thought, as the skepticism, even at times pessimism, about the prospects of civil society present in Augustine often flow from his anthropology and exegesis of Scripture. Sin, war, evil, injustice, and other privations of goodness are a reality for Augustine in the earthly city, and are only remedied by Christ. For this reason, as we have discussed, I subscribe to the belief that his pessimism is not total, as he maintains the possibility for grace to work in the human soul. Also, Augustine's concern with humanity's end is of central importance, as we have already seen in our discussion. Augustine's worldview and his view of this world's fulfillment flow directly from his theology. Therefore, the absence of theology, which is true in some of the interpretations we have surveyed, can present a skewed interpretation of Augustine's actual vision of social and political life.

This criterion also necessitates another one, namely the use of Augustine's corpus. While his *City of God* is obviously central to this discussion, his *Epistulae* and theological tracts are no less relevant to his vision of man's nature and destiny. While a variance is present within Augustine's texts based on his own development, his theology remains connected to a larger tradition. As a result, his exegesis, theological essays, and correspondence are also important. An integrated interpretation of Augustine, therefore, must take account of his theological and historical context so as not to present his thought anachronistically. This integration also prevents the association of Augustine with subsequent trends utilizing his thought, and allows the vision of the Bishop of Hippo to receive fair treatment without becoming the "straw man" of Western civilization. Criticism of Augustine's vision is certainly possible, but it cannot be done simply by using our terms, our times, and our intellectual context.

Another essential authoritative element of any interpretation of Augustine's vision must be a serious reception within his thought of the reality and separation of his two cities. The heavenly city is not a production of human efforts, nor is it some fantasy or utopian ideal, but rather for Augustine it is a true and distinct *civitas*. It stands in contrast by its very nature to the earthly city, which is embodied in the political entities that emerge in human society. The heavenly city, which is Augustine's fundamental concern, evokes in its own citizens a loyalty that remains supreme over any human institution or desire. It is the fulfillment of Augustine's anthropology, ecclesiology, and is understood only by virtue of his Christology. It is also the true object of his political and social reflection. His concern with earthly political affairs is limited to how they touch the lives of his flock and affect the prospect of their heavenly citizenship. Augustine certainly allows for the independent exercise of temporal authority, but places on the Christian the obligation to assure that involvement in temporal affairs does not justify his eternal end. This understanding allows for a separation between Augustine and his later interpreters, especially in the later merging of secular and sacred authority.

While many commentators have disagreed with Augustine or have maintained different philosophical principles, the fact remains that Augustine's own vision should be represented authentically in accord with his theological context if the adjective "Augustinian" is used. The use of Augustine's name also evokes the Christian tradition he defended and advanced. I believe Robert Dodaro is correct in asserting at the beginning of his work, "The question 'How did Augustine conceive the just society?' involves aspects of his thinking about Christ, human knowledge, the church, and scriptural hermeneutics, as well as political thought and ethics."[114] Numerous commentators have captured the latter concern, namely the "political thought and ethics," but fewer have truly sought to engage the true

114. Dodaro, *Christ and the Just Society*, 1.

locus of Augustine's vision, namely his theology. Obviously, how commentators put forward their own vision of political and social life is certainly their concern, but in putting forward Augustine's vision his theological and historical context must be respected. The debates over the meaning of certain elements of this context, while at times inevitable, must at least recognize his categories and acknowledge the theological nature of his concepts. Without such respect for Augustine's vision, the adjective "Augustinian" can become paradoxical by being placed next to positions unthinkable to Augustine himself. Indeed, what could be a debate over the meaning of his concepts becomes a manipulation of his thought. Any recovery, therefore, of Augustine's vision must include a recovery of an authoritative Augustinian identity.

It is evident, therefore, in our discussion of the hermeneutic of retrieval that a century of debate has led to the emergence of a number of central themes. The very possibility of discovering political applications within Augustine's thought has been the continued subject of debate from the very beginning of political Augustinianism. Also, we examined the theological nature of Augustine's thought, especially its eschatological, ecclesiological, and Christological foundations. Central to contemporary discussion of Augustine's political thought is also his understanding of grace and Christian virtue. In light of Robert Markus's work, it has been necessary to examine the source of social consensus in Augustine and the reception of Marrou's assertion of a *tertium quid*. Finally, the hermeneutical question of what constitutes an authentic Augustinian interpretation has been examined, and we have pinpointed the necessary acknowledgement of Augustine's theological context, the utilization of certain primary sources, and preservation of his vision of two cities as necessary elements of any Augustinian interpretation. It is now necessary to examine another hermeneutic of Augustinian interpretation, namely those who dissent from Augustine and his continued influence.

The Hermeneutic of Refutation

Having discussed the hermeneutic of retrieval, the major themes that such a hermeneutic requires, and the essential points of an authentic Augustinian vision of political and social life, we must turn to another hermeneutic of Augustine's work: refutation. Not all of Augustine's contemporary commentators seek to retrieve his principles; instead, some authors have sought to identify, criticize, and replace his influence in public life. Reading Augustine's works, their opinions in chorus seek to show the culpability and problematic legacy of Augustine on a number of ideological and historical fronts. Indeed, unlike the hermeneutical issues we have discussed above, these authors do not claim to be "Augustinian," but rather stand in protest of any continued influence of Augustine in Western thought, let alone the "retrieval" of such an influence. William Connolly summarizes this position, and indeed the hermeneutic as a whole, in the opening of his work *The Augustinian Imperative*:

> I approach Augustinian texts, then, not as an Augustinian, nor as one who reduces a text to its specific historical context, nor as one who reduces it to a pile of arguments available for critical examination. I approach Augustine from a critical distance, from a (post-) Nietzschean perspective that seeks to reassess and modify effects of the Augustinian legacy on the present . . . . I seek to disturb Augustinianism from an ethical perspective that is both indebted to it and at odds with it.[115]

There are three claims, therefore, that I believe summarize the arguments at the center of this hermeneutic: a fundamental social

---

115. Connolly, *The Augustinian Imperative*, xviii.

instability and trauma caused by Augustine's concepts of guilt and confession, a problematic anthropology and vision of sexuality, and a subversion of the temporal or natural order to the supernatural order.

Augustine's Conception of Guilt and Confession

This critique largely argued by William Connolly, as we have previously discussed, is based on the identification of "penitential machinery" in Augustine leading to a sense of morality based in "obedience to transcendental command" and "attunement to an intrinsic design of things."[116] Connolly's arguments, which we have discussed in chapter three, seek to overcome what he perceives as the "moral self confidence" of Augustine's arguments and the "conservative" hermeneutic of justifying Augustine by utilizing his very presuppositions, namely monotheism. Where others, such as Markus and Ward, have at times attempted a dialogue of Augustine's ideas with post-modern thought, Connolly embraces the latter in order to remove the former. Nietzsche and Foucault, therefore, provide for Connolly the alternative vision to Augustine and allow for a "progressive" advancement beyond a confessional morality.

Connolly embraces Nietzsche's understanding of the "cruelty installed in the morality of good and evil, a cruelty installed in those moral economies that take themselves to embody the will of god, a Law of laws, an Intrinsic Purpose of Being, or a fictive Contract."[117] Augustine's moral system, Connolly argues, is based around piety, which is the "key Augustinian weapon on behalf of morality."[118] In this way, things that are, in Connolly's terminology, "uncanny" in morality become impious acts against a "god," and

116. Ibid., xviii.
117. Ibid., 132.
118. Ibid.

hence anxiety and guilt become reinforcing dynamics of the moral system. Connolly embraces an alternative put forward by Foucault, namely an "ontological universal," which is a "contestable projection," or a moral reading of experience continually updated and reviewed because of the changing nature of language and the relative nature of experience. However, while agreeing with Nietzsche and Foucault on the contestation and disturbance of ethical systems, Connolly does admit the impossibility of creating a moral foundation from their sensibilities. Their ideas simply do not serve as a basis for an ethical system. He commiserates this in writing, "They lack 'compossibility' not because of 'weakness of will' or 'the crooked timber of humanity,' where the primordial 'fault' resides within the self, but because the accentuation of one element in this combination at any time necessarily impedes the other at that time."[119]

The reason, in my opinion, such post-modern sensibilities do not function as a moral foundation of a "post-modern" ethic is much more than simply their "lack of 'compossibilitiy.'" There is rather a fundamental need to ground community and human sociality, for which Nietzsche, Foucault, Connolly and their disciples cannot account. James Schall describes this problem in contemporary thought, "What is thus lacking is precisely a notion of community that can bear both diverse personalities and their common relationship to one another."[120] Kristen Deede Johnson has responded to Connolly's ideas in her work, *Theology, Political Theory, and Pluralism: Beyond Tolerance and Difference*, and notes that Connolly admits to the need for an ontological shift in political theory, but "seeks to avoid any implication of 'logos' that a fundamental logic, principle or design of being exists in or underlies the world."[121]

---

119. Ibid., 150. There is here also the issue of moral relativism alluded to by these shifting "moral readings" of one's experience.
120. Schall, *Christianity and Politics*, 107.

Foucault's "ont*a*logical universal" is in itself recognition of the fundamental problem that plagues this school. Connolly also confirms this diagnosis by observing in his emphasis on political epistemology an underlying "social ontology."[122] As Kristen Deede Johnson points out Connolly's mission is like that of Foucault, namely to question the fundamental "uncritical acceptance that contributes to the continuation of fundamentalization over pluralization."[123]

However, I believe what Connolly overlooks or potentially seeks to ignore is the reason why such a "social ontology" is still invoked, even after the "post-modern project." The fact remains that the philosophical principles put forward by him and his forebears provide no possibility of grounding human community or unifying human beings. Connolly's vision of Augustine, therefore, as a manipulator of religion for moral ends, assumes that Augustine and any Christian believer is either delusional or unwilling to "critically accept" reality. Connolly's vision is, therefore, diametrically opposed to that of Augustine's, as faith in Connolly's view is reduced to narrative. There is a complete rejection here of any sense of truth and the basic ontological system, which Augustine held and which is still at Christianity's core. Augustine believed that there is Truth, and that we have been given access to it through Christ, and hence with grace can achieve our highest good. Augustine's moral principles are not a manipulation of religion, but in fact emerge from his faith and his theological vision.

The fundamental vision of Connolly is, therefore, inconsistent and irreconcilable with the believing Christian, which he sees as potentially a fundamentalist. However, the Christian cosmology that

---

121. Kristen Deede Johnson, *Theology, Political Theory, and Pluralism: Beyond Tolerance and Difference* (Cambridge: Cambridge University Press, 2007), 116.
122. Ibid., 118.
123. Ibid.

Augustine works under and promotes remains based around the fact that, as Schall summarizes, "The natural law presumes ethics/Ethics presumes metaphysics. Metaphysics does not presume, but it does not exclude revelation. And revelation is primarily a thing of intelligence, so that it might reach human life in individual persons, in John, Paul, and Mary."[124] In Connolly's view, this particular vision is what is to be refuted or, at least, seriously challenged. Therefore, inasmuch as Augustine is responsible for promoting this Christian vision, he, like the vision itself, is considered problematic.[125] As Joan Lockwood O'Donovan argues, what is insisted upon by Connolly and others is the "denial of a *common moral universe* in which objective spiritual goods mediate and determine the self-transcending of individual wills in their mutual relationships."[126]

However, in understanding this element of Augustinian criticism and the perennial problem for contemporary thinkers presented by this lack of a "common moral universe," we can understand the influences behind various contemporary applications of Augustine's work. I believe it is in Connolly that we find, for example, the counterpoint to which Radical Orthodoxy, especially Milbank, Ward, and Hanby, seek to respond. This connection is well documented in the work of Kristen Deede Johnson, who notes that "'Milbank's 'Augustinian' theology also leads him to question the 'secular' and to counter the predominance of morality based in law or command with an 'ethic of gift.' Though these concerns are similar to

---

124. Schall, *Christianity and Politics*, 240.
125. It is impossible here to reconcile these two perspectives, and it is far beyond the scope of this thesis. However, it must be stated that the contemporary questions raised by Connolly are of primary importance in understanding the rise and context of *Radical Orthodoxy*. It can be said, therefore, that the first element of this hermeneutic of refutation is the object of John Milbank's response in *Theology and Social Theory*. See Milbank, *Theology and Social Theory*, 278-290.
126. Joan Lockwood O'Donovan, "The Challenge and Promise of Proto-modern Christian Political Thought," in *Bonds of Interpretation: Christian Politics Past and Present* (Grand Rapids, MI: Eerdmans, 2004), 141.

those of Connolly, Milbank believes that a tenable ethic needs to be grounded in an abundance and plenitude that go much deeper than that which can be drawn from Nietzsche."[127]

Ultimately, this question of establishing a common ethic and grounding social relationships remains central in political and ethical theory, and has led to Augustine's increased contemporary relevance. I find it no surprise that Johnson ends her examination of Connolly and other postmodern political theorists by noting the need to turn to Augustine and theology. There is a common recognition of the void that is left by the post-modern rejection of Christian social ontology. Johnson, therefore, summarizes well the appeal of a theological shift to answer this question, a shift that is truly Augustinian. She notes, "Could it be that a Trinitarian ontology would enable us to imagine communities of harmony that respect the universal *and* the particular? We would do well to walk through the ontological door opened by agonistic political theorists and walk towards Christianity's ontology of peace as a possible way to expand our political and pluralist imagination."[128]

Two Contentious Areas of Augustinian Debate: Platonism and Sexuality

The question often emerges as to whether Augustine's outlook necessarily implies a Platonic philosophical outlook as well. The response to such queries must be an affirmative one, as there remains a clear Platonic influence in the political and social thought of St. Augustine. However, this influence is often simplified to a discussion of dualism and its implications on the "two cities." These generalized connections do little justice to the true Platonic influence upon

127. Johnson, *Theology, Political Theory, and Pluralism*, 138.
128. Ibid., 139.

Augustine's concept of *res publica* and his theological anthropology in general. As James Wetzel has noted, Plato's philosophy opens Augustine to the "reality beyond the sensible."[129] The highest good in that reality is for Augustine, God. The power of the supreme good, the power of God, is nothing less than the transformation of God's "beholder."[130] This notion of transformation is at the core of Augustine's view of grace, as in seeking God himself one both seeks the supreme good and by God's power receives it. As Wetzel makes clear, "God is good guaranteeing its own reception in the human will."[131] For this reason, Augustine understands justice both in the individual soul and in the commonwealth at large in terms of "rightly ordered love," namely a love of the good.[132]

In the midst of the contemporary equivocation of freedom and rights, Augustine's understanding stands as a contrast. He recognized that human freedom originated not in earthly goods, but in the "supreme value outside of humanity."[133] As a result, when the supreme good, God, is loved one is rightly able to love the creatures dependent on God, as well. As Joan Lockwood O'Donovan explains, this rightly ordered love can only occur when "the transcendent, universal, and supreme Good" is loved and hence creatures are loved by virtue of their dependence on God.[134] O'Donovan and others note that the implication of this concept is important in Augustine, as the privatization of good (so valued in contemporary society) and the seeking of things other than God lead to disordered love and hence the erosion of communal bonds.

---

129. Wetzel, *Augustine and the Limits of Virtue*, 4.
130. Ibid.
131. Ibid., 9.
132. Joan Lockwood O'Donovan, "Natural Law and Perfect Community: Contributions of Christian Platonism to Political Theory," *Modern Theology* 14, no.1 (Jan 1998), 26.
133. Wetzel, *Augustine and the Limits of Virtue*, 11.
134. O'Donovan, "Natural Law and Perfect Community," 26.

In order to assure that the will is ordered towards God and that we are cooperating with God's grace, Augustine, saw the continual need for conversion. There remains the need to strive by God's grace to perfect our freedom and hence redirect our will back towards the supreme good, God. As Wetzel points out, the goal of this continual transformation is to be transformed into the image of the good we know and rid ourselves of the limitations to our freedom caused by sin.[135] It is here that Augustine's Platonism is so uniquely manifest, as a lack of virtue is not caused by a lack of knowledge, but indeed a refusal to acknowledge the good.[136] It is this failure that causes "the destruction of community, of the common good," as O'Donovan notes, "because it involves radical loss of the shared spiritual possession of and acting toward being, meaning, and value."[137] As she rightly summarizes, "Such were the ideas bequeathed by St. Augustine about community, property, and justice, about ordered and disordered love, that, as part of the greater patristic inheritance, formed medieval moral and political orientations."[138]

As numerous authors have noted, Augustine's Platonic context influenced his understanding of order and disorder. However, this distinction was particularly evident in Augustine's discussion of sexuality. James Weidenaar, in his analysis of Book XIV of *City of God*, has noted the particular focus of Augustine on sexual appetite as compared to others : "While the others might rise up in rebellion against the soul and apart from reason, sexual lust, as Augustine conceives of it, is distinguished by the fact that it presents not only a *challenge* to the will of the soul, but an *overpowering* and *irresistible* challenge . . . Sexual lust *rules* the soul."[139] Laurie Jungling has argued

---

135. Wetzel, *Augustine and the Limits of Virtue*, 11.
136. Ibid.
137. O'Donovan, "Natural Law and Perfect Community," 26.
138. Ibid.

that Augustine's connection of disorder and personal concupiscence affected his view of human sexuality: "Once the first humans broke the order, sexual concupiscence became one way that brokenness was experienced."[140] Observing the progression in Augustine's thought, Jungling argues that Augustine saw sexuality as disordered, "though acceptable for procreation and excused within the marriage of man and woman."[141] Augustine used sexuality as evidence of fallen humanity, a fact bemoaned by Jungling and other contemporary theologians: "Sex became a theological concept as symbol, as evidence, and as a paradigm of human sinfulness."[142]

Similar criticism of Augustine is present in William Connolly's analysis of the Augustinian imperative, as he bemoans the "unexamined faith in an intrinsic moral order of gender and sex."[143] Elaine Pagels, in her work *Adam, Eve, and the Serpent: Sex and Politics in Early Christianity*, has directly connected Augustine's interpretation of Genesis 1-3 with a loss of a Western sense of political freedom, writing "Augustine went further: Adam's sin not only caused our mortality but cost us our moral freedom, irreversibly corrupted our experience of sexuality (which Augustine tended to identify with original sin), and made us incapable of genuine political freedom."[144] For Pagels, Augustine's pessimism and his rejection of any trace of human "self-government" opens the door to imperial

139. James B. Weidenaar, "Augustine's Theory of Concupiscence in *City of God*, Book XIV," *Calvin Theological Journal* 30, (1995), 57-58.

140. Laurie A. Jungling, "Passionate Order: Order and Sexuality in Augustine's Theology," *Word and World* 27, no.3 (Summer 2007), 318.

141. Ibid., 323.

142. Ibid., 324.

143. Connolly, *The Augustinian Imperative*, 27. As in the discussion of just war, there remains an independent collection of secondary literature on Augustine's view of sexuality. Our brief presentation of this theme is to demonstrate this element of the hermeneutic of refutation, and is in no way an exhaustive study.

144. Elaine Pagels, *Adam, Eve, and the Serpent: Sex and Politics in Early Christianity* (New York: Vintage Books, 1989), xxvi.

power and secular rule.[145] She explains this connection between original sin and government further:

> Augustine's dark vision of a human nature ravaged by original sin and overrun by lust for power rules out uncritical adulation and qualifies his endorsement of imperial rule . . . Augustine places secular government at the center of human society, indispensable for the best as well as the worst among its members. For a Christian, civic obligations rank second, certainly, to one's obligation to God (or, as this usually meant in practice, to the church). Yet apart from direct conflict of interest, even the bishop must render appropriate obedience to secular authority . . . Augustine's theory enabled his contemporaries to come to terms both with the fact of Christian empire and with its intractably human nature.[146]

While Augustine is often decried as a formative thinker in a negative Western conception of sexuality, Mathijs Lamberigts has sought to respond to this criticism in his study, "A Critical Evaluation of Critiques of Augustine's View of Sexuality."[147] Lamberigts cites a classic formulation of this incrimination of Augustine in Uta Ranke-Heinemann, who wrote in her work *Eunuchs for the Kingdom of Heaven*, "The man who fused Christianity together with hatred of sex and pleasure into a systematic unity was the greatest of the Church Fathers, St. Augustine."[148] Eugene TeSelle, as well, has argued that Augustine is "guilt-ridden over sexuality," and hence sets Christian ethics on an errant path.[149] From a bioethical perspective, James Drane also echoes this common criticism: "Because of Augustine's prestige, Catholic moral teachings on sexuality in general and in particular on procreativity have been marked by an unhealthy

---

145. Ibid., 105.

146. Pagels, *Adam, Eve, and the Serpent*, 118.

147. See Mathijs Lamberigts, "A Critical Evaluation of Critiques of Augustine's View of Sexuality," in *Augustine and His Critics: Essays in Honor of Gerald Bonner*, ed. Robert Dodaro & George Lawless (New York: Routledge, 2000).

148. Ibid., 176.

149. TeSelle, *Toward an Augustinian Politics*, 87.

Puritanism."[150] This critique of Augustine's vision of sexuality has usually been tied to what is perceived as an oppressively pessimistic anthropology that flows from a strong platonic dualism. Drane echoes this chorus by accusing Augustine of being influenced by his Manichean roots, writing "For [the Manicheans], all matter and flesh were in the realm of darkness and evil. To be moral one had to avoid both sex and procreation. Augustine, in response to this Manichean absurdity, approved of sexuality and sexual relations, but only if they were procreative."[151]

Such lines of criticism are now routinely heard, and have become commonplace in the academy. Augustine has been criticized routinely over the past four decades by feminist theologians as well, who attribute to him much of the social ills befalling women in Western society. Many of them, as well, embrace a "hermeneutic of refutation" in their attempted extrication of Augustine's legacy from Christian theological anthropology. Rosemary Radford Reuther in her study "Augustine: Sexuality, Gender, and Women," examined both Augustine's personal history and theology to locate the origins of his views, and she concludes:

> Augustine sees this relation of male ruling intellect to feminine desire as intrinsic to the order of the cosmos as God intended. Thus it belongs to the original order of things . . . The libidinous woman out of the control of male authority and acting on her own is the prime social expression of this disordered state, mirroring the dominion of desire over reason within the male.[152]

Reuther goes on to note how in Augustine's vision, virginity remains the "ideal state of Christian life," a fact concretized by the perpetual

---

150. James F. Drane, *A Liberal Catholic Bioethics* (Münster: Lit Verlag, 2010), 123.
151. Ibid., 123.
152. Rosemary Radford Reuther, "Augustine: Sexuality, Gender, and Women," in *Feminist Interpretations of Augustine*, ed. Judith Chelius Stark (University Park, PA: Pennsylvania State University Press, 2007), 56-57.

virginity of the Blessed Virgin Mary.[153] Furthermore, Augustine's image of God is a *pater familias*, lacking any motherly traits.[154] Indeed, Reuther argues, only in heaven can women overcome "gender hierarchy." However, she notes that even this comes "at the price of the excising in women of all that has to do with their specific female functions, sex and childbearing."[155] In concluding her study, Reuther admits that Augustine's views flow from those of his age, but adds, "Women and men in the Western Christian tradition have suffered for a millennium and a half from the ways Augustine's views on these matters have been treated as normative."[156]

In evaluating this line of dissent, the feminist critique of Augustine that we have just laid out falls into the same hermeneutical problem that we see in other commentators, namely, a failure to fully contextualize Augustine's vision and to separate Augustine from his later interpreters. Augustine's vision of sexuality, and indeed his anthropology, are influenced not just by the exegesis of Genesis, but also by a strong sense of human *caritas and cupiditas*. William Babcock has rightly placed the conflict of these two terms as central in Augustine's anthropology, as Babcock notes, "It is *cupiditas*, the *amor* for things that can be lost against one's will, that gives birth to this desperate sense that others constitute a threat to self. Fearing loss, it seeks to secure against loss by removing or by dominating others so as to eliminate the threat they represent . . . ."[157] It is *cupiditas*, therefore, that demeans the self by causing the mind to become "entangled" in irrational things and obscuring the human capacity to understand truth and falsehood.[158] Physical and sexual desires are for

---

153. Reuther, "Augustine: Sexuality, Gender, and Women," 62.
154. Ibid., 63.
155. Ibid., 64.
156. Ibid., 64.
157. William S. Babcock, "*Cupiditas* and *Caritas*: The Early Augustine on Love and Human Fulfillment," in *Augustine Today*, ed. Richard John Neuhaus (Grand Rapids, MI: Eerdmans, 1993), 15.

Augustine not in themselves evil, but become problematic when they lead to a very loss of the unique human faculties that separate us from all other creatures.

Mathijs Lamberigts also helps aid the contextualization of Augustine on this issue by examining Augustine's works against Julian of Eclanum, including *De nuptiis et concupiscentia* and *Contra Iulianum*. Lamberigts notes that Augustine's definition of *concupiscentia* was not simply a synonym of sexual desire, but of any desire contrary to the Holy Spirit.[159] The Genesis account is significant because it demonstrates that after original sin, shame enters the world as the result of "disorderliness." It is here that Augustine's vision of sexuality is influenced, as "the desire to go one's way or exert one's own will constituted *indications* that, after the Fall, self-control was no longer an easy manner . . . the hierarchal order in the human person had been disrupted."[160] It is for this reason that Pagels, citing *City of God* Book XIII. 21, asserts, "Augustine, on the contrary, having denied that human beings possess any capacity whatever for free will, accepts a definition of liberty far more agreeable to the powerful and influential men with whom he himself wholeheartedly identifies . . . it is the serpent who tempts Adam with the seductive lure of liberty. The forbidden fruit symbolizes, he explains, 'personal control over one's own will.'"[161]

However, as Lamberigts points out, the problem with such an argument is that it oversimplifies Augustine's concept of concupiscence. The *concupiscentia carnis* is not simply problematic in Augustine because of the body, but indeed because of its effects on the soul: "As a rational being, the human person realises that he or

---

158. Babcock, "*Cupiditas* and *Caritas*: The Early Augustine on Love and Human Fulfillment," 16.
159. Lamberigts, "Augustine's View on Sexuality," 180.
160. Ibid., 181.
161. Pagels, *Adam, Eve, and the Serpent*, 120.

she ought to take action in the process of unrest brought on by the *concupiscentia carnis*. It is precisely this absence of the will to conform itself to reason . . . that Augustine considered negative . . ."[162] There is, therefore, a parallel that I believe one can draw between Augustine's ideas on the effects of the *libido dominandi* and his understanding of concupiscence and its effects on the individual person and society as a whole. In reality, therefore, the two discussions are directly related by a common anthropology.

Just as we have seen in the discussion of Augustine's societal vision, an element untreated and often ignored here is the role of grace. The human person, male and female, for Augustine was not simply a stagnant fixed reality, but, if open, could experience the effects of God's grace. While Augustine held little hope for human beings on their own to resist disordered impulses and *cupiditas*, his vision of the person under grace differed greatly. As Lamberigts notes, "He considered it the duty of every believer who desired to grow in faith to resist sexual desire. Grace had a crucial role to play in the struggle, given that it worked in a liberating and beneficial way for the human person."[163] Like Babcock, Lamberigts correctly seeks to recover from his critics the positive nature of desire in Augustine.

For Augustine, it is not that human desire is evil in itself, but it is evil when it is seeking something other than God: "The central concept in Augustine's evaluation of *concupiscentia* is the criterion of faith. Since desire as such distracts the human person from his or her true purpose and, in a certain sense, commands the entire person, it cannot be from God but must belong to the world of the flesh, which is at war with the spirit."[164] The primary goal of the human person for Augustine remained beatitude in God forever,

162. Lamberigts, "Augustine's View on Sexuality," 181.
163. Ibid., 185.
164. Ibid., 186.

and anything that deviated one from that goal was to be avoided and seen as a hindrance. As Lamberigts concludes, "[Augustine] was firmly rooted in a tradition—partly confirmed by the Bible—in which the satisfaction of sexual desires as an end in itself was rejected."[165] However, I agree with Lamberigts that it is an oversimplification to view Augustine alone as the "Father of the whole of western history's dealings with sexuality."[166] Such an oversimplification while creating an easy target, in reality prevents an integral reading of Augustine's theology. It obscures the breadth and complexity of his theological anthropology, and risks becoming a "straw man" attacked by anachronisms.

Refuting Augustine's Subversion of the Temporal Order

The third major critique within this hermeneutic of refutation is based in the theory that Augustine subverts the temporal or natural order to the supernatural order. In this view, Augustine allows the Church, the dispenser of supernatural grace through the working of the Holy Spirit, to become the supreme authority on earth and absorb temporal power. I will not deal with this third element as extensively as the two previous arguments, for we have already touched upon this theme in our first and third chapters. However, it is clear that the most famous contemporary proponent of this view is Henri-Xavier Arquillière, who expounds upon this theory in his work *L'augustinisme politique*. Although not seeking to refute Augustine, as we have discussed, Arquillière's theory helped to advance the connection between Augustine and his medieval interpreters, and obscured the theological nature of his vision of the just society.[167]

165. Ibid., 188.
166. Ibid.

John Neville Figgis, who wrote before Arquillière argued, "Augustine never identified the *Civitas Dei* with any earthly State. But he had prepared the way for other people to do this."[168] Figgis cites early twentieth century historians of his day, such as Lord James Bryce, who argued, "It is hardly too much to say that the Holy Roman Empire was built upon the foundation of the *De Civitate Dei*."[169] While even Figgis rejected this latter view as too extreme, the notion that Augustine has prepared the way for a Christian empire has endured. However, as Henri de Lubac and others have shown in response to "political Augustinianism," such a narrative is a contrived theory that oversimplifies the history of Augustinian interpretation in the Middle Ages.[170]

It is interesting that Augustine is often blamed for a project openly taken up by Eusebius of Caesarea. In fact, Augustine's understanding of the temporal and sacred order stands in sharp contrast to that of Eusebius. Joseph Ratzinger argues that it is Eusebius who combines the eschatological language of Christianity with the imperial language of the state. Unlike Augustine, Eusebius advances the empire towards a concept of "political theocracy."[171] While Eusebius embraces this unification of orders, Augustine introduces a "sacramental" conception of the Kingdom present in the world and

---

167. This is laid out convincingly in Douglas Kries, "Political Augustinianism," in *Augustine Through the Ages: An Encyclopedia*, ed. Allan Fitzgerald, O. S. A., (Grand Rapids, MI: Eerdmans, 2002), 657-658. "Arquillière argued that medieval political thinkers who looked to Augustine for guidance tended to absorb the natural order of the state within the supernatural order of the church. He thus viewed political Augustinianism as the logical extension of doctrinal Augustinianism" (657).

168. Figgis, *The Political Aspects*, 84.

169. Ibid.

170. De Lubac argues, "The extraordinary upheavals of history that occasioned so many confontations with entirely new situations are scarcely mentioned, or seem unworthy of consideration. The Augustinian 'supernaturalism' suffices to explain everything about this grandiose construction of which Gregory VII was the 'spiritual architect' and which was brought to culmination by Hugh of St. Victor and St. Bernard." De Lubac, *Theological Fragments*, 259.

171. Ratzinger, *L'unità delle nazioni*, 113.

consistently rejects any confusion of the Church and the state. Ratzinger argues this point quite clearly: "His *civitas Dei* is not a purely ideal community of all people that believe in God, but it also lacks any similarity to an earthly theocracy, even with a world constituted of Christians, it is rather a sacramental-eschatological entity, that lives in this world as a sign of the future world."[172] Ratzinger directly rejects any declaration of Augustine as "father of a theocratic conception of the Church," noting that "one cannot simplistically define Augustine as responsible for the errant interpretation that later is connected to future events."[173]

This sacramental-eschatological language of Augustine applies also to his view of the Christian, who resides in the world. As Miikka Ruokanen has explained, "That small measure of justice in social life is solely due to the correct reference of the citizens of the city of God . . . In contrast to others, the Christian, at least, knows and recognizes the correct orientation, even though the realization remains imperfect."[174] With this in mind, we must now turn to the question of what Augustine has to say to the Christian statesman in our time, and how the Christian can truly maintain a focused direction towards their heavenly home while remaining an active citizen of the earthly city.

Augustinian Lessons for Contemporary Christians

The Contemporary Debate

Having laid out and synthesized the various political and social interpretations of Augustine in contemporary theology and their

---

172. Ibid.
173. Ibid., 115.
174. Miikka Ruokanen, *Theology of Social Life in Augustine's De Civitate Dei*, 145.

hermeneutical foundations, we are left with considering the relevance of this discussion, and indeed the relevance of St. Augustine himself, to our current historical and political context. A number of recent events have caused renewed reflection over the role of Christianity in Western society, most especially the drafting of the constitution of the European Union and the terrorist attacks both in Europe and the United States at the beginning of this new millennium. These events in addition to political election cycles in the United States and in Europe have led to an increased discussion of the Christian roots, and the presence of Christianity itself, in the West. As in past generations, these events have also led to an increased discussion of St. Augustine and his implications for our historical context.

In the United States, this debate over the role of Christianity, and religion in general, in the public square has increasingly intensified. This has occurred, in my opinion, due to two related factors. The first is an increasing level of dissent and a growing reliance on a relativist moral system evident in the contemporary discussion of a variety of moral issues, including abortion, euthanasia, same-sex marriage, capital punishment, and other issues. For example, when dissenting from the Catholic Church's position on any number of these issues, a Catholic serving in public office will often express a separation of one's "personal views" from the demands of "public office." Others invoke the rights of "conscience" in order to justify a separation of personal morality from public service. However, the conception of conscience that emerges is one that often neglects its relationship to truth, and abandons its goal as stated in *Dignitatis Humanae*, namely "to seek the truth in matters religious in order that he may with prudence form for himself right and true judgments of conscience, under use of all suitable means."[175]

Quite often, the freedom of conscience in contemporary political discourse bears no relationship to truth or to the natural moral law, both of which are essential elements to the definition put forward in *Dignitatis Humanae*. Nevertheless, such a division of personal opinion from one's role in public office has emerged as part of a larger relativistic context. Indeed, the ethical ideals of Nietzsche and Foucault, which have been promoted by Connolly and others, have taken their hold in Western society and culture. Such relativism has aided in an all too common divorce of conscience from truth and freedom from responsibility. This has often rendered ethical discourse in the public square a cacophony lacking a common language or end. The Congregation for the Doctrine of the Faith noted the deleterious presence of such relativism, and clarified in its "Doctrinal Note on Some Questions Regarding the Participation of Catholics in Political Life," that such relativism must not define the Christian notion of freedom:

> Such relativism, of course, has nothing to do with the legitimate freedom of Catholic citizens to choose among the various political opinions that are compatible with faith and the natural moral law, and to select, according to their own criteria, what best corresponds to the needs of the common good. Political freedom is not—and cannot be—based upon the relativistic idea that all conceptions of the human person's good have the same value and truth, but rather, on the fact that politics are concerned with very concrete realizations of the true human and social good in given historical, geographic, economic, technological and cultural contexts.[176]

The second dynamic, which is connected to this growth of relativism, is the increasing trend of religion's privatization, or to use a common term in our discussion, the secularization of public life.

---

175. *Dignitatis Humanae*, 3.
176. Congregation for the Doctrine of the Faith, *Doctrinal Note on Some Questions Regarding the Participation of Catholics in Political Life* (November 24, 2002), *AAS* 96 (2004): 359-370, n. 3.

Here, we can observe an interpretation of the relationship between religion and public life as mutually exclusive. Religion, in this viewpoint, has no standing in public discourse, the formation of public policy, or even in the negotiation of the ethical principles that govern society. The separation of Church and state is viewed here as a dividing wall built to prohibit any perceived "interference" of religion in the public square. Religion from this perspective is a private matter, and the public realm (politics, the academy, or any social institution) must remain neutral and devoid of its influence. Social consensus, moral principles, and indeed, conceptions of truth, goodness, and beauty, must all be found outside of metaphysics and the Christian tradition. In fact, the divine law, which was called by *Dignitatis Humanae* as "eternal, objective, and universal," is seen as passé or, in many parts of the academy, a taboo.

In response to these trends and within such a context, I do not believe it is mere coincidence that two prominent Catholic prelates have recently made recourse to St. Augustine of Hippo. Both Francis Cardinal George and Archbishop Charles Chaput have recently invoked Augustine, and more specifically his *City of God*, to respond to the contemporary challenges facing the Church in such a hostile context. Cardinal George, in his work *The Difference God Makes: A Catholic Vision of Faith, Communion, and Culture*, credits Augustine with asserting a "social dimension" to the ontology of *communio* and participation, which emerged from Trinitarian theology. George notes that Augustine was "interested in neither accommodating nor compromising with the Roman system . . . on the contrary, he excoriates Rome as an unjust society and holds up Christianity itself as the only valid basis for a just form of social arrangement."[177]

---

177. Francis Cardinal George, O.M.I., *The Difference God Makes: A Catholic Vision of Faith, Communion, and Culture* (New York: Crossroad Publishing, 2009), 6.

Cardinal George, therefore, sees in Augustine an important model, as he advocates that the City of God has a clear counter-cultural role. George also argues that Augustine rejects a social structure where the state orders public life, and the Church is relegated to a corner of society in the care of spiritual goods. George writes, "The problem is not how to reconcile the competing concerns of the spiritual and the secular; the problem is orthodoxy, that is to say, getting our metaphysics and our praise of God in order, so that we can live in a just, rightly ordered society."[178] Therefore, as we have discussed previously, the larger contemporary challenge from an Augustinian perspective is the loss of an ontological sense of sociality, and hence an embrace of an individualism which allows for a compromise with the earthly city. It is not a coincidence that the lack of social ontology and the rise of individualism are continual themes throughout this discussion, as the Doctor of Grace points to a common diagnosis, and reminds us that in Christ alone will we find the remedy.

Archbishop Charles Chaput examines St. Augustine in his work, *Render Unto Caesar: Serving the Nation by Living Our Catholic Beliefs in Political Life.* In his view, Augustine's vision posits that the state has the minimal responsibility of "not hindering the practice of the Catholic faith."[179] However, Archbishop Chaput sees Augustine as going further, arguing that the state should aid in the advancement of the Gospel. Indeed, a compromise would be reached by Gelasius I in 494 of a duality of powers with an "ultimate priority of religious matters." In Chaput's view, "The practical autonomy of civil authority and religious authority—became the Christian sense of church and state in the West for centuries."[180] In contemporary

---

178. George, *The Difference God Makes.*, 8.
179. Chaput, Charles J. *Render Unto Caesar: Serving the Nation by Living Our Catholic Beliefs in Political Life* (New York: Doubleday Publishing, 2008), 69.
180. Chaput, *Render Unto Caesar,* 69.

history, however, Chaput identifies the "Address to the Greater Houston Ministerial Association on September 12, 1960," made by President John F. Kennedy, the nation's first Catholic president, as a break with the traditional Catholic understanding of civil and religious autonomy.[181]

In this speech, Kennedy argues that the separation of Church and state is "absolute." He separates personal beliefs from public duty and invokes the role of conscience, while neglecting to speak of the need for its formation or its fundamental goal of truth. Kennedy stated:

> I believe in an America where the separation of church and state is absolute—where no Catholic prelate would tell the President (should he be Catholic) how to act, and no Protestant minister would tell his parishioners for whom to vote—where no church or church school is granted any public funds or political preference—and where no man is denied public office merely because his religion differs from the President who might appoint him or the people who might elect him.[182]

This address allowed Kennedy to buttress his campaign against Protestant suspicions of his Catholicism. Chaput and other commentators have noted that Kennedy's speech and its subsequent interpretation have helped obscure the idea of a Christian vocation in public life. Augustine recognized the proper role of political authority, but he cautioned the Christian in public life that his office did not negate the obligations of his Christian faith and the need to focus on eternal ends. This "absolutizing" of Church-state separation stands in contradiction to a vision of Christian life determined first and foremost by the Christian's eternal fulfillment, and it excludes the influence of the Gospel from the principles of governance and the

181. John F. Kennedy, "Address of Senator John F. Kennedy to the Greater Houston Ministerial Association, September 12, 1960," The John F. Kennedy Library and Museum, http://www.jfklibrary.org/Research/Ready-Reference/JFK-Speeches/Address-of-Senator-John-F-Kennedy-to-the-Greater-Houston-Ministerial-Association.aspx (3 May 2012).
182. Ibid.

formation of conscience. As Chaput argues, "It began the project of walling religion away from the process of governance in a new and aggressive way. It also divided a person's private beliefs from his or her public duties. And it set 'the national interest' over and against 'outside religious pressures or dictates.'"[183] A Protestant response to Kennedy's speech published in the editorial section of *The Christian Century* demonstrates the contrast Kennedy's speech marked with previous teaching.:

> It is difficult to see how a Roman Catholic candidate could have gone farther or said more and remained a member of that church. The statement strengthens the evidence that Senator Kennedy could resist political pressures from his church. It also helps the voter to evaluate more reasonably the major issues: international relations, foreign aid, civil rights, schools, defense, slums, depressed areas, agriculture, a worthy national purpose.[184]

There is an irony in this editorial response, as it describes President Kennedy's Catholic faith, or as it says "his church," as almost a hindrance to discussing important social issues and ethical challenges. Whereas it is the Christian's conscience informed by faith and his soul strengthened by grace, which moves him or her to act virtuously in response to those in need and in situations of crisis. This is the difficulty in Robert Markus's neutral *saeculum*, and its contrast to Augustine's call for the Christian in authority to seek and exercise virtue. The promotion of neutrality towards religious values, the gradual loss of social ontology, and the "walling off" of religion from public life are all effects of this "absolute separation." They

---

183. Charles J. Chaput, "JFK's Houston Speech Undermined Religion in Public Life," *Origins* 39, no. 40 (March 18, 2010): 652. While *Origins* has assigned a title to this speech, the Archbishop's title I believe captures the true nature of his address, namely "The Vocations of Christians in American Public Life."

184. "Kennedy Clarifies Stand to Houston Ministers," *Christian Century* 77, no.39 (Sept. 28, 1960), 1109.

have created an environment, in which discussion of social issues has become mutually exclusive to any reference to faith and its formation of conscience. Therefore, just as a need has emerged to "retrieve" Augustine's vision within the discussion of "political Augustinianism," Cardinal George, Archbishop Chaput, and others see a need to recover the meaning of the lay vocation in the life of each Christian, especially those who bear public responsibilities. This vocation of the laity "in temporal affairs" was profoundly stated at the Second Vatican Council and its *Dogmatic Constitution on the Church, Lumen Gentium*:

> But the laity, by their very vocation, seek the kingdom of God by engaging in temporal affairs and by ordering them according to the plan of God. They live in the world, that is, in each and in all of the secular professions and occupations. They live in the ordinary circumstances of family and social life, from which the very web of their existence is woven. They are called there by God that by exercising their proper function and led by the spirit of the Gospel they may work for the sanctification of the world from within as a leaven.[185]

This call to be "leaven" from within society is not fueled by indifference, but rather the desire through the exercise of virtue to accomplish real concrete good. Such good is sought while remaining knowledgeable that it will be limited within an often violent and sinful world. It is not surprising that Archbishop Chaput cites Robert Dodaro's analysis of Augustine's political and social vision, as relevant for our contemporary situation. Indeed, Chaput argues that Augustine's call for Christians in public office to embrace their vocation, namely to conform their lives to the Gospel and accomplish real good by virtue of their lives, can be extended to all believers.[186]

---

185. *Lumen Gentium* (LG), 31.
186. Chaput, "JFK's Speech," 654.

Chaput, therefore, applies the theological retrieval of Augustine to the contemporary situation of Christians:

> What Augustine believes about Christian leaders, we can reasonably extend to the vocation of all Christian citizens. The skills of the Christian citizen are finally very simply: a zeal for Jesus Christ and his Church; a conscience formed in humility and rooted in Scripture and the believing community; the prudence to see which issues in public life are vital and foundational to human dignity, and which ones are not; and the courage to work for what's right. We don't cultivate these skills alone. We develop them together as Christians, in prayer, on our knees, in the presence of Jesus Christ.[187]

The Christian Citizen

The discussion of the Christian in public life allows us to reflect upon some of the concrete elements of Augustine's vision that bear relevance to our contemporary situation. Our discussion, therefore, will touch upon both the Christian citizen and subsequently the Christian politician.

While the concept of citizenship is noticeably absent from public discussion, it is of primary importance in applying Augustine's vision to our contemporary situation. Archbishop Chaput notes an important Augustinian principle, namely that Christian political involvement was to be primarily the task of the Christian layman who, citing John Courtney Murray, S. J., allows the Holy Spirit to enter the City of Man through "his energetic spirit of justice and love that dwells in the man of the City, the layman."[188] Citizenship in the heavenly kingdom is of supreme importance in Augustine's vision,

187. Ibid., 654.
188. Ibid., 653.

but it does not exclude the earthly obligations of civic responsibility. Voting, the payment of taxes, military service, and obedience to the rule of law, are all to be undertaken by the Christian. Indeed, all of these tasks, as banal at times as they might seem, are opportunities to accomplish good by the exercise of virtue.[189] However, none of these obligations must be seen as equal to the heavenly calling of the Christian, who must object to them if they threaten the ultimate end, heavenly citizenship. For this reason, the recently published *Compendium of the Social Doctrine of the Church* makes clear, "It is a grave duty of conscience not to cooperate, not even formally, in practices which, although permitted by civil legislation, are contrary to the Law of God."[190]

To discern and to act appropriately where a conflict emerges between these two citizenships, the Christian must rely upon a well-formed conscience that is ordered to truth. Augustine, as we have discussed in the interpretation of Joseph Ratzinger, placed religion under truth, and removed it from a relativist political context. The conscience, as well, must be viewed in a similar light, namely ordered to what is true and good. The fact remains, however, that the Christian, in order to properly discern and respond to the ethical dilemmas that emerge in the exercise of civic responsibilities, requires a well-formed conscience that seeks the good and strives towards virtue. Yet, such formation is made difficult by the individualist and materialist tendencies that pervade contemporary culture. Pope John Paul II pointed this out directly in his 1998 encyclical, *Fides et Ratio*:

Faced with contemporary challenges in the social, economic, political

---

189. While we have discussed the issue of just war and conscientious objection in the work of Paul Ramsey and Jean Bethke Elshtain, I will not dwell on it further due to the scope of this work. However, the contemporary discussion of this area of Augustinian interpretation has certainly been treated in Jean Bethke Elshtain, *Just War Against Terror: The Burden of American Power in a Violent World* (New York: Basic Books, 2003).

190. *Compendium of the Social Doctrine of the Church* (CSDC), 399.

and scientific fields, the ethical conscience of people is disoriented . . . Conscience is no longer considered in its prime reality as an act of a person's intelligence, the function of which is to apply the universal knowledge of the good in a specific situation and thus to express a judgment about the right conduct to be chosen here and now. Instead, there is a tendency to grant to the individual conscience the prerogative of independently determining the criteria of good and evil and then acting accordingly. Such an outlook is quite congenial to an individualist ethic, wherein each individual is faced with his own truth different from the truth of others.[191]

Conscience is not based on relative desire, but ultimately on the human adhesion to the divine law, which is both grasped by reason (the natural law) and mediated by Revelation. This also demonstrates the problem of an "absolute" separation of Church and state, as the Christian's discernment of morality, especially on various issues that bear serious moral implications, necessarily includes the voice of the "community of believers," the Church. While the preference of many is to rely on, what John Paul II has called, "individual truth," this has caused many to become unable or unwilling to speak on moral issues and, in many cases, has simply led to apathy. The Church, however, while not seeking to infringe upon the autonomy of political authority, must speak out when the "religious or moral implications" of a particular program or policy contradict the divine law and threaten the common good.[192] The role of the Magisterium, therefore, while often unpopular in light of the predominance of individualist ideals, must be seen as an aid in the formation of the Christian's conscience and in responding to moral dilemmas that emerges in the public square.

Another area of Augustinian relevance to Christians in contemporary Western society is the importance of relying upon

191. *Fides et Ratio,* 98.
192. *CSDC,* 424.

and strengthening the family and the local community. Indeed, in applying Augustine's vision to our contemporary situation, our expectations for the political and economic systems of our time are necessarily tempered. The capacity for such structures to promote virtue, secure an earthly peace, and work for the common good are oftentimes limited by human sinfulness and pride. However, this does not imply abandoning such common efforts, but rather securing a proper set of expectations and an understanding that all such structures remain "works in progress." Pope Benedict XVI affirmed this in his encyclical, *Caritas in Veritate*:

> Man's earthly activity, when inspired and sustained by charity, contributes to the building of the universal *city of God*, which is the goal of the history of the human family. In an increasingly globalized society, the common good and the effort to obtain it cannot fail to assume the dimensions of the whole human family, that is to say, the community of peoples and nations, in such a way as to shape the earthly city in unity and peace, rendering it to some degree an anticipation and a prefiguration of the undivided *city of God*.[193]

Augustine also urges us to refocus our efforts on local levels of community, most especially the family. Jean Bethke Elshtain noted that, in front of a pessimistic reading of Augustine's political vision, we must always keep in mind the other "countervailing influences," namely the institutions and relationships built around human friendship. These "mark our dependence on one another, our need for trust, our capacity to mark new beginnings and to hope . . ."[194] She calls such institutions "containers for human social life," and places them within Augustine's call for *caritas*.[195] Such a connection has also been made recently in the *Compendium of Social Doctrine*,

---

193. Pope Benedict XVI, *Deus Caritas Est*, 7.
194. Elshtain, *Augustine and the Limits of Politics*, 38.
195. Ibid.

"No legislation, no system of rules or negotiation will ever succeed in persuading men and peoples to live in unity, brotherhood, and peace; no line of reasoning will ever be able to surpass the appeal of love."[196]

Reflecting upon the 1983, *Charter of the Rights of the Family*, the Church's affirmation that family must be given priority over society and the state reflects the Augustinian interpretation of Jean Bethke Elshtain and others.[197] Such priority is based upon the principle of subsidiarity, which demands that "public authorities may not take away from the family tasks which it can accomplish well by itself or in free association with other families."[198] This should cause us to reconsider the level of involvement and the role of families in the education of children, the care of the elderly, the use of community resources, and other public tasks. The role of the state, however, is not to be excluded, as it is tasked with aiding families in the carrying out of such responsibilities. The family is not to be seen, therefore, as a luxury or even a private good, but rather it should be given prominence in society, as the first and primary expression of human sociality and the place where *caritas* is best displayed. The Christian citizen, in cultivating a loving home and reaching out to other families, truly helps to build up and improve society by promoting and modeling Christian virtue. Encouraging signs have emerged, which demonstrate a decline in divorce for those married in the last two decades. [199] It remains in the best interest for human society to

196. *CSDC*, 207.
197. *CSDC*, 214.
198. *CSDC*, 214.
199. For a recent scientific study of this trend see Betsey Stevenson and Justin Wolfers, "Trends in marital stability," in *Research Handbook on the Economics of Family Law*, ed. Lloyd R. Cohen & J. Wright (Cheltenham, UK: Edward Elgar, 2011): 96–108. "The more recent data give us greater confidence in forecasting that subsequent marriages are less likely to end in divorce. Indeed, the divorce probabilities of the 1990s marriage cohort are now only a little above those who married in the 1960s, when comparing couples with similar marriage durations. It is worth noting that these cohorts will likely live longer than previous cohorts, giving them a longer period of time to be "at risk" of divorcing. Thus, declining divorce probabilities at each year of marriage yield a reasonably clear forecast of longer and more stable marriages, although rising

encourage such trends, and promote family life as an exercise also of good citizenship.

The Christian Politician

Our discussion has also illuminated some important Augustinian principles for the Christian serving in public office. Archbishop Chaput's application of Robert Dodaro's work to the contemporary situation of Christians in public office is an important step forward. It must be stated that Augustine saw Christians in public office as potentially a positive opportunity for good to be done and virtue exercised. Robert Dodaro has noted, "In Augustine's view, the Christian statesman's primary objective in governing piously should be to assist his subjects to love God in the truest way possible. This fundamental aim should guide all of his endeavors to advance the temporal welfare of his subjects, whether he seeks to assist those in material need or to discipline those who undermine public security."[200] Therefore, the positive effects that Christians can have in public office emerge precisely because they are informed by and adhere to the Gospel. As we have discussed, Augustine does not have illusions that such Christian public officials are common, but rather maintains generally, as Fortin and Kaufman have reminded us, a wary outlook. Such pessimism is at the core of the tension between the two cities, and Augustine's recognition that sinfulness and vice will persist throughout the course of human history until its completion.

Nevertheless, Christian politicians like Macedonius do at times emerge, and when they do, the Church has a responsibility to evangelize and to encourage them, as Augustine did Macedonius.

---

longevity complicates any assessment of the relative likelihood of marriage ending by divorce rather than death" (103).

200. Dodaro, *Christ and the Just Society*, 210-211.

Such is the task of the local bishop even today, namely to preach prophetically and to evangelize those within his flock, especially those who hold positions of authority. Here, I believe, we can ascertain the solution to Dodaro's insistence on transformative virtue and Fortin and Kaufman's pessimism, namely the pastoral relationship of the bishop and the faithful. Augustine's concern for Macedonius was at its core a pastoral relationship. While some will debate the paradigmatic nature of their correspondence, the pastoral nature of their relationship remains irrefutable. As a result, even today that pastoral concern remains an important example and model for the local bishop and the Catholic politician within his diocese. Aware that many politicians might not be open to such a relationship or will even reject its ecclesiological foundations, what must be undeterred is the mission to evangelize and preach in season and out of season (2 Tim 4:2).

Unfortunately, such openness is not observed today among many Catholic politicians in the United States, Europe, and elsewhere, as some have relegated Catholic moral teaching to a collection of "private views." Many dissent openly and publicly from the Church's moral teaching and its Magisterium on numerous ethical issues, including abortion, euthanasia, physician-assisted suicide, same-sex marriage, capital punishment, the treatment of immigrants and refugees, and other issues. In the discussion of these issues, adhesion to the Gospel and to the moral tradition of the Church is often portrayed as a betrayal of political autonomy and even an attack on "freedom." Statements are at times made affirming "personal" belief in the Church's teaching, but such faith often does not lead to public action.

As we have discussed, many have justified their political positions by invoking the "absolute separation of Church and state," and the separation of "private beliefs" and public duties. However, in making such distinctions, many politicians and public officials have also excluded the influence of the natural moral law and revealed truth, preferring instead to base decisions on relativist principles. The Church's teaching on moral issues based upon the natural law and the Gospel is often ignored or outwardly rejected. In response the Congregation of the Doctrine of the Faith has clarified the responsibilities of a Catholic in political office:

> When political activity comes up against moral principles that do not admit of exception, compromise or derogation, the Catholic commitment becomes more evident and laden with responsibility. In the face of fundamental and inalienable ethical demands, Christians must recognize that what is at stake is the essence of the moral law, which concerns the integral good of the human person. This is the case with laws concerning abortion and euthanasia (not to be confused with the decision to forgo extraordinary treatments, which is morally legitimate).[201]

The Congregation's instruction affirms the call of Augustine for all Christians in every station of life, including those in political authority, to keep before their eyes their ultimate fulfillment in the heavenly city. Remaining always attentive to "what is at stake," and the "integral good of the human person." Archbishop Chaput notes the lay character of these political responsibilities, "Christian political engagement, when it happens is never *mainly* the task of the clergy. That work belongs to lay believers who live most intensely in the world."[202] While remaining a task reserved to the laity, quite often the Christian politician is tempted to govern apart from faith instead of being informed by it. This is the pitfall opened up by a neutral *saeculum*, where the principles of faith must be checked at the door prior to entering the public square. Rather, the Christian politician

---

201. Congregation for the Doctrine of the Faith, "The Participation of Catholics in Political Life," 4.
202. Chaput, "JFK's Speech," 653.

in Augustine's view must be inspired and informed by faith and true virtue, which comes from a relationship with Christ. Chaput rightly states, "Human law teaches and forms as well as regulates; and human politics is the exercise of power—which means both have moral implications that the Christian cannot ignore and still remain faithful to his vocation as a light to the world (Mt. 5:14-16)."[203] Indeed, Augustine maintains that both politicians and clergy remain vulnerable to sin and temptation, but both also find their common path to virtue in the humility of knowing their imperfection and their willingness to do penance for their sins. Such humility, which was so counter-cultural in the ancient world, remains no less counter-cultural today.

Augustine also reminds all Christians that the results that government and every social institution can accomplish will always be imperfect. Indeed, the perfectly just society is a goal attained not in this world, but only by Christ in the heavenly city. This theological truth is also important for the Christian in public office, as it tempers expectations in what legislation can accomplish, and prevents the misplacement of Christian hope in human institutions. If political goals alone become the complete focus of the Christian in public service, then the desires of the politician will seek nothing more than the vainglory and self-glorification Augustine detested in Roman society. This is a veritable temptation for the Christian politician, both in Augustine's day and in our own. It is a temptation that has been brought to light in the formation of political positions on the major ethical questions of our day. Such positions are often not the

---

203. Ibid. This is affirmed by the Congregation for the Doctrine of the Faith at the opening of its *Doctrinal Note on Some Questions Regarding the Participation of Catholics in Political Llife*,"By fulfilling their civic duties, 'guided by a Christian conscience' in conformity with its values, the lay faithful exercise their proper task of infusing the temporal order with Christian values, all the while respecting the nature and rightful autonomy of that order, and cooperating with other citizens according to their particular competence and responsibility" (1).

result of a genuine and conscientious discernment of truth and the common good, but rather political calculations seen as necessary to win another election or reach higher office. It is for this reason that, while recognizing the potential good that a Christian can accomplish in public office, Augustine also cautions against placing anything before our fundamental and primary citizenship, namely citizenship in the heavenly city.

Motivation is not a secondary concern for Augustine when dealing with a Christian in public office, as is evident in Augustine's correspondence with Macedonius. While recognizing that perfect virtue is unattainable in this world, as Dodaro notes, "Augustine is confident that as long as the statesman's desire to govern with true piety leads him to understand the aims of civic virtues in harmony with the love of God, and provided that he receives with humility the grace that Christ bestows on him, his virtues gradually increase in strength while they also converge in the love of God."[204] Faced with enormous pressures and numerous temptations, which have certainly not decreased since Augustine's own lifetime, the strengthening of virtue is only brought about by true piety and the humble reception of grace. Therefore, the Christian politician's union with Christ's mystical body, the Church, is a source of strength and assistance not just interiorly, but also in the decisions of governance.

The reception of the Sacraments and the grace that flows through the mediation of Christ and the work of the Holy Spirit provide the Christian politician, jurist, and public official, then and now, with the only true way of growing in virtue and renewing their lay vocation. It is through encountering Christ in this way that motivations are corrected, pride is checked, and a true sense of Christian vocation is restored. The vocation of the Christian politician is not outside

---

204. Dodaro, *Christ and the Just Society*, 211–212.

of the Church; like all vocations, it builds upon and flows from the Christian's first and primary vocation, namely the call to holiness given to us in Baptism.[205] Benedict XVI, in his encyclical, *Deus Caritas Est*, reaffirmed this connection and builds upon the 1988, Post-Synodal Apostolic Exhortation of his predecessor, John Paul II, *Christifideles Laici*. "The direct duty to work for a just ordering of society, on the other hand, is proper to the lay faithful. As citizens of the State, they are called to take part in public life in a personal capacity. So they cannot relinquish their participation 'in the many different economic, social, legislative, administrative and cultural areas, which are intended to promote organically and institutionally the *common good*."[206]

The Christian politician, therefore, should envision his or her public duties not apart from the Church, but rather as a fulfillment of a lay vocation within the Church for the good of the human community. However, this implies communion with Christ's mystical body, and moving beyond an oversimplified and absolutist vision of the role of faith in public life that prevents the informing of conscience, the strengthening of virtue, and the broadening of compassion for the most vulnerable and neediest among us. The larger concern for Augustine, therefore, is not the public separation of the Church and state, but rather the separation and divisions within the heart of the Christian in public office, which can confuse desire and misplace Christian hope.

What is offered by Augustine, and indeed by the Church's social teaching is not a general condemnation of Christian politicians, but

---

205. *LG*, 39. "This holiness of the Church is unceasingly manifested, and must be manifested, in the fruits of grace which the Spirit produces in the faithful; it is expressed in many ways in individuals, who in their walk of life, tend toward the perfection of charity, thus causing the edification of others; in a very special way this (holiness) appears in the practice of the counsels, customarily called 'evangelical.'"
206. Pope Benedict XVI, *Deus Caritas Est*, 29.

an encouragement towards an authentic understanding of their service, as a living out of the vocation of the laity. However, such a vision can only be embraced, as Augustine points out, when one is dedicated to true piety and strengthened by grace. Indeed, *Gaudium et Spes* expresses this encouragement clearly, and provides a positive vision often forgotten in today's political context. This vision, I hope, has been reinforced by our discussion of Augustine's political and social vision, and will become a renewed mission among Christians, especially those in public service:

> Those who are suited or can become suited should prepare themselves for the difficult, but at the same time, the very noble art of politics, and should seek to practice this art without regard for their own interests or for material advantages. With integrity and wisdom, they must take action against any form of injustice and tyranny, against arbitrary domination by an individual or a political party and any intolerance. They should dedicate themselves to the service of all with sincerity and fairness, indeed, with the charity and fortitude demanded by political life.[207]

207. GS, 75.

Conclusion

It is has been the goal of this study to survey comprehensively the interpretations of Augustine's social and political thought, examine the related hermeneutical questions involved, and connect Augustine's vision with the contemporary situation facing the Christian citizen and politician. It is apparent throughout this study that the socio-political lens in which Augustine's work has been viewed after Arquillière remains problematic. This hermeneutic, as we have discussed, has isolated certain elements of Augustine's corpus to characterize his thought. While often preferred in the academy, it misrepresents the theological nature of Augustine's thought and the meaning behind his two cities. It is true that Augustine bears concern for public life and advocates for the utilization of earthly goods, but always out of concern for eternal ends. It appears that only such an integral understanding of his thought allows for a proper reading of Augustine, especially when he writes in Book XIX of his *City of God:*

> A household of men who live by faith looks forward to the blessings which are promised as eternal in the life to come; and such men make use of earthly and temporal things like pilgrims: they are not captivated by them, nor are they deflected by them from their progress towards God.[1]

---

1. *CD* (XIX, 17), 945.

The way in which the Christian utilizes earthly goods also alludes to the way in which Augustine's thought can be applied wholeheartedly to the social and political realm, namely in the exercise of virtue and the concrete life of the statesman. This argument put forward by Robert Dodaro remains, in my opinion, the most effective and comprehensive solution, as it permits both a guarded Augustinian outlook towards the prospect of bettering earthly society and the potential for the activity of grace in the life of the public official. This response, which Dodaro notes, emerges from Augustine's reflections on the responsibilities of Macedonius in light of a Neoplatonic theory of virtue, "[a]llows Augustine to see how it is possible for statesmen to deepen their love of God as 'citizens of the heavenly city' without abandoning their political offices in order to become philosophers or monks."[2] Such an affirmation is contested by Fortin and Kaufman, who provide us with a cautionary and more pessimistic vision of the Christian's ability to live virtuously in public life. However, such pessimism, which I do not believe necessarily excludes Dodaro's position, is an important caution in light of the temptations that accompany such positions of authority. This understanding is also consistent with magisterial teaching since *Gaudium et Spes*. While admitting the autonomy of the political and ecclesial spheres, such autonomy does not necessitate the "absolute" separation of Church and state popular in contemporary political discussions. Indeed, Augustine argued for the possible good that could be achieved from a politician remaining open to grace and striving to conform to Christ in the carrying out of public responsibilities.

The *tertium quid*, the point of encounter between the two cities proposed by Marrou, is taken up by Markus, but rendered a neutral shared space. However, in my opinion and the opinion of others

---

2. Dodaro, "Augustine on the Statesman and the Two Cities," in *A Companion to Augustine*, ed. Mark Vessey (Oxford: Blackwell Publishing, 2012), 396.

such neutrality is a step too far if one is attempting to remain faithful to Augustine's vision. The virtue that flows from supernatural grace and the connection to Christ's mystical body cannot be compartmentalized from the duties of the public official. In fact, such Christian virtue is necessary to produce the limited good that is possible in human society, and to avoid the temptations posed by pride and self-glorification in the political arena. However, Augustine also does not justify the opposite view, in which the autonomy of the sacred and temporal is lost. Such an extreme, which can be drawn from Milbank and others, appears inconsistent with the later Augustine who insists on the concept of *ecclesia permixta*. Indeed, such a position to the other extreme gives credence to Augustine's many critics in their accusations that he subverts the temporal order. Such an accusation, as Joseph Ratzinger has pointed out, is more fittingly applied to Eusebius of Caesarea, and is inconsistent with Augustine's acknowledgment of the importance of the political and temporal order. This balanced solution focused on virtue, which is consistent with the work of James Schall, Ernest Fortin, and Robert Dodaro, is still unpopular with those who prefer a "secularist" reading of Augustine. However, it is also unpopular with others, like Peter Iver Kaufman, who believe Augustine's pessimism is the dominant strain of his social and political discourse. However, such disagreement is natural when faced with the fact, observed by Miikka Ruokanen, that Augustine is both an ontological optimist, seeing in creation the beauty and perfection imbued in it by the Creator, and a moral pessimist, believing that disorder caused by sin has marred human nature and stains also human institutions.[3]

I believe a service has been done by Francis Cardinal George and Archbishop Charles Chaput in extending a virtue-centered

---

3. Ruokanen, *Theology of Social Life*, 157.

understanding of the role of the Christian politician to the Christian citizen as well. The Christian citizen, like the statesman, if conformed to the truly just society formed by Christ can live and fulfill civil responsibilities while remaining focused on the goal of heavenly citizenship. While perfection remains beyond our grasp, even in light of sin and moral failings, Augustine offers a path of humility and penance in order to maintain eternal goals. Such a concept of citizenship, as we have seen, explains the loyalty of the Christian martyrs to their faith in spite of punishment and death. While the challenges of secularism, relativism, individualism, and even postmodern nihilism all militate against such an understanding of Christian citizenship and statesmanship, it also appears that our time bears some similarity with the context of Augustine's own lifetime. Augustine's context was shaped by the ideological and theological challenges of Donatism, Pelagianism, and Stoicism. Then, like now, the Christian will be challenged, even publicly, to maintain faith in the face of hostility, especially political and social pressures. Indeed, unpopularity, ridicule, and even persecution might accompany the openly Christian politician or citizen in certain contexts or on certain issues. However, despite those pressures, I believe Augustine's undertones are captured in the formula for citizenship proposed by Archbishop Chaput addressing Catholics in the United States:

> It's time for all of us who claim to be 'Catholic' to recover our Catholic identity as disciples of Jesus Christ and missionaries of his Church. In the long run, we serve our country best by remembering that we're citizens of heaven first. We're better Americans by being more truly Catholic—and the reason why, is that unless we love our Catholic faith authentically, with our whole heart and our whole strength, we have nothing worthwhile to bring to the public debates that will determine the course of our nation.[4]

---

4. Charles Chaput, "Church and State Today: What Belongs to Caesar, and What Doesn't," *Journal of Catholic Legal Studies* 47, no.3 (2008), 7.

Finally, I believe Augustine's ideas, while openly opposed by many thinkers who adhere to a hermeneutic of refutation, will be a fixture in the political and social conversation for generations to come. While authors like Connolly and others have sought a systematic removal of Augustine's influence and ethics from Western thought, their post-modern ideology has led to nihilism. Nothing has been constructed from their efforts, and none of their proposals are able to rebuild what their nihilism negates, namely social consensus, human relationships, and even interpersonal communication. In their systems, all such efforts are rendered futile. Jean Bethke Elshtain diagnosed this problem well in her important article, "While Europe Slept":

> And secularism—a rigid cultural ideology that mocks religion as superstition and celebrates technological rationalism as the only proper and intelligent way to think and to be in the world—has developed into nihilism, into a world in which we can no longer make judgments of value and truth in defense of human dignity and flourishing.[5]

Augustine's vision, therefore, continues to remain relevant because it is a remedy, a way forward outside of the nothingness embraced often in contemporary thought. Augustine's presupposition of a social ontology is shown even in his rendering of Cicero's *res publica*. This is because, as Elshtain notes, Augustine realized that it was not human interest that built society, but *caritas*.[6] Such a belief, however, stems from a concept of sociality, or human inter-connectedness, which flows from Augustine's theology of the Trinity. And so, we are reminded by Augustine that just as perfect charity is modeled to us in Christ, the true and perfect society is built not by us, but by Him.

---

5. Jean Bethke Elshtain, "While Europe Slept" *First Things* 191 (March 2009), 34.
6. Elshtain, "Why Augustine?," 11.

Bibliography

I. Magisterial Sources

1.1 Acts of the Apostolic See

Acta Apostolicae Sedis. Vols. 1ff. Vatican City: Typis Polyglottis Vaticanis, 1909–Present.

1.2. Conciliar Documents

Acta Synodalia Sacrosancti Concilii Oecumenici Vaticani II. Vols. I–VI. Vatican City: Typis Polyglottis Vaticanis, 1970–1998.

Vatican Council II. Dogmatic Constitution on the Church *Lumen Gentium*. *AAS* 57. 1965.

Official English translation in *The Documents of Vatican II with Notes and Index: Vatican Translation*, Strathfield, Australia: St. Pauls Publications, 2009.

———. Pastoral Constitution on the Church in the Modern World *Lumen Gentium*. *AAS* 58.

1966. Official English translation in *The Documents of Vatican II with Notes and Index: Vatican Translation*, Strathfield, Australia: St. Pauls Publications, 2009.

———. Declaration on Religious Freedom *Dignitatis Humanae AAS* 58. 1966. Official English translation in *The Documents of Vatican II with Notes and Index: Vatican Translation*, Strathfield, Australia: St. Pauls Publications, 2009.

1.3. Papal Encyclicals

John Paul II. Encyclical Letter *Fides et Ratio. AAS* 91. 1999. Official English translation published by Libreria Editrice Vaticana, Vatican City, 1998.

Benedict XVI. Encyclical Letter *Caritas in Veritate. AAS* 101. 2009. Official English translation published by Libreria Editrice Vaticana, Vatican City, 2009.

———. Encyclical Letter *Deus Caritas Est. AAS* 98. 2006. Official English translation published by Libreria Editrice Vaticana, Vatican City, 2006.

1.4. Apostolic Exhortation

John Paul II. Post-Synodal Apostolic Exhortation *Christifideles Laici. AAS* 81. 1989. Official English translation published by Pauline Books & Media, Boston, 1988.

1.5. Papal Addresses

Benedict XVI. *Address to Federal Parliament in Berlin's Reichstag Building: Politics at the Service of Rights and Justice.* Original German text in *AAS* 103. 2011. Official English translation in *L'Osservatore Romano Weekly Edition in English*, September 28, 2011.

———. *Responses to the Questions Posed by the Bishops of the United States of America*, National Shrine of the Immaculate Conception in Washington, D. C. (April 16, 2008). Original English text in *AAS* 100 (2008): 314-319.

1.6. Congregational Documents and Other Sources

Congregation for the Doctrine of the Faith. *Doctrinal Note on Some Questions Regarding the Participation of Catholics in Political Life. AAS* 96. 2004. Official English translation published by Libreria Editrice Vaticana, Vatican City, 2003.

———. *Instruction on Certain Aspects of the "Theology of Liberation." AAS* 76. 1984. Official English translation published by Libreria Editrice Vaticana, Vatican City, 1984.

Catechism of the Catholic Church. Vatican City: Libreria Editrice Vaticana, 1994.

Pontifical Council for Justice and Peace. *Compendium of the Social Doctrine of the Church.* Washington D. C.: USCCB Publishing, 2004.

Holy See. *Charter of the Rights of the Family.* Official English translation in *L'Osservatore Romano Weekly Edition in English.* November 28, 1983.

II. Augustinian Sources

Augustine of Hippo. *The City of God Against the Pagans.* Edited by R. W. Dyson. Cambridge: Cambridge University Press, 1998.

———. *Sermones.* Patrologiae Cursus Completus, Series Latina 38, ed. J. P. Migne. Paris: 1881.

III. Primary Authors

Arquillière, Henri-Xavier. *Saint Grégoire VII: Essai Sur Sa Conception Du Pouvoir Pontifical*. L'eglise Et L'état Au Moyen Âge, Iv. Paris: J. Vrin, 1934.

———. ed. *L'augustinisme Politique: Essai Sur La Formation Des Théories Politiques Du Moyen-Age*. 2. éd., rev. et augm. ed, Études De Philosophie Médiévale. Paris: J. Vrin, 1933.

Combès, Gustave. *La Doctrine Politique de Saint Augustin*. Paris: Plon, 1927.

Connolly, William E. *Why I Am Not a Secularist*. Minneapolis, MN: University of Minnesota Press, 2002.

———. *The Augustinian Imperative: A Reflection on the Politics of Morality*. Newbury Park, CA: SAGE Publications 1993.

———. *Identity\Difference: Democratic Negotiations of Political Paradox*. Minneapolis: University of Minnesota Press, 1991.

de Lubac, Henri. *Augustinianism and Modern Theology*. Translated by Lancelot Sheppard and Introduced by Louis Dupre. New York: Herder & Herder, 2000.

———. *Theological Fragments*. Translated by Rebecca Howell Balinski. San Francisco: Ignatius Press, 1989.

———. *Théologies D'occasion*. Paris: Desclée de Brouwer, 1984.

Deane, Herbert. *The Political and Social Ideas of St. Augustine*. New York: Columbia University Press, 1963.

Dodaro, Robert. "Augustine on the Statesman and the Two Cities." In *A Companion to Augustine*, 386-397. London: Blackwell Publishing Ltd., 2012.

———. "Augustine's Use of Parallel Dialogues in his Preaching of Nonviolence." In *Ministerium sermonis: Philological, Historical and Theological Studies on Augustine's Sermones ad populum*, Instrumenta Patristica et Mediaevalia 53, 327-344. Edited by G. Partoens, A. Dupont, M. Lamberigts. Turnhout: Brepols, 2009.

———. "Ecclesia and Res Publica: How Augustinian are Neo-Augustinian Politics?" In *Augustine and Post Modern Thought: A New Alliance Against Modernity?* Edited by L. Boeve, M. Lamberigts, M. Wisse. Leuven: Peeters Press, 2008.

———. "Tra le due città: azione politica in Agostino da Ippona." In *Fede e storia: IRC e coscienza storica,* 9-25. Edited by Filippo Morlacchi. Roma: Lateran University Press, 2007.

———. "Augustine and the Debate Concerning 'Political Augustinianism'." Unpublished Address delivered at Ave Maria University. Naples, FL: 2005.

———. *Christ and the Just Society in the Thought of Augustine.* Cambridge: Cambridge University Press, 2004.

———. "Political and Theological Virtues in Augustine, Letter 155 to Macedonius," *Augustiniana* 54 (2004): 431-474.

———. "Augustine's Secular City." In *Augustine and his Critics.* Edited by R. Dodaro and G. Lawless. London: Routledge, Chapman & Hall, 1999.

———. Review of *Theology of Social Life,* by Miikka Ruokanen. *Journal of Theological Studies* 45, no. 1 (April 1994): 344-347.

Dyson, R. W. *Normative Theories of Society and Government in Five Medieval Thinkers St. Augustine, John of Salisbury, Giles of Rome, St. Thomas Aquinas, and Marsilius of Padua.* Lewiston: Edwin Mellen Press, 2003.

———. *The Pilgrim City: Social and Political Ideas in the Writing of Saint Augustine of Hippo.* Woodbridge: Boydell Press, 2001.

Elshtain, Jean Bethke. "While Europe Slept." *First Things* 191 (March 2009): 33-36.

———. Review of *The Desire of the Nations,* by Oliver O'Donovan. *Theological Studies* 58, no. 4 (December 2004): 749-751.

———. "How Does—Or Should?—Theology Influence Politics?" *Political Theology* 5, no. 3 (July 2004): 265-274.

———. *Just War Against Terror: The Burden of American Power in a Violent World*. New York: Basic Books, 2003.

———. "Why Augustine? Why Now." *Theology Today* 55, no. 1 (April 1998): 5-14.

———. *Augustine and the Limits of Politics*, Frank M. Covey, Jr. Loyola Lectures in Political Analysis. Notre Dame, IN: University of Notre Dame Press, 1995.

Figgis, J. Neville. *The Political Aspects of St. Augustine's City of God*. London: Longmans, Green, & Co., 1921.

Fortin, Ernest L. *Classical Christianity and the Political Order: Reflections on the Theologico-Political Problem*. Edited by J. Brian Benestad. Vol. 2 of *Ernest Fortin: Collected Essays*. Lanham, MD: Rowman & Littlefield Pub., 1996.

———. "The Political Thought of St. Augustine." In *History of Political Philosophy*, 3rd ed., eds. L. Strauss and J. Cropsey, (Chicago: University of Chicago Press, 1987): 176-205.

———. "Augustine's City of God and the Modern Historical Consciousness." *The Review of Politics* 41 (1979): 739-746.

———. "Augustine, Thomas Aquinas, and the Problem of Natural Law." *Mediaevalia* 4 (1978): 179-208.

———. *Political Idealism and Christianity in the Thought of St. Augustine*. Villanova, PA: Villanova University Press, 1972.

———. Review of *The Political and Social Ideas of St. Augustine*, by Herbert Deane. *Cross Currents* 14, no. 4 (1964): 482-484.

Gilson, Étienne. *The Christian Philosophy of Saint Augustine*. Translated by L. E. M. Lynch. New York: Random House, 1960.

———. Foreword for *Saint Augustine, The City of God: Book I-VII*. trans. D. Zema, S. J., and G. Walsh, S. J., New York: Fathers of the Church, Inc., 1950.

———. *Introduction a l'Étude de Saint Augustin*. Paris: Librairie Philosophique J. Vrin, 1943.

———. *The Spirit of Medieval Philosophy: Gifford Lectures 1931-1932*. trans. A. H. C. Downes. London: Sheed and Ward, 1936.

Gregory, Eric. "Augustinians and New Liberalism." *Augustinian Studies* 41, no. 1 (2010): 315-32.

———. *Politics and the Order of Love: An Augustinian Ethic of Democratic Citizenship*. Chicago: University of Chicago Press, 2008.

Hanby, Michael. *Augustine and Modernity*. New York: Routledge, 2003.

Kaufman, Peter I. "Christian Realism and Augustinian (?) Liberalism." *Journal of Religious Ethics* 38, no. 4 (2010): 699-724.

———. "Augustine and Corruption." *History of Political Thought* (2009): 46-59.

———. *Incorrectly Political: Augustine and Thomas More*. University of Notre Dame Press, 2007.

———. "Augustine, Martyrs, and Misery." *Church History* 63, no. 1 (March 1994): 1-15.

———. *Redeeming Politics*. Princeton, NJ: Princeton University Press, 1990.

———. *Augustinian Piety and Catholic Reform*. Macon, GA: Mercer University Press, 1983.

Lettieri, Gaetano. *Il senso della storia in Agostino d'Ippona*. Roma: Borla, 1988.

Markus, Robert A. Review of *Politics and the Order of Love: An Augustinian Ethic of Democratic Citizenship*, by Eric Gregory. *Scottish Journal of Theology* 64 (2011): 248-250.

———. "Political Order as Response to the Church's Mission." *Political Theology* 9, no. 3 (July 2008): 319-326.

———. *Christianity and the Secular*. Notre Dame, IN: University of Notre Dame Press, 2006.

———. Review of *Christ and the Just Society in the Thought of Augustine*, by Robert Dodaro. *Journal of Ecclesiastical History* 57, no. 1 (January 2006): 105-106.

———. "Evolving Disciplinary Contexts for the Study of Augustine, 1950-2000: Some Personal Reflections." *Augustinian Studies* 32, no. 2 (2001): 189-200.

———. *The End of Ancient Christianity.* Cambridge: Cambridge University Press, 1990.

———. *Saeculum: History and Society in the Theology of Saint Augustine.* 2nd ed. Cambridge: Cambridge University Press, 1989.

———. ed. *Augustine: A Collection of Critical Essays.* New York: Anchor Books, 1972.

———. *Saeculum: History and Society in the Theology of Saint Augustine.* Cambridge: Cambridge University Press, 1972.

Marrou, Henri-Irénée. *Théologie de l'Histoire.* Paris: Seuil, 1968.

———. "Civitas Dei, civitas terrena: num tertium quid?" In *Studia Patristica: Papers Presented to the Second International Conference in Patristic Studies held at Christ Church, Oxford,* edited by K. Aland and F. L. Cross, 342-50. Berlin: Akademie Verlag, 1957.

———. *St. Augustine and His Influence Through the Ages.* Translated by Patrick Hepburne-Scott. New York: Harper Torchbooks, 1957.

———. "Théologie de l'Histoire." In *Augustinus Magister: Congres International Augustinien, Paris: 21-24 Septembre 1954 Actes.* Paris: Études Augustiniennes, 1954.

———. *Saint Augustin et la fin de la culture antique.* Paris: Biblioth. de Fècole, 1949. Reprint, 1949.

Mathewes, Charles. *The Republic of Grace: Augustinian Thoughts for Dark Times.* Grand Rapids, MI: Eerdmans, 2010.

———. "A Worldly Augustinianism: Augustine's Sacramental Vision of Creation." *Augustinian Studies* 41, no. 1 (2010): 333-48.

———. *A Theology of Public Life.* Cambridge: Cambridge University Press, 2007.

———. "An Augustinian Look at Empire." *Theology Today* 63, no. 30 (2006): 292-306.

———. "Augustinian Anthropology: Interior intimo meo." *The Journal of Religious Ethics*, 27, no. 2 (Summer 1999): 195-221.

Milbank, John. "Enclaves, or Where is the Church?" *New Blackfriars* 73, no. 861 (June 1992): 341-352.

———. "'Postmodern Critical Augustinianism': A Short Summa in Forty Two Responses to Unasked Questions." *Modern Theology* 7, no. 3 (April 1991): 225-237.

———. *Theology and Social Theory: Beyond Secular Reason.* Oxford: Blackwell Publishers, 1990.

———. "An Essay Against Secular Order." *Journal of Religious Ethics* 15, no. 2 (1987): 199-224.

Niebhur, Reinhold. *An Interpretation of Christian Ethics.* New York: Meridian, 1956.

———. *Christian Realism and Political Problems.* New York: Charles Scribner's Sons, 1953.

———. *The Children of Light and the Children of Darkness.* New York: Charles Scribner's Sons, 1950.

———. *The Nature and Destiny of Man: A Christian Interpretation.* Vol. 1, *Human Nature.* New York: Charles Scribner's Sons, 1941.

O'Donovan, Oliver. *The Ways of Judgement.* Grand Rapids, MI: Eerdmans, 2005.

———. *Bonds of Imperfection: Christian Politics, Past and Present.* Edited by Oliver O'Donovan and Joan Lockwood O'Donovan. Grand Rapids: Eerdmans, 2004.

———. *Common Objects of Love: Moral Reflection and the Shaping of Community.* Grand Rapids: Eerdmans, 2002.

———. "Behold, the Lamb!" *Studies in Christian Ethics* 11, no. 2 (1998): 91-110.

———. *The Desire of the Nations: Rediscovering the Roots of Political Theology*. Oxford: Oxford University Press, 1996.

Ramsey, Paul. "Human Sexuality in the History of Redemption." *Journal of Religious Ethics* 16, no. 1 (Spring 1988): 56-86.

———. *The Just War: Force and Political Responsibility*. Lanham, MD: University Press of America, 1983.

———. "Some Rejoinders." *Journal of Religious Ethics* 4 (Fall 1976): 185-237.

———. "The Vatican Council on Modern War," *Theological Studies* 27, no. 2 (June 1966): 179-203.

———. *Nine Modern Moralists*. Englewood Cliffs, NJ: Prentice Hall, 1962.

———. *War and the Christian Conscience*. Durham, NC: Duke University, 1961.

———. ed. *Faith and Ethics: The Theology of Reinhold Niebuhr*. New York: Harper and Row, 1957.

———. "God's Grace and Man's Guilt," *The Journal of Religion* 31, no. 1 (January 1951): 21-37.

———. *Basic Christian Ethics*. Louisville, KY: Westminster John Knox Press, 1950.

Ratzinger, Joseph. *Church, Ecumenism, and Politics: New Endeavors in Ecclesiology*. Translated by Michael Miller et al. San Francisco: Ignatius Press, 2008.

———. *Europe Today and Tomorrow*. Translated by Michael Miller. San Francisco: Ignatius Press, 2007.

———. *Introduction to Christianity*. Translated by J. R. Foster. San Francisco: Ignatius Press, 2004.

———. *L'unita Delle Nazioni. Una Visione Dei Padri Della Chiesa*. Brescia: Morcellina, 1973.

———. *Die Einheit der Nationem. Eine Vision der Kirchenväter*. Salzburg-München: Universitätsverlag Anton Pustet, 1971.

———. *Volk und Haus Gottes in Augustins Lehre von der Kirche.* München: K. Zink, 1954.

Ruokanen, Mikka. "Augustine's Theological Criticism of Politics." *Studia Patristica* 33 (1997): 236-38.

———. *Theology of Social Life in Augustine's De Civitate Dei.* Göttingen: Vandenhoeck and Ruprecht, 1993.

Schall, James V. *The Mind That Is Catholic: Philosophical and Political Essays.* Washington D. C.: Catholic University of America Press, 2008.

———. Review of *Augustine and the Limits of Politics*, by Jean Bethke Elshtain. *Theological Studies* 58, no. 2 (June 1997): 389.

———. *Christianity and Politics.* Boston: St. Paul's Editions, 1981.

Ward, Graham. *The Politics of Discipleship: Becoming Postmaterial Citizens.* Grand Rapids, MI: Baker Academic, 2009.

———. *Cities of God.* Edited by John Milbank, Catherine Pickstock and Graham Ward, Radical Orthodoxy. New York: Routledge, 2000.

Wetzel, James. "Splendid Vices and Secular Virtues: Variations on Milbank's Augustine." *Journal of Religious Ethics* 32 no. 2, (Summer 2004): 271-300.

———. *Augustine and the Limits of Virtue.* Cambridge: Cambridge University Press, 1992.

———. "The Recovery of Free Agency in the Theology of St. Augustine." *Harvard Theological Review* 80 (1987): 101-25.

Williams, Rowan. *Faith in the Public Square.* London: Bloomsbury Publishing, 2012.

———. *Why Study the Past?: The Quest for the Historical Church.* Grand Rapids, MI: Eerdmans, 2005.

———. "Politics and the Soul: A Reading of the City of God." *Milltown Studies* 19/20 (1987): 55-72.

IV. Studies and Commentaries

Adeney, Frances S. "Jean Bethke Elshtain: Political Theorist and Postmodern Prophet." *Religious Studies Review* 27, no. 3 (July 2001): 243-249.

Bedouelle, Guy. "Le Désir De Voir Jérusalem. Histoire Du Theme Des Deux Cités." *Communio* XI, no. 3 Mai-Jun (1986): 38-52.

Benestad, J. Brian. "An Introduction to the Work of Ernest Fortin." *Communio* 26, (Spring 1999): 39-54.

Bowlin, John. "Parts, Wholes, and Opposites: John Milbank as *Geisteshistoriker.*" *Journal of Religious Ethics* 32, no. 2 (Summer 2004): 254-270.

Brezzi, P. "Considerazioni Sul Cosidetto 'Agostinismo Politico.'" *Augustinianum* 25, no. 1-2 (1985): 235-54.

Brown, Peter. "Introducing Robert Markus." *Augustinian Studies* 32, no. 2 (2001): 181-187.

———. *Augustine of Hippo: A Biography*. Berkeley: University of California Press, 2000.

———. *Authority and the Sacred: Aspects of the Christianisation of the Roman World*. Cambridge: Cambridge University Press, 1997.

———. *Religion and Society in the Age of Saint Augustine*. New York: Harper and Row, 1972.

Burt, Donald X., O. S. A., *Friendship and Society: An Introduction to Augustine's Practical Philosophy*. Grand Rapids, MI: Eerdmans, 1999.

Chaput, Charles J. "JFK's Houston Speech Undermined Religion in Public Life." *Origins* 39, no. 40 (March 18, 2010): 651-654.

———. *Render Unto Caesar: Serving the Nation by Living Our Catholic Beliefs in Political Life*. New York: Doubleday Publishing, 2008.

———. "Church and State Today: What Belongs to Caesar, and What Doesn't." *Journal of Catholic Legal Studies* 47, no. 3 (2008): 3-8.

Chroust, Anton-Hermann. "The Philosophy of Law of St. Augustine." *The Philosophical Review* 53, no. 2 (1944): 195-202.

Cohen, Lloyd R. & J. Wright, eds. *Research Handbook on the Economics of Family Law*. Cheltenham, UK: Edward Elgar, 2011.

Congar, Yves, O. P. *L'Eglise dans le monde de ce temps: Tome I*. Paris: Les Éditions du Cerf, 1967.

Cooper, John W. *The Theology of Freedom: The Legacy of Jacques Maritain and Reinhold Niebuhr*. Macon, GA: Mercer Press, 1985.

Culler, Jonathan D. *On Deconstruction: Theory and Criticism after Structuralism*. Ithaca, NY: Cornell University Press, 2007.

Cullman, Oscar. *Christ and Time: The Primitive Christian Conception of Time and History*. Philadelphia: Westminster Press, 1950.

Davis, Scott. "'Et Quod Vis Fac': Paul Ramsey and Augustinian Ethics." *The Journal of Religious Ethics* 19, no. 2 (1991): 31-69.

Diggins, John Patrick, *Why Niebuhr Now?* Chicago: University of Chicago Press, 2011.

Doak, Mary. "The Politics of Radical Orthodoxy: A Catholic Critique." *Theological Studies* 68 (2007): 368-393.

Doering, Bernard. "Jacques Maritain: A Beggar for Heaven on the Byways of the World." *Theology Today* 62 (2005): 306-316.

Doody, John, Kevin Hughes, Kim Paffenroth, eds. *Augustine and Politics*. Lanham, MD: Lexington Books, 2005.

Dougherty, Jude P. *Jacques Maritain: An Intellectual Profile*. Washington, D. C.: Catholic University Press, 2003.

Drane, James F. *A Liberal Catholic Bioethics*. Münster: Lit Verlag, 2010.

Dunn, Charles, ed. *The Future of Religion in American Politics*. Lexington: University of Kentucky Press, 2009.

Ellul, Jacques. *The Meaning of the City*. Grand Rapids, MI: Eerdmans, 1970.

Fitzgerald, Allan, O. S. A., ed. *Augustine Through the Ages: An Encyclopedia*. Grand Rapids, MI: Eerdmans, 2002.

Fox, Richard W. *Reinhold Niebuhr: A Biography*. New York: Pantheon Books, 1985.

George, Francis Cardinal. *God in Action: How Faith in God Can Address the Challenges of the World*. New York: Doubleday Publishing, 2011.

——. *The Difference God Makes: A Catholic Vision of Faith, Communion, and Culture*. New York: Crossroad Publishing, 2009.

Gutiérrez, Gustavo. *A Theology of Liberation*. Translated and edited by Caridad Inda and John Engleston. Maryknoll, NY: Orbis Books, 1988.

Halvorson, John V. "The Kingdom and Realism in Ministry." *Word and World* II, no. 2 (1982): 109–116.

Harris, Charles E. Jr. "Love as the Basic Moral Principle in Paul Ramsey's Ethics." *The Jounral of Religious Ethics* 4, no. 2 (1976): 239–258.

Hauerwas, Stanley. *After Christendom? How the Church Is to Behave if Freedom, Justice, and a Christian Nation Are Bad Ideas*. Nashville TN: Abingdon Press, 1991.

Hollerich, Michael J. "John Milbank, Augustine, and the 'Secular'." *Augustinian Studies* 30, no. 2 (1999): 311–26.

——. "Augustine as a Civil Theologian." In *Augustine: Presbyter Factus Sum*, edited by J. T. Lienhard, E. C. Müller and R. J. Teske, 57–69. New York: Peter Lang, 1993.

Hollingworth, Miles. *The Pilgrim City: St. Augustine of Hippo and His Innovation in Political Thought*. London: T&T Clark International, 2010.

Jehasse, J., and A. McKenna, eds. *Religion Et Politique: Les Avatars De L'augustinisme. Actes Du Colloque Organisé Par L'institut Claude Longeon Du 4 Au 7 Octobre 1995*. Saint-Étienne: Publications de l'Université de Saint-Étienne, 1995.

Johnson, Kristen Deede. *Theology, Political Theory, and Pluralism: Beyond Tolerance and Difference*. Cambridge: Cambridge University Press, 2007.

Jungling, Laurie A. "Passionate Order: Order and Sexuality in Augustine's Theology." *Word & World* 27, no. 3 (Summer 2007): 315–324.

Kliever, Lonnie D. "The Christology of H. Reinhold Neibuhr." *The Journal of Religion* 50, no. 1 (January 1970): 33-57.

Kegley, Charles W., Robert Bretal, eds. *Reinhold Niebuhr: His Religious, Social, and Political Thought.* New York: Macmillan, 1956.

Kotsko, Adam. "'That They Might Have Ontology': Radical Orthodoxy and the New Debate." *Poltical Theology* 10, no. 1 (2009): 115-124.

Kries, Douglas. "Political Augustinianism." In *Augustine Through the Ages: An Encyclopedia,* edited by Allan D. Fitzgerald, 357-358. Grand Rapids, MI: Eerdmans, 1999.

Lovin, Robin. *Reinhold Niebuhr and Christian Realism.* Cambridge: Cambridge University Press, 1995.

Malotky, Daniel James. "Reinhold Niebuhr's Paradox: Groundwork for Social Responsibility." *The Journal of Religious Ethics* 31, no. 1 (Spring 2003): 101-123.

Mandonnet, Pierre-Félix. *Siger de Brabant et l'Averroïsme latin au XIII° siècle. Étude critique et documents inédits par Pierre Mandonnet, O. P.* Fribourg: Libraire de l'Université, 1989.

Mariani, Ugo. "L'agostonismo Politico." In *Sanctus Augustinus Vitae Spirituali Magister.* Roma: Analecta Augustiniana, 1956.

Maritain, Jacques. *The Social and Political Philosophy of Jacques Maritain: Selected Readings.* Edited by J. Evans and L. Ward. New York: Charles Scribner's Sons, 1955.

———. *La Personne et le Bien Commun.* Paris: Desclée de Brouwer, 1947.

———. *The Person and the Common Good.* trans. John J. Fitzgerald. New York: Charles Scribner's Sons, 1947.

McIlroy, David H. "The Right Reason for Caesar to Confess Christ as Lord: Oliver O'Donovan and Arguments for the Christian State." *Studies in Christian Ethics* 23, no. 3 (Aug. 2010): 300-315.

———. "Idols and Grace: Re-Envisioning Political Liberalism as Political Limitism." *Political Theology* 11, no. 2 (2010): 205-225.

McLynn, Neil B. "Augustine's Roman Empire." *Augustinian Studies* 30, no. 2 (1999): 29-44.

McKenzie, Michael. "Christian Norms in the Ethical Square: An Impossible Dream?" *Journal of the Evangelical Theological Society* 38, no. 3 (September 1995): 413-427.

Meynell, Hugo Anthony, ed. *Grace, Politics, and Desire: Essays on Augustine.* Calgary: University of Calgary Press, 1990.

Mulcahy, Bernard, O. P. *Aquinas's Notion of Pure Nature and the Christian Integralism of Henri de Lubac: Not Everything is Grace.* New York: Peter Lang Publishing, 2011.

Murphy, Francesca A. *Art and Intellect in the Philosophy of Étienne Gilson.* Columbia, MO: University of Missouri Press, 2004.

Neuhaus, Richard John, ed. *The Naked Public Square.* Grand Rapids, MI: Wm. B. Eerdmans, 1996.

———. ed. *Augustine Today.* Grand Rapids, MI: Wm. B. Eerdmans, 1993.

Nicholls, David. *The Pluralist State: The Political Ideas of John Neville Figgis and His Contemporaries.* New York: St. Martin's Press, 1994.

Nitrola, Antonio. *Trattato di escatologia vol. 1: Spunti per un pensare escatologico.* Torino: Edizioni San Paolo, 2001.

O'Donovan, Joan Lockwood, "Natural Law and Perfect Community: Contributions of Christian Platonism to Political Theory." *Modern Theology* 14, no. 1 (Jan. 1998): 19-42.

Pagels, Elaine. *Adam, Eve, and the Serpent: Sex and Politics in Early Christianity.* New York: Vintage Books, 1989.

———. "The Politics of Paradise: Augustine's Exegesis of Genesis 1-3 versus that of John Chrysostom." *The Harvard Theological Review* 78, no. 1-2 (Jan-Apr. 1985): 67-99.

Pasquale, Gianluigi, O. F. M. Cap. *La Ragione della Storia: Per una filosofia della storia come scienza.* Torino: Bollati Boringhieri, 2011.

————. *Teologia della Storia della Salvezza nel Secolo XX.* Bologna: Edizione Dehoniane Bologna, 2001.

Pieper, Josef. *The End of Time: A Meditation on the Philosophy of History.* Translated by Michael Bullock. San Francisco: Ignatius Press, 1999.

Rawls, John. *Political Liberalism.* New York: Columbia University Press, 1996.

————. *A Theory of Justice.* Cambridge, MA: Harvard University Press, 1971.

Rees, Geoffrey. "The Anxiety of Inheritance: Reinhold Niebuhr and the Literal Truth of Original Sin." *Journal of Religious Ethics* 31, no. 1 (March, 2003): 75-99.

Reuther, Rosemary. "Augustine and Christian Political Theology." *Interpretation* 29, no. 3 (1975): 252-65.

Richardson, Graeme, "Integrity and Realism: Assessing John Milbank's Theology." *New Blackfriars* 84, no. 988 (June 2003): 268-280.

Riché, Pierre. *Henri Irénée Marrou: Historien Engagé.* Paris: Les Éditions du Cerf, 2003.

Rist, John. *What is Truth? From the Academy to the Vatican.* Cambridge: Cambridge University Press, 2008.

Saak, Eric. *Highway to Heaven: The Augustinian Platform Between Reform and Reformation, 1292-1524.* Leiden: Brill Publishing, 2002.

Santurri, Edmund N. "Global Justice after the Fall: Christian Realism and the 'Law of Peoples.'" *Journal of Religious Ethics* 33, no. 4D (2005): 783-814.

Schilling, Otto. *Die Staats- und Soziallehre des hl. Augustinus.* Freibourg: Herder, 1910.

Schlabach, Gerald W. "Is Milbank Niebuhrian despite himself?" *Conrad Global Review* 23, no. 2 (Spring 2005): 33-40.

————. *For the Joy Set Before Us: Augustine and Self-Denying Love.* Notre Dame, IN: University of Notre Dame Press, 2001.

Skerrett, K. Roberts. "The Indispensable Rival: William Connolly's Engagement with Augustine of Hippo." *Journal of American Academy of Religion* 72, no. 2 (June 2004): 487–506.

Stark, Judith Chelius. *Feminist Interpretations of Augustine*. University Park, PA: Pennsylvania State University Press, 2007.

Stringfellow, William. *An Ethic for Christians and Other Aliens in a Strange Land*. Waco, TX: Word Books, 1973.

Tanner, Kathryn. *The Politics of God: Christian Theologies and Social Justice*. Minneapolis: Fortress Press, 1992.

TeSelle, Eugene. *Living in Two Cities: Augustinian Trajectories in Political Thought*. Scranton, PA: University of Scranton Press, 2005.

———. "Toward an Augustinian Politics." *Journal of Religious Ethics* 16, no. 1 (Spring 1988): 87–109.

Trainor, Brian T. "Augustine's Glorious City of God as Principle of the Political." *The Heythrop Journal* 51 (2010): 543–553.

Troeltsch, Ernst. *Augustin, die christliche Antike und da Mittelalter*. Munich: R. Oldenbourg, 1915.

Tucker, Maurice. *John Neville Figgis: A Study*. London: S. P. C. K., 1950.

Van Oort, Johannes. *Jerusalem and Babylon: A Study Into Augustine's City of God and the Sources of His Doctrine of the Two Cities*. Leiden: E. J. Brill, 1991.

Vessey, Mark. ed. *A Companion to Augustine*. London: Blackwell Publishing Ltd., 2012.

Von Gierke, Otto F. *Das deutsche Genossenschaftsrecht*. Graz: Akademische Druck–u. Verlagsanstalt, 1868.

Von Heyking, John. *Augustine and Politics as Longing in the World*. Columbia, MO: University of Missouri Press, 2001.

Walker, Graham. "Antique Modernity: Augustine's 'Liberalism' and the Impasses of Modern Politics." In *Saint Augustine the Bishop*. Edited by

Fannie LeMoine and Christopher Kleinhenz, 201-02. New York: Garland Publishing, 1994.

Weidenaar, James B. "Augustine's Theory of Concupiscence in *City of God*, Book XIV." *Calvin Theological Journal* 30 (1995): 52-74.

Weithman, Paul J. "Augustine's Political Philosophy." In *The Cambridge Companion to Augustine*. Edited by Eleonore Stump and Norman Kretzman, 234-252. Cambridge: Cambridge University Press, 2001.

———. "Toward an Augustinian Liberalism." In *The Augustinian Tradition*. Edited by Gareth Matthews, 304-322. Berkeley: University of California Press, 1999.

———. "Augustine and Aquinas on Original Sin and the Function of Political Authority." *Journal of the History of Philosophy* 30, no. 3 (July 1992): 353-376.

Yeager, D. M. "On Making the Tree Good: An Apology for a Dispositional Ethics." *The Journal of Religious Ethics* 10, no. 1 (1982): 103-120.

Index